Community Care for Older People

A Comparative Perspective

Susan Tester
Lecturer in Social Policy, University of Stirling

Consultant Editor: Jo Campling

First published in Great Britain 1996 by
MACMILLAN PRESS LTD
Houndmills, Basingstoke, Hampshire RG21 6XS
and London
Companies and representatives
throughout the world

A catalogue record for this book is available
from the British Library.

ISBN 0–333–54933–3 hardcover
ISBN 0–333–54934–1 paperback

First published in the United States of America 1996 by
ST. MARTIN'S PRESS, INC.,
Scholarly and Reference Division,
175 Fifth Avenue,
New York, N.Y. 10010

ISBN 0–312–15912–9

Library of Congress Cataloging-in-Publication Data applied for

10   9   8   7   6   5   4   3   2   1
05   04   03   02   01   00   99   98   97   96

Copy-edited and typeset by Povey–Edmondson
Okehampton and Rochdale, England

Printed in Malaysia

For Charlie and Nathalie

Contents

List of Tables

Acknowledgements

Many people have contributed to this study in various ways during the past few years. I am grateful for all their help, even though it is not possible to name them all here. Financial support for study visits was provided by the Council of Europe, the Marjory Warren Funds and the University of Stirling Research Fund. Thanks are due to all those who helped me to organise my study visits to France, Germany, the Netherlands and the United States of America. Ulla Rydberg gave much help and companionship at the University of Florida; her untimely death was a great sadness. I am most grateful to all the policymakers, professionals, care workers and service users in the institutes and agencies visited, who gave their time to answer my questions and explain policies and practice to me.

My task of producing the book was assisted by the helpful comments of those who read draft chapters, including George Giarchi, Christine Hallett, Hannelore Jani, Barbara Klein, Otto von Mering, Robert Pinker, Willi Rückert and, especially, Barbara Meredith and Henk Nies who provided detailed comments on all chapters. Christopher Turner gave support and encouragement through the long process of writing. Sue Dyer helped with preparation of the typescript. I am grateful to my editor, Jo Campling, for suggesting the book and for her patience in awaiting its completion. Thanks are also due to Frances Arnold and Catherine Gray at the publishers and to the anonymous reader for helpful comments on the first draft. I appreciate all the help received from all those involved; responsibility for the accuracy of the contents, however, remains my own.

SUSAN TESTER

List of Abbreviations

AAA	Area Agency on Aging (US)
AARP	American Association of Retired Persons (US)
ACE	Age Concern England (UK)
ADL	Activities of Daily Living
AMA	Association of Metropolitan Authorities (UK)
AoA	Administration on Aging (US)
AWBZ	*Algemene Wet Bijzondere Ziektekosten* (Exceptional Medical Expenses Act, Netherlands)
BMFuS	*Bundesministerium für Familie und Senioren* (Federal ministry for families and older people, Germany)
CCAS	*Centre Communal d'Action Sociale* (municipal social services centre, France)
CEC	Commission of the European Communities
DHHS	Department of Health and Human Services (US)
DHSS	Department of Health and Social Security (UK)
EC	European Community
EU	European Union
FRG	Federal Republic of Germany
GDP	Gross Domestic Product
GDR	German Democratic Republic
GHS	General Household Survey (UK)
GP	General practitioner
HMO	Health Maintenance Organisation (US)
HMSO	Her Majesty's Stationery Office (UK)
KDA	*Kuratorium Deutsche Altershilfe* (Germany)
NHS	National Health Service (UK)
NISW	National Institute for Social Work (UK)
OAA	Older Americans Act (US)
OECD	Organisation for Economic Cooperation and Development
OPCS	Office for Population Censuses and Surveys (UK)
PSSRU	Personal Social Services Research Unit (UK)
RADAR	Royal Association for Disability and Rehabilitation (UK)

RIAGG   *Regionale Instelling voor Ambulante Geestelijke Gezondheidszorg*
          (Regional institute for outpatient mental health services)
          (Netherlands)
SSI   Social Services Inspectorate (UK)
SSN   *Servizio Sanitario Nazionale* (National Health Service, Italy)
SUA   State Unit on Aging (US)
SWSG   Social Work Services Group (UK)
UK   United Kingdom
US   United States
USL   *Unità Sanitarie Locali* (local health units, Italy)
VA   Veterans Administration (US)

1
Introduction

Caring for dependent older people has rapidly gained visibility as a major social policy issue for the 1990s. In the changed socio-economic and political context of the postmodern world, devising appropriate and acceptable responses to the needs of ageing populations is a crucial challenge. The twentieth century has seen a remarkable increase in longevity in advanced industrial societies. Life expectancy at birth rose by over 28 years for females and 24 years for males between 1900 and 1980 in OECD countries (OECD, 1988a: 12,14); populations aged as falling mortality and fertility rates led to increasing proportions of older people. The proportion of people aged over 65 in the populations of OECD countries is projected to have doubled from an average of below 10 per cent in 1950 to over 20 per cent in 2050 (OECD, 1994a: 37).

Increased life expectancy is a positive achievement, yet population ageing is often perceived as a burden, especially by governments concerned about costs of social welfare service provision for older people. Since the 1970s governments in Europe and North America have expressed fears about population ageing at times of economic crisis. Reforms are being implemented in most industrial societies to address the issue of increasing pension and health care costs entailed by rising numbers in the oldest age groups. The greatest increase in social expenditure will be for pensions (OECD, 1988a: 36). However, alarm about these increases may be ill-founded, since to counteract pressures from the older age groups there will be less need for education and family benefits for the declining population of children.

Most OECD countries promote policies for 'ageing in place': that is, that older people with physical or mental disabilities or illnesses should be helped to live in their own homes, or in home-like settings close to their communities, for as long as possible (OECD, 1994a: 37). This is the basis for most programmes described as 'community care' in the Anglo-Saxon world. The systems and their focus are, however, undergoing changes, partly in response to perceptions about demographic ageing. Changing forms of service provision and finance affect the lives of those older people who need care and support. Within the heterogeneous older population such changes affect people differently according to factors such as age, gender, socio-economic class and 'race' (see note on p. 25).

These effects transcend national borders, reflecting similarities and differences in populations and in governmental responses. Policies may be informed by 'borrowing' or 'learning from' other countries with similar political priorities and socio-economic or demographic profiles. In the 1980s policies from the US influenced Conservative governments in the United Kingdom (UK). Within the European Union (EU) there has been an increasing interest in the social structures and institutions of member states and a growing awareness of the prospect of population mobility within the EU. Where care for older people is concerned, emerging issues include retirement in different countries, mobility of professionals working with older people, and cross-national service provision by non-governmental service providers. Such issues increase the need for basic knowledge of the health and welfare structures of other countries. This book seeks to enhance such knowledge.

Aims and methods

Comparative information about community care systems was rarely available until the early 1990s (for example, Jamieson, ed., 1991; Evers and van der Zanden, eds., 1993). This book provides, in accessible form, a background to systems and cultures of social and welfare service provision in Europe and North America, as a basis for more detailed comparative studies on community care for older people. In this chapter a framework is developed for the analysis of community care systems for older people in industrial societies, following an analysis of definitions, concepts and components of community care, models of welfare provision and some of the factors that influence welfare and community care policies. The origins, substance and outcomes of different aspects of community care for older people in a selection of countries are then compared.

The countries studied are France, Germany, Italy, the Netherlands, the United Kingdom and the United States. To cover this wide topic adequately with a greater number of countries was considered impossible. The reasons for selection were somewhat arbitrary, and the countries are taken as case studies rather than as a representative sample. The scope was limited by availability of published material and influenced by existing contacts and opportunities for study visits to the US and north western European countries, the areas most commonly compared in social gerontology. To avoid exclusive focus on these areas, however, a southern European country, Italy, was included. The six countries have similar socio-economic conditions, but different types of welfare regime. The proportions of people aged over 65 in the populations of the countries vary, ranging from 12.7 per cent in the US to 15.8 per cent in the UK, as shown in Table 1.1.

All six countries are members of the Organisation for Economic Cooperation and Development (OECD). The European countries selected are all member states of the EU, since the book was planned at a time of growing interest in the then European Community (EC) in anticipation of the introduction of the single European market in 1993. Interest in older people in the EC also burgeoned in the early 1990s with the first EC programme for older people initiated in 1991, the setting up of the EC Commission policy observatory on ageing and older people, and the activities of the European year for older people and solidarity between generations in 1993. Since 1989, however, events in eastern Europe have had far-reaching implications for Europe that overshadow the narrower concerns of the internal market. An eastern European dimension to the study was included as former East Germany, the German Democratic Republic (GDR), was incorporated into the Federal Republic of Germany (FRG) in October 1990 with the unification of Germany.

Table 1.1 *Proportions of older people in populations of countries studied, 1990*

	France	Germany[a]	Italy	Nether-lands	United Kingdom	United States
Total population inhabitants (thousands)	57,050	64,036	57,783	15,065	57,370	262,200
% of people aged 65+ *in population*	14.1	15.4	15.4	12.9	15.8	12.7
% of people aged 75+ *in population*	7.0	7.2	6.3	5.3	7.0	5.2
% of people aged 80+ *in population*	3.8	3.8	3.1	3.0	3.7	2.9

[a] former FRG.

Cross-national comparisons

Comparing community care systems of a selection of countries with different characteristics can offer the opportunity to gain a deeper and broader view of social policy issues than would result from a single country study. The researcher has to look at the broad context of the system being studied, which makes it possible to find out much more about the various factors which impinge on each other (Hantrais, 1989: 11). To understand a particular aspect of social policy, such as community care for older people, it is necessary to know how it fits into the wider social welfare systems and cultural expectations of the country concerned.

One advantage of cross-national comparisons is that they may facilitate problem solving by showing how other countries are trying to tackle similar issues. In addition to describing varying policy responses to such issues, cross-national comparisons may help in the search for explanations for such responses and enable the researcher to establish what is specific to a country or system and what is generalisable (Higgins, 1981: 12–14; 1986: 222–3; Jones, 1985: 4). Comparisons thus provide useful evidence from a range of sources for the formulation of theories about social policy responses or systems.

The difficulties of conducting cross-national comparisons in social policy are, however, as well recognised as is the value of such studies. Methodological problems of cross-national social policy research include questions about what to compare, and how to compare like with like. It is difficult to find equivalent concepts and terms when these are often specific to the culture or context (Jones, 1985). Bolderson comments that: 'Instances may be truly comparable and meaningful when they are particular and closely specified, but they are then incapable of generalisation without numerous qualifications' (1988: 271). More practical considerations concern obtaining comparable data, when statistics are often compiled for different purposes using varying definitions. Such difficulties may be compounded by the researcher's lack of knowledge of countries and languages. It is thus important to acknowledge the many theoretical and practical problems in any cross-national comparison and to exercise caution when interpreting findings (Higgins, 1986).

The range of methods open to cross-national policy analysts is as wide as that for any other area of social research. A truly comparative cross-national survey is both difficult, for the reasons discussed above, and expensive. Jones (1985: 20) distinguishes between comparable and comparative sources which may be 'factual' or 'commentary' including national or cross-national compilations of statistics and policy studies. The present study draws on all these types of published material, but it must be acknowledged from the outset that there is a lack of comparative data on many of the specific questions covered, and particularly on long-term social care for older people. The author's previous research in the UK, and short study visits to France, Germany, the Netherlands and the US, provide background knowledge and experience. During these visits discussions were held with policymakers, service providers and academic researchers; visits were made to various forms of service provision, and literature and documentation on policies and procedures were collected. Given limited resources, as wide a range as possible of sources and methods was thus used in preparation of this book. The limitations of undertaking such a study without conducting a purpose-designed comparative survey are, however, fully recognised.

Community care: definitions and concepts

The difficulties of cross-national comparison become immediately apparent when attempting to define 'community care'. The term has been used in the UK for four decades usually to denote care in non-institutional settings, and policies advocating community care in this sense have been adopted widely in English-speaking countries. But the meaning of the concept 'community care' has never been as clear as the rhetoric which advocates it. The ambiguous and changing meanings of community care are discussed further below. The problem for European comparative studies is that in other European languages the concept of community care is not used in this sense. As Jamieson points out: 'From a purely linguistic point of view, it is a very Anglo-Saxon concept, whose exact equivalent cannot always be found in other languages' (1989: 446). The equivalent terminology in other European languages usually means support for people in their own homes, for example the French '*maintien à domicile*'. For this reason cross-national European studies have preferred to use terms such as 'home care' or 'home-based care' (for example Jamieson, ed., 1991). In the US the focus is on 'long-term care', whether institutional or 'community-based'. In Anglo-Saxon countries terms such as community-based are understood, but 'community' is not used in this sense in Europe. In English 'community' has many meanings, but its use in conjunction with 'care' is vague and misleading, and therefore unhelpful for comparative purposes.

Irrespective of the terminology used, the basic element of the policy is simply to help older people who need care to continue to live in their own homes (or carers' homes) for as long as possible. This, of course, is not a new idea, since the great majority of older people have always lived in their own homes, and, it must be stressed, most do not need any form of care. The crucial new dimension was the formulation of explicit policies on community care (Jamieson, 1989: 450).

In the UK the meaning of the concept of community care has never been clearly defined by governments. The 'community' element of the concept in government policy has changed over the years from meaning care provided by agencies *in* the community rather than in institutions, to care provided *by* the community, in practice usually care by the family (see, for example, the policy paper *Growing older*, DHSS, 1981). A consensus about the worth of vaguely-defined community care has been maintained in Britain for several decades because it sounded like 'a good thing', in contrast to institutional care, and because the meaning was not questioned. Need for community care was not measured and resources were not made available to implement the policy fully. The consensus seems to have been mainly based on rhetoric, as Walker (1989) argues.

Writers such as Titmuss (1968) have commented that the use of this cosy sounding concept has covered up the underlying issues and realities, implying that a friendly community was providing services, when in reality care was mainly provided by the family. In a lecture in 1961 Titmuss warned that:

> We may pontificate about the philosophy of community care; . . . but unless we are prepared to examine at this level of concrete reality what we mean by community care, we are simply indulging in wishful thinking. (1968: 106)

By the late 1980s the gap between rhetoric and reality was still wide, as described by the Griffiths review: '. . . in few areas can the gap between political rhetoric and policy on the one hand, or between policy and reality in the field on the other hand have been so great' (Griffiths, 1988: iv).

In British government policy documents the number of services included as community care seems to have increased over the years (see, for example, *The way forward*, DHSS, 1977: 8). Community care used to be contrasted with institutional care, but some institutions are now included as community care. The Wagner report sees residential care as: 'an element in a range of community care services' (National Institute for Social Work, 1988: 11). In *People first* the Department of Health and Social Security for Northern Ireland (1990: 11) uses community care to mean simply 'care outside hospital'. A further complication in the UK in the early 1990s was the use of 'community care' as synonymous with the community care reforms implemented from 1991–3, to be discussed below. This usage suggested that community care was a new phenomenon, rather than a goal that had existed for nearly forty years. Definitions of community or home care for older people with care needs have also been shifting in other countries, following trends discussed later in this chapter.

Community care is a term widely used in English speaking countries, but must be recognised as a broad concept susceptible to vague definitions. It is used in this book in its widest sense, which includes housing, domiciliary health and welfare services, health services outside the home, day care services, and the social, leisure and educational facilities that help to maintain the older person's quality of life. In other words it means simply care for older people who live in their own homes, irrespective of whether those homes are in ordinary housing, carers' homes, specialised or small scale residential settings. For the purpose of cross-national comparison covering countries with different languages and systems, the wide concept must be divided into basic components. It is, in practice, more useful to examine such components across different systems than to attempt to compare broad goals and systems described by such terms as 'community care'.

Types and components of community care

There are four main aspects to be considered in the categorisation of care services. First, which caring tasks or services are offered? Second, in what settings is this help provided? Third, who provides it? And fourth, who pays for it?

First, then, older people may benefit from one or more of a range of services which are not always considered to be part of community care. A basic essential is *suitable housing*, in ordinary, specialised or some residential settings. *Financial support*, such as pensions and welfare benefits, is also crucial. Then more specifically caring services could include *basic care* to help with daily living, mobility and self care, and, for people with physical or mental health problems, *medical care, nursing or therapy* services. To promote more general wellbeing, *counselling or emotional support* could be given, and *social, educational and leisure* activities could be taken up. *Transport* services may be essential for use of health care and social facilities. *Information* about the whole range of services and opportunities is a key factor in access to appropriate care (see also Meredith, 1995: 19–20).

Second, turning to the settings in which such services could be offered, ways of defining differences between types of care are examined by Higgins (1989), who suggests that there is no clear distinction between institution and community, and that many care settings have elements of both. Institutional care can take place in the community, for example in hostels for people with mental illness who have moved from a large institution to a smaller one. Much community care takes place in institutions, for example day hospital or respite care, but most care takes place in the home, provided by the family. Higgins suggests that the simplest way of categorising care is to ask where people sleep at night, in an institution or at home? Services may then be divided into those available *in a home*, for example an institution such as a hospital, or a home in the community such as a hostel or nursing home; *from home*, for example day care or respite care; or *at home*, such as domiciliary care by agencies or family. In this model there is no need for the concept community, which Higgins finds unhelpful (Higgins, 1989: 5–7).

As discussed above, the imprecisely defined 'community' element of community care, based mainly on rhetoric, is of little use in comparative analysis. However, Higgins' distinction between 'institution' and 'home' is also problematic. The place where people usually sleep at night is their home, whether or not it is considered to be an institution. If a distinction is to be made between institution and home, the concept 'institution' must also be clearly defined. To categorise settings in which help is provided, a two-fold typology, based on Higgins' 'from home' and 'at home' will be more useful. The type of home, such as ordinary housing, group home, nursing home, may then be specified where relevant. The main distinction between settings in which care is provided will thus be whether the service is received in the home where the person usually lives, or whether they leave that home to receive it, for example in a day care setting.

Third, although until fairly recently much of the literature on care for older people in industrialised countries has focused on care provided by agencies, it is now recognised that by far the largest proportion of care (about 75–80 per cent) is provided by the informal sector, that is family, friends and neighbours, mainly women. Similarly, although much attention has been devoted to state-provided services, most countries have pluralist systems of care provided by governmental and non-governmental agencies, formal organisations and informal carers. The balance of the various sectors in what is now described as the mixed economy of welfare in the systems of the selected countries is detailed later. For the purposes of definition, at this stage it is necessary to identify types of service providers for the various caring tasks or services which comprise community care. The main providers are informal carers, the state, private profit-making agencies, voluntary or non-governmental non-profit-making organisations, employers and trade unions (Higgins, 1986).

Informal carers are likely to be mainly involved in providing basic care to help with daily living, mobility and self care, although some also give highly skilled nursing care. The state may provide financial support, accommodation, health and social care, through social security, health and welfare systems organised at national, regional and local levels. Private commercial enterprises may, for example, be major providers of housing and residential care, medical services, pensions and leisure activities. The non-profit sector in various forms provides, for example, social and medical care, housing, leisure and transport services, in some countries playing the major role in health and welfare provision. Employers and trade unions, while providing occupational welfare services mainly for current employees, may have a role in providing or administering pensions and other financial benefits and welfare services for former employees and retired members. Various factors determine the roles played in service provision by each sector in different political, economic and welfare systems.

Fourth, the provision of care is financed through different sources and methods. The financer of services is not necessarily the provider, although this has been a common assumption, as Glennerster (1992: 4–5) points out. Glennerster emphasises the distinctions between public and private provision and public and private financing and shows that there are few clear cut examples of services entirely publicly or privately provided *and* funded. For example care homes for older people are often provided by private agencies but partly funded from public sources. The main financers of community care services are the individual and family, the state, insurance funds, employers, trade unions and charities. The finance may have been raised or reallocated from other sources such as through taxation and may be channelled through various routes to purchase services from different providers (Glennerster, 1992). The complex policies and practices of financing community care services are discussed further in chapter 2.

It is thus important in categorising care services to distinguish clearly between particular tasks or services, care settings, providers and financers.

Community care in the context of welfare provision

Two main strands in comparative social policy have tended to develop separately: macro-theoretical studies of the welfare state and empirical research on particular aspects of policy or practice (Higgins, 1986: 221). Few examinations of substantive areas relevant to community care for older people have been related to broader theoretical comparative literature. This study is not concerned with the reasons for the development of welfare states in general but examines differences between types of welfare regime and the relevance of such differences to care systems for older people.

One of the main approaches of macro-theoretical comparative work has been to devise and explain types of welfare state regime based on North American or West European capitalist welfare systems. Titmuss proposed a three-fold typology: the 'residual welfare', 'industrial achievement–performance' and 'institutional–redistributive' models (Titmuss, 1974: 30–1). Esping-Andersen (1990) identified three clusters of regime types which correspond approximately to those of Titmuss: the 'liberal' welfare state, the 'conservative–corporatist' welfare state and the 'social democratic' regime type. In identifying these welfare state regimes Esping-Andersen examines the different roles played by the state, the market and the family and the interaction between them. He also considers the extent of 'de-commodification', that is how well state welfare allows people to live without relying on participation in the market through paid work.

Esping-Andersen suggests that the 'liberal' welfare state, corresponding to Titmuss' 'residual' model, provides minimal benefits with strict criteria, aimed at poor people, and encourages market reliance for the majority. The 'conservative–corporatist' welfare state (Titmuss' 'industrial achievement–performance' model) aims to preserve status differentials based on performance in the market through insurance welfare, is influenced by the church, and emphasises family responsibilities with limited state involvement. The 'social democratic' model ('institutional' welfare state) promotes high standard flat rate universal state services based on citizenship, and is committed to and dependent on a high level of employment (Esping-Andersen, 1990: 26–8).

Esping-Andersen uses aspects of social security programmes to measure the extent of 'de-commodification' and ranks 18 OECD welfare states in order. The three clusters thus identified correspond to the three welfare regime types; the 'liberal' welfare states have the lowest de-commodification score, 'conservative–corporatist' countries form a middle group and 'social democratic' welfare states score highest (Esping-Andersen, 1990: 52).

Esping-Andersen and others who devise models of welfare state regime stress that countries do not fall neatly into one of these categories but tend predominantly to one type while combining elements of others. Some authors agree with Esping-Andersen's three main categories but add a fourth into which anomalous countries fit more closely. For example the UK is classified as a 'labourite' welfare state by Mitchell (1991), or as 'liberal collectivist' by Ginsburg (1992) whose other three types are 'corporate market economy', such as the US, 'social market economy', for example Germany, and 'social democratic', such as Sweden.

Jones (1985) suggests two dimensions for comparison: level of social spending and type of social policy, that is 'welfare *capitalist*' (corresponding to Titmuss' 'industrial achievement–performance' model) or '*welfare* capitalist' ('institutional-redistributive' model). Another type of welfare regime which Leibfried (1993) adds to Esping-Andersen's three is the 'rudimentary welfare state' of Europe's 'Mediterranean rim', exemplified by Greece and Spain. Italy also has some characteristics of this type.

The welfare regime types of the six welfare capitalist countries studied are discussed further below. However, the relevance of such categories to the topic of community care for older people has yet to be explored. As Ginsburg (1992: 24) points out, most comparative research has focused on social security systems rather than health or social care.

Comparative social policy analysts criticise categorisations of welfare state regimes as inadequate in the changed political, economic and ideological context of the 1990s. First, as they are based on western capitalist systems, the models may not be relevant to the changing welfare systems of post-communist regimes of Eastern Europe which, before 1989, had 'bureaucratic state collectivist' systems of welfare (Deacon, 1992). Deacon suggests that these regimes may adopt non-European patterns of welfare based on South American, Japanese or South East Asian systems.

Second, critical approaches to comparative social policy point out that existing models of welfare state regimes have failed to address issues of gender, 'race' and age, focusing attention on the white working male, as has mainstream social policy in general (Williams, 1989; Ginsburg, 1992; Deacon, 1992). Ginsburg (1992: 19) stresses that although empirical research suggests differences between countries in 'welfare status of racialized groups . . . there has been no attempt to theorize these cross-national differences and the experiences of racialized groups in modern welfare states'. For example 'race' is not included in Esping-Andersen's analysis (Ginsburg, 1992: 23).

⮕ The neglect of gender differences is particularly relevant to the study of community care since it is women who are primarily involved as unpaid and paid carers, whether working in family, state or market ⮕sectors. Thus Esping-Andersen (1990) has been criticised because, although his analysis of welfare regime types includes the relationship between work and welfare, work is assumed to be *paid* work. His concept of de-commodification refers to freedom from dependence on paid work in the market, and unpaid work is excluded from the analysis. The gender implications of paid and unpaid work, de-commodification and dependence are not addressed.

As Langan and Ostner (1991), Taylor-Gooby (1991) and Lewis (1992) point out, experiences of commodification and de-commodification differ according to gender. The commodification of workers in the market place customarily depends on the support of unpaid workers, usually women, in the private sphere. If women are de-commodified, that is not relying on paid work, it usually means that they are carrying out unpaid work in the home and may not have access to full time employment. Thus

> The role of social rights in de-commodification differs according to gender, in general protecting men's position in the labour market while disadvantaging women by restricting their access to certain areas of employment. (Langan and Ostner, 1991: 131)

In none of Esping-Andersen's regime types do women have the same career opportunities as men. This is partly because it is assumed that they have particular propensity to caring work which tends to be of lower status than men's work. This perpetuates the gender division of unpaid care as it is usually more beneficial for families to rely mainly on men's higher earnings (Taylor-Gooby, 1991). Lewis (1992: 161) points out that 'women have typically gained welfare entitlements by virtue of their dependent status within the family as wives' and that all welfare regime types are based on the male breadwinner family model. Thus it is suggested that models of welfare regimes such as Esping-Andersen's should be developed to incorporate the relationship between welfare policy and unpaid caring work in the private sphere as well as paid work in the public sphere (Taylor-Gooby, 1991).

Such criticisms of the categorisation of welfare state regimes reflect the more general criticism of comparative social policy, that it has given too much attention to state welfare at the expense of that provided through the market or informal sectors. In the changed context of the 1990s comparative social policy focused more closely on the concepts of welfare pluralism and the welfare mix, and on the shifting balance in different countries' welfare mixes between the roles of the state, market, family and voluntary sectors (for example, Evers and Svetlik, 1993). This approach could be more useful for the analysis of community care policies for older people than the more restricted application of categories of welfare state regime, as Hugman (1994: 155) suggests.

Welfare and community care policies

Many interrelated economic, political and ideological factors affect both the wider context of welfare and the specific formulation and implementation of community care policies for older people (see for example Higgins, 1981). The type of welfare state regime and the roles of state, market, non-profit organisations and family in welfare provision that have developed historically in a country are rarely static but evolve in response to a combination of interconnected influences. The structure and organisation of government at different levels and the extent of centralisation or decentralisation are also important determinants.

The wider context of social policy is particularly dependent on the economy and economic policy. Major changes in principles and practice of social welfare often follow economic crises and recessions; for example there was widespread debate on the future of the western welfare state in the aftermath of the world oil crisis in the 1970s. Demographic factors, such as ageing populations and increasing numbers of very elderly people, entailing rising pensions and health care costs, combine with economic and other factors to affect politicians' responses to social policy issues.

The perspectives and actions or non-actions on social welfare issues taken by governments are influenced by party politics and ideologies, and by the political power exercised by interest groups, the working class, trade unions, professionals and so on. For example, dependent older people and their carers have traditionally exercised much less power than the professionals involved in their care, particularly the medical profession, which has led to the predominance of the medical model in many systems (Jamieson, 1989: 447). Mishra (1993: 27) comments on the change from class politics to a more plural influence of interest groups that cross class lines, such as those based on gender and age. The influence of age-related groups has been manifest mainly in the US, but Wilson (1993) suggests that there may be scope for such influence in Europe through the EU rather than at national level.

Ideological, cultural and religious perspectives on the welfare state influence the roles played by the state, market, non-profit sector and family in welfare provision, social preferences for different forms of care, and the outcomes of welfare policy. In general the Protestant and Catholic churches have encouraged self-help and provision by the family, church and community groups rather than by the state (Higgins, 1981: 87). Ideological influences on social policy vary according to political regime types, for example the three identified by Esping-Andersen (1990), 'liberal', 'conservative' and 'socialist', corresponding to his three welfare regime types.

'Liberal' politics place responsibility on the individual and family to provide for themselves, with a residual role for the state and main provision through private agencies. This perspective was influenced by the Protestant ethic in countries such as the US and UK; more recently it has gained renewed prominence through the rise of the New Right in the late 1970s and 1980s. 'Conservative–corporatist' regimes are influenced both by conservative politics and by the Catholic church's teachings on the family and the principle of 'subsidiarity' which limits the role of state and formal organisations to tasks which the family and community organisations are unable to perform. 'Socialist' or 'social democratic' regimes, however, are more likely to place strong emphasis on the role of the state.

Such broad political perspectives and ideologies underpin stated government policies, for example on community care. This concept can be shown to meet both 'humanitarian' and 'organisational' aims, as identified by Macintyre (1977). From a 'humanitarian' perspective, concerned with the interests of older people themselves, community care policies were first formulated in the context of criticisms of institutional care and the view that it is preferable for those needing care to live in their own homes. Thus community care is based on concepts of independence, social integration and normalisation, aimed at helping people to be part of their community, and to live as independently and in as 'normal' a social environment as possible. The other main policy aim of community care, from an 'organisational' perspective, concerned with costs to society, is to minimise these costs, since community care is argued to be cheaper than institutional care. This argument, however, depends on the availability of unpaid informal carers. The outcomes of community care policies for older people also depend on the systems through which they are organised and provided (Illsley and Jamieson, 1990), and on the extent to which stated policies are actually implemented in practice.

These main influences on welfare and community care policy are discussed further below and in subsequent chapters. Further issues for discussion are identified in the following overview of trends in community care.

Trends in community care in Western Europe and North America

Economic and political developments in the late 1970s and 1980s, such as recession and the election of governments committed to New Right ideology, led to a new emphasis on restricting health and welfare expenditure. Measures to contain health care costs and address the issue of rising pension costs were taken by most West European and North American governments. Projected increases in the proportion of very elderly people were used to justify reforms to care systems, and the promotion of care in the community provided mainly by the informal sector rather than by formal agencies. Policies emphasised targeting services to those most in need and increasing efficiency, using economic criteria and market practices which were new to some social welfare services, such as introducing to health care systems management techniques used in industry.

A common trend in welfare states was a move towards welfare pluralism, with shifts in the balance of the welfare mix leading to increased emphasis on provision by non-state sectors, and leaving the state to finance, regulate and coordinate care provided by the market, community organisations and informal carers (Baldock, 1993; Evers, 1993). Another outcome of this trend was the tendency towards dual systems whereby the market and insurance systems provide for those in continuous full time employment, while those with a weaker relationship to or outside the labour market have to rely on means-tested assistance systems, community organisations and informal care. Thus it has been suggested that there is a tendency towards convergence of welfare states on the 'conservative–corporatist' model (Abrahamson, 1992). This means that in countries like the UK which previously relied mainly on state provision services became more fragmented.

Decentralisation and increasing consumer participation and choice are further aspects of the trend to welfare pluralism. Countries such as France and Italy moved in the 1980s towards decentralisation of state services (Chamberlayne, 1991–2: 15). Self-help groups were promoted and funded for example in Germany during the 1980s (Mayo, 1994). Such trends were reflected in community care policies promoting flexibility and consumer choice. Whereas previously the user was expected to fit into standardised services, the emphasis moved to devising 'packages of care' to meet the needs of individuals, and 'care management' of the services to be coordinated for them. Another aspect of this trend was to recognise informal carers more explicitly than before and to involve and interact with them in providing care (Baldock and Evers, 1992).

Economic and ideological rationales combine in the policy of 'substitution' of less institutional, less technical and less formal services for institutional and expensive forms of care. This implies a move away from long-term hospital and nursing home care even for the most dependent older people, and the provision of more social (as distinct from medical) care in people's own homes. With the emphasis on efficiency and targeting, a further implication of this policy is that community care services are increasingly focused on those who would otherwise need institutional care, at the expense of those with lower priority needs who have to rely on private or informal care.

The following brief overview of the main trends in welfare and community care policy in the six selected countries provides a background for the more detailed discussion of the issues in subsequent chapters. As an indicator of comparative levels of social spending, public expenditure on social protection as a proportion of gross domestic product (GDP) in the countries studied is given in Table 1.2.

It must be recognised, however, that comparisons between countries may mask wide differences within those countries, between federal states, regions and localities. This is particularly the case in federal systems such as Germany and the United States, or countries such as Italy which are decentralised regionally. In a more detailed study it could be useful to compare regions or localities and to generate comparative data which are rarely available at these levels at present.

As an example of the limitations of categorising welfare states, *France* does not fit neatly into any welfare regime type. The social insurance

Table 1.2 *Public expenditure on social protection[a] as a percentage of GDP*

	France	Germany[b]	Italy	Netherlands	United Kingdom	United States
1980	23.85	25.40	19.75	27.16	21.30	14.10
1985	27.86	25.15	22.68	28.78	24.12	14.31
1990[c]	26.49	23.47	24.53	28.78	22.34	14.58

[a] includes health and social security (pensions and benefits) expenditure.
[b] former FRG.
[c] 1990 data estimated.
Source: OECD, 1994a.

system leads Esping-Andersen (1990) to consider its welfare regime 'conservative–corporatist', and Jones (1985: 82) to find elements of the welfare *capitalist* type. Jones, however, places France, a 'high social spending' country, mid-way between welfare *capitalism* and *welfare* capitalism, because there is also a strong emphasis on family benefits. The Catholic church has influenced policy and played a role in non-state welfare provision. Traditionally the state has had a strong role through Napoleon's centralised administrative system, modified by President Mitterrand's decentralisation measures introduced from 1982.

In the 1960s France's social policies on older age were based on the new goal of social integration rather than care in institutions. To further this aim, community care policies were formulated following publication of the Laroque (1962) report on old age. Home care services were initiated and a range of social, health, housing and income maintenance measures introduced to promote social integration. The concept of a positive and active '*troisième âge*' (third age) became current; institutional care was associated with a '*quatrième âge*' (fourth age) of dependence (Henrard et al., 1990). Ageing issues were included in the Sixth Economic and Social Plan 1971–5, and a programme of community care was set out in a 1972 circular (*Ministère des Affaires Sociales*, 1972). The Seventh Plan 1976–80 firmly stated the policy of helping older people to remain in their own homes through home care services, third age clubs, restaurants and day centres.

The Ninth Plan 1984–8 advocated decentralisation of social services, with the objectives of localising services, reducing bureaucracy and making services more responsive to consumer demands. The Braun report (Braun and Stourm, 1988) reiterated priority for support in people's own homes, with better coordination between medical and social care. In 1991 a parliamentary commission report (Boulard, 1991) and a planning commission report (Schopflin, 1991) made recommendations to the government for reforming the care systems for older people.

The *Federal Republic of Germany (FRG)* is a prime example of the 'conservative–corporatist' welfare state regime (Esping-Andersen, 1990); Jones (1985: 82) classifies it as 'welfare *capitalist*' and 'high social spending'. The FRG operates as a social market economy rather than a welfare state, with the market taking the leading role. Main influences are the principles of subsidiarity and self-help, conservative views about preserving status relations and the Catholic church's teachings on family responsibility. In the FRG the central state has a limited role in welfare policy and the federal states (*Länder*) have considerable autonomy. Most service provision is by the non-state sectors, including the Catholic and Protestant churches. In 1990 the former German Democratic Republic was incorporated into the FRG, whose welfare systems were gradually introduced to replace the existing bureaucratic state collectivist system.

The main feature of German social policy is the social insurance system introduced by Bismarck in the 1880s. Social support services are less developed than those covered by social insurance and are provided mainly under the means-tested social assistance system. Plans for older people are formulated at federal, state and municipal levels. During the 1980s care in the community policy was emphasised. Chancellor Kohl's policy of change (*Wendepolitik*) in 1982 included the strong promotion of self-help (Mangen, 1991: 111).

In 1984 the social assistance law gave community services priority over care in institutions. In 1988 the reform of health services act (*Gesundheits-reformgesetz*) introduced insurance cover for nursing and housekeeping for people heavily dependent on care, who had previously been excluded from statutory health insurance. These reforms, implemented in 1991, however, did not solve the basic problem of poor provision for dependent people with long-term care needs not covered by the medical insurance and care systems. Long-term care insurance had been under discussion for many years; in June 1992 the government legislated for compulsory care insurance to be introduced in 1995–6.

Italy's welfare state is also considered 'conservative–corporatist' by Esping-Andersen (1990); it has a social insurance system, and has been strongly influenced by the Catholic church and the principle of subsidiarity. The high reliance on family care and the church, particularly in the south and other areas poorly covered by services, leads Leibfried (1993) to see in Italy elements of the 'rudimentary' welfare state of Europe's Mediterranean rim. There were incremental moves towards a more 'social democratic' model in the 1970s, with radical reforms to welfare services, influenced by working class movements. Universal services were introduced, including a national health service from 1978 and a generous pension system; responsibilities were decentralised to the regions and local authorities. The national health service aimed to provide integrated decentralised health services organised by local health units. These reforms, however, were not fully implemented in practice. During the 1980s there was increasing use of the commercial and non-profit sectors, cooperatives and volunteers in the provision of social welfare.

Stated policy on care for older people since the 1970s emphasised social integration and preventive services to delay or avoid admission to residential care. Since the late 1980s, however, developments in institutional care and the building of new residential homes were planned and financed (Bianchi, 1991: 111). Home care services, including nursing, home help and social care, developed slowly and unevenly under the social services system, the responsibility of local authorities. Reforms to the social services under Law 142, 1990, allowed for wider scope for the market and non-profit sector; the reform of the national health service under Law 421 and Decree 502, 1992, to be implemented from 1995, introduced an internal market to the health care system (Saraceno and Negri, 1994).

The Netherlands, often compared with Sweden, is considered a 'social democratic' welfare regime, with high social spending. It developed a generous social security system and comprehensive universal welfare services, in spite of dominance by Christian democratic politics more likely to produce the 'conservative–corporatist' type of welfare (van Kersbergen and Becker, 1988). Elements of both the social insurance model, favoured by Christian democrats, and the universal model, advocated by social democrats, were implemented (Roebroek, 1989). The system derived from traditional 'pillarisation': vertical divisions of society, between Catholics and Protestants, socialists and liberals, with their own organisations and political parties. A process of 'de-pillarisation' since the end of the 1960s has, however, partly broken down these divisions. The influence of the churches, applying the subsidiarity principle, ensured that responsibility for welfare remained with the family, church and the pluralist system of non-state organisations, based on traditional divisions.

Since the second world war the Netherlands has had a higher proportion of older people living in institutions than other European countries. In the late 1960s policy moved towards community care with support services in people's own homes. During the 1980s there was increased concern over the coordination of health and welfare services, and since 1983 there has been greater emphasis on reducing the proportion of older people in institutional care. The key principle became 'substitution' of community care for institutional care and less formal for more technical services.

By the late 1980s the welfare system was becoming more selective, influenced by New Right views. Reforms to the health insurance system, based on the Dekker Report (1987) and Simons Plan, were proposed. These would cover a wide range of care services and increase the role of the market. Measures were to be phased in from 1991–5; following a change of government, however, many of the Dekker/Simons proposals were not implemented. The report of the Welschen Committee, set up in 1993 to advise on care for older people, proposed a new structure for dividing the costs of health care and housing (*Commissie Modernisering Ouderenzorg*, 1994).

The *United Kingdom* is the most difficult of the six countries to classify in Esping-Andersen's typology because its welfare system has elements of both the universal social democratic type and the selective liberal type in 'unstable combination' (Taylor-Gooby, 1991: 96). Esping-Andersen (1990: 33) sees the UK as tending to the liberal type, exemplified by the US and other Anglo-Saxon countries, where Protestant and other religious groups resisted the expansion of state welfare. The UK is classified as 'low social spending' '*welfare* capitalist' by Jones (1985: 82). The universal system envisaged by Beveridge was never funded on a generous level and elements of selectivity have increasingly been introduced.

Government reports began to advocate community care policies for older people in the late 1950s. The aim was to provide care by health and welfare workers in people's own homes rather than in institutions. By the early 1980s the emphasis had changed to care *by* the community, that is by unpaid carers, usually female relatives (Finch and Groves, 1980). During the 1980s government reports focused on management, coordination and funding problems in the care systems. The Griffiths review (1988) proposed reforms to the system, taken up in the policy paper *Caring for people* (HMSO, 1989a) and the National Health Service and Community Care Act 1990.

The reformed community care system was implemented in stages from 1991 to 1993. Influenced by New Right ideas, it was intended to develop the mixed economy of care by extending the roles of the market, non-profit organisations and informal sectors, while reducing the state's role in direct service provision. The local authority was given responsibilities for planning, coordination and regulation of the system, and a new funding system was introduced to limit state financial support for residential care. The reformed system was intended to make services more responsive to individual assessed needs and increase choice, and, in effect, to encourage 'substitution' of community for institutional care and informal for formal types of provision (Davies, 1991: 2).

The *United States of America* is a prime example of the 'liberal' or 'residual' welfare state, relying on the market and family, with means-tested assistance as a last resort. In Jones' model (1985: 82) it is a 'low social spending' 'welfare *capitalist*' type. The central state plays a minimal role as the constitution limits government intervention; in the federal system individual states have much autonomy. Many different religious, ethnic, professional and other interest groups are influential and have an interest in limiting the role of the state, whereas there has been little involvement of working class movements (Higgins, 1981). The voluntary sector and self-help groups have played an important role in service provision. Age related interest groups have more influence in the US than in Europe, and have successfully lobbied for improvements to care systems.

Care services for older people are provided mainly through medical agencies and funding such as Medicare and Medicaid, rather than social agencies. There is no national long-term care programme or funding system for community care services. Individual states have their own community care policies; there is great diversity in levels and types of provision. During the 1980s there was much research on and innovation in community care services, for example the introduction of case management. The Reagan administration, however, sought to reduce the federal role in the government of social welfare, to encourage the use of the for-profit sector in health and social care, and to promote family care. The Federal government attempted to expand Medicare to cover long-term care through the Medicare Catastrophic Coverage Act 1988, to be financed through income tax. Pressure from higher income older people led to the repeal of the act. The Pepper Commission (1990) report on long-term care reform proposed expanded funding for nursing home care and home health care. Further legislation to expand Medicare to help cover long-term care costs in the community and in nursing homes was introduced in 1990 (Waxman, 1990). In 1993 the Clinton administration put forward a health care reform plan to insure all citizens for a package of minimum health care benefits. Attempts to legislate for a health care reform plan, however, proved unsuccessful in 1994.

Origins, substance and outcomes of community care policies: framework for analysis

The preceding overview of the economic, political and ideological context and influences on community care policies has identified the main issues to be addressed in this book. As a basis for analysis of the different aspects of community care in the subsequent chapters, these issues are now summarised, using the framework of three key components of social policy: origins, substance and outcomes (Ginsburg, 1992).

Origins

The origins element examines the various determinants of welfare and community care policies and services. First, in the context of different welfare state regime types the development of policies on particular aspects of care for older people is examined. Second, the changing economic, demographic, political, ideological and cultural influences on these policies are identified and explored. Third, consideration is given to the levels of government at which such policies are made. Fourth, the principles, values and assumptions on which policies are based, the reasons for these assumptions and the extent to which they are explicit or implicit are identified. For example, there are questions about the influence of principles such as subsidiarity, the prevalence of 'humanitarian' or 'organisational' aims in stated policies, assumptions about the dependence of older people, or the role of the family and availability of unpaid carers. On the basis of the comparison of all these factors it may be possible to suggest explanations for the difference between countries in care policies and systems.

Substance

The substance questions consider the ways in which the components of community care are provided, funded and organised. In examining the practice of community care it must be recognised that the stated policies are not necessarily those that are implemented at different levels, whether central, regional or local. First, the various services and benefits that contribute to a particular component of care, such as housing or home care are identified. Second, the settings in which such services are offered are examined. Third, the balance of the welfare mix in terms of the sectors responsible for service provision, and the levels at which responsibilities are vested are considered. Fourth, the financers and funding sources for each service are identified. Fifth, the organisational and procedural aspects of the care systems, such as arrangements for coordination between the sectors in the welfare mix, and linkages between community-based care and long-term care in general and other structures relevant to older people's lives are discussed. Developments in the patterns of care provision in different countries resulting from changing policies, influences and principles are examined.

Outcomes

The outcomes element attempts to identify the implications and impact of policies and systems for different groups of older people and their carers. Again it must be recognised that the outcomes may not be those intended by policymakers, and, further, that outcomes may be the result of government inaction rather than explicit policy in relation to different groups.

First, the impact and appropriateness of policies for people of different gender, 'race', socio-economic class, age, different geographical areas, and types of area such as rural or urban are assessed. Second, issues concerning access to services are explored, for example access to information and to referral and assessment systems, and the costs of access to different types of care. Third, the rights and responsibilities of the service users and carers, and the extent of choice and participation in services experienced by different groups are considered. Fourth, outcomes arising from the systems of provision and funding, for example those that result from professional and organisational fragmentation and lack of coordination, or from the dominance of the medical model rather than social care, are identified. This enables an assessment to be made as to whether issues concerning outcomes are affected by changes in patterns of services discussed above, for example the extent to which trends to more pluralistic forms of provision increase inequalities of access, as suggested by Baldock and Evers (1992: 306).

This framework for analysis, summarised in Table 1.3, attempts to be comprehensive. It must be recognised from the outset that it is unlikely that all of the questions can be addressed for each component of community care. There is as yet inadequate comparative research on this topic and other studies have found that many of the data required are not available. For example Doty (1988), in her comparison of long-term care in 18 countries, found that although statistics on rates of institutionalisation were collected systematically, it was more difficult to obtain data on community-based non-medical services. Ginsburg found a lack of comparative data on class, 'race' and gender in relation to the aims and outcomes of social policy, and describes the information available as 'pinpricks of light' (Ginsburg, 1992: 1). He points out that statistics collected, for example by OECD, rarely include such variables in their analysis.

Approaches and structure of the book

Since mainstream perspectives on social policy have neglected issues concerning gender, 'race' and age, the book takes a critical approach. It takes account of social divisions by class, gender and 'race' which are particularly relevant to community care, affecting access to care resources for different groups of older people and influencing their experiences of ageing. For example gender divisions in the labour market and in welfare policies have implications for older women needing care, for women as low status workers in welfare services, and for those female relatives who are expected to provide unpaid care.

The tendency towards more pluralistic provision and dual welfare services, based on private provision and insurance rights for wealthier older people and lower status means-tested assistance for poor people and marginalised groups, may perpetuate social divisions. Without the care services, however, the inequalities would be greater, as Ginsburg (1992: 2) points out in stressing the 'contradictory nature of the welfare state in both mitigating and furthering social inequalities and divisions'.

Whilst highlighting such effects of community care policies, the book provides a background understanding of the policies and procedures of various components of care systems in the selected countries, taking a comparative approach to each topic. Chapter 2 examines pensions, social security and health insurance systems and their links with health care, social care and the funding of community care services. Chapter 3 considers various housing options and living arrangements for older

Table 1.3 *Framework for analysis of origins, substance and outcomes of community care*

> *Origins*
> 1 Development of policies
> 2 Influences on policies
> 3 Levels of policy making
> 4 Principles, values and assumptions

> *Substance*
> 1 Services and benefits provided
> 2 Settings in which services provided
> 3 Sectors responsible for provision
> 4 Funding sources
> 5 Organisation, procedure, coordination

> *Outcomes*
> 1 Impact of policies for different
>   groups/areas
> 2 Differences in access to services
> 3 Rights and responsibilities, choice
>   and participation of users and carers
> 4 Outcomes arising from systems of
>   provision/funding

people. In chapter 4 health and social care offered by formal and informal carers to people in their homes is reviewed. Chapter 5 turns to health services provided outside the home in health centres, clinics and hospitals. Day care, leisure and educational services outside the home are considered in chapter 6. Chapter 7 examines the issues concerning coordination of all these services and developments in arrangements for designing packages of care for individuals. Chapter 8 provides a summary of the main themes and conclusions on the key areas of origins, substance and outcomes of community care policies.

Note: 'Race' is in inverted commas because this is a conventional way in social policy literature of avoiding biological connotations in this term.

2
Financing of Services and Benefits

Financial considerations are fundamental to questions on the origins, substance and outcomes of care systems under different welfare regime types. Where service provision is concerned, the level of resources and the sources and methods of funding all affect the structures of the systems and the quantity and quality of services. For individual dependent older people access to financial resources such as pensions, benefits and capital affects need for and access to other care services. Financial incentives within the systems, for example those that encourage use of medical rather than social care, influence which caring systems are used and the type of services received.

This chapter sets the background to these crucial issues, examining first the development of policies on welfare finance in general, focusing on the main pensions and health care systems and the principles on which they are based. It then outlines the bases on which the main components of community care are funded in the countries studied. In the final part of the chapter the implications of these funding systems for the outcomes of services for different groups of older people are discussed.

Background to current welfare funding systems

Development of welfare finance policies

Three welfare state regime types identified by Esping-Andersen (1990) were discussed in chapter 1: the 'conservative–corporatist', 'liberal' and 'social democratic' types. Broadly corresponding to these welfare regimes, Esping-Andersen identified three 'pension regimes' from analyses of data on the mix of public and private pensions in OECD countries.

First, 'corporative state-dominated insurance' systems, for example that of Germany, emphasised preserving status relations through 'highly occupationally segregated' social security, special privileges for civil servants and a marginal role for the private market. Second, in 'residualist' systems such as that of the US, a higher proportion of total pension expenditure was on private market pensions than in other systems. Third, in 'universalistic state-dominated systems', 'population-wide social rights took precedence', for example in countries such as Sweden. The UK was a 'mixed case' in which an overall pattern was not established. (Esping-Andersen, 1990: 85–7).

The pensions systems of France, Germany and Italy could thus be broadly categorised as 'corporative state-dominated'. They have statutory earnings-related pensions insurance schemes, with privileged systems for civil servants. France and Germany have different types of health insurance scheme, whereas a system of occupational insurance funds in Italy was replaced in 1978 by a national health service (*Servizio Sanitario Nazionale*, SSN).

The US, with a 'residualist' pension regime, has federal statutory earnings-related pensions insurance. The relatively low pensions provided under this state social security system are supplemented by a wide range of private pension plans. Private health insurance is the main system of health care funding, while for the over-65s Medicare provides health insurance for some services.

The Netherlands, which tends towards the 'universalist state-dominated' pension regime, has a national insurance system with basic flat rate pensions for all residents. Supplementary occupational pension schemes are compulsory in many industries, voluntary in others. The social insurance system provides compulsory health insurance for people below a fixed income limit; those not covered take up voluntary health insurance.

The UK's pension system is atypical because it has elements of both the 'universalistic' and the 'residualist'. There is a national insurance basic flat rate pension, and a supplementary state earnings-related pension scheme (SERPS), introduced in 1978, which is compulsory, but from which people may contract out in favour of an occupational or private pension scheme. The level of the pension, even with the small supplement, is low. There is a national health service (NHS).

Since the pensions and health care to which people are entitled through these main social security and social insurance systems do not cover the whole population, all six countries have, to some extent, dual welfare systems in which there are also more stigmatised social assistance schemes. Such means-tested, discretionary assistance is for poorer people and marginalised groups who have a weaker relationship to the labour market than the core workers who are strongly protected by social insurance. In some countries the insurance/assistance divide is stronger than in others, and in some cases the balance has changed in response to recent economic, political and ideological trends.

During the period of expansion of welfare states from around 1950 to the mid 1970s public expenditure on welfare services in West European and North American countries increased in a context of economic growth, low inflation and high employment. The economic crises of the 1970s following the 1973 oil crisis engendered attempts to curtail welfare expenditure when public sector deficits arose as expenditure continued to increase more quickly than economic growth and tax revenues. In countries influenced by New Right ideology public expenditure cuts were also pursued as part of the overall objective of reducing the state's role in welfare. Attempts to restrict public expenditure were made particularly in the high spending areas of pensions and health care.

The main strategies used to control pensions expenditure were tightening eligibility criteria and restricting the level of upratings. For example, in Germany the pension formula was modified in 1977, and changes in 1981, 1982 and 1983 reduced entitlement to pensions (Alber, 1986). Similarly in Italy there were restrictions to the indexing of pensions in 1978 and restrictions in entitlements to minimum pensions in 1981 and 1983 (Ferrera, 1986). From 1980 pensions in the UK were uprated in line with prices rather than earnings, and in 1986 changes in eligibility criteria weakened SERPS, whereas private personal pensions were promoted.

Attempts to contain expenditure on health care included controlling supply side costs through cash limits or restricted lists of prescription drugs, and restricting demand, for example by increasing charges to patients. In Germany the 'concerted action' (*Konzertierte Aktion*) strategy introduced in 1977 attempted to limit fees charged by doctors to insurance companies by linking these negotiated fees to earnings levels; prescription charges were increased in 1977, 1981 and 1982 and patient charges for hospital care were introduced in 1982 (Alber, 1986). In Italy prescription charges were introduced in 1978 and increased along with other health service charges in 1981, 1982 and 1983 (Ferrera, 1986). Similarly in the UK prescription charges and other patient payments such as dental charges were increased considerably during the 1980s.

However, as shown in Table 2.1, total health expenditure as a proportion of gross domestic product continued to increase in the six countries during the 1970s; it also rose during the 1980s, although at a slower rate, except in Germany.

Most analyses of attempts to control public expenditure from the mid 1970s to the mid 1980s suggest that although the rate of increase was reduced, a gradual increase in aggregate public spending continued, partly in response to rising numbers of unemployed people, pensioners, lone parents and so on. Despite New Right rhetoric, welfare states were not dismantled during this time; it was a period of consolidation rather than retrenchment (Alber, 1986; Morris, 1988; Mishra, 1990). However, the cumulative effect of small incremental changes has been to erode some of the basic welfare state services, for example in the UK and US (Mishra, 1990).

Another aspect of the 'post-crisis' rethinking of welfare state policies was the trend towards welfare pluralism, reducing the role of the state in welfare provision and increasing the roles of the market, non-profit organisations and the informal sector. The implication of this trend for the financing of services was that, on the whole, the state continued to fund services by reallocating resources to other service providers. In the case of privatisation and decentralisation of services, however, another effect was that central state funding was withdrawn or reduced, leaving the individual or family, local agencies or charities to bear the costs. As

Table 2.1   *Total expenditure on health as a percentage of GDP*

	France	Germany[a]	Italy	Netherlands	United Kingdom	United States
1970	5.8	5.9	5.2	6.0	4.5	7.4
1980	7.6	8.4	6.9	8.0	5.8	9.2
1985	8.5	8.7	7.0	8.0	6.0	10.5
1990	8.8	8.3	8.1	8.2	6.2	12.4
1991	9.1	8.5	8.3	8.3	6.6	13.4
Average annual growth rate (%)						
1970–80	2.64	3.65	2.86	2.99	2.52	2.31
1980–90	1.56	−0.11	1.65	0.15	0.72	2.95

[a] former FRG.
© OECD, 1993. OECD Health Data Version 1.5. Reproduced by permission of the OECD.

Mishra (1990: 111) points out, reducing the state's role in service provision is not merely a question of 'rearranging the division of labour in social welfare' but means that people may no longer be entitled to services, if the state does not ensure that non-state sectors are able to deliver or pay for services.

Although welfare state expenditure continued to increase in the 1980s, there was a tendency towards more selectivity in services which became more targeted to people on low incomes or those most dependent on care. Further, changing employment patterns mean that fewer people are in regular long-term employment and entitled to insurance benefits. Those on the periphery of the labour market are thus more dependent on means-tested assistance systems, whereas core workers are covered by social insurance and also better able to afford private insurance and provision in the more pluralist systems (Chamberlayne, 1991/92). Selective services are also more likely than universal ones to be cut back because it is more politically acceptable to reduce stigmatised services that do not benefit the majority; Mishra (1990: 42) therefore suggests that there has been 'differential retrenchment of the welfare state'. This trend leads to an increasing emphasis on dual welfare and a stronger divide between insurance and assistance systems.

The measures taken to contain expenditure on pensions and health care in the 1980s had limited success. Health care costs continued to increase, for example in Germany despite the 'concerted action', and in the US in spite of the Reagan and Bush administrations' policies to control health care costs. Discussion on costs of pensions, health and social care for older people continued and policies were formulated for major reforms in the 1990s designed mainly to control public expenditure. The world economic recession of the early 1990s led to further reviews of welfare services and cuts in welfare funding to reduce public deficits in all six countries. In Germany the costs of 1990 unification also had far-reaching implications for the level of funding available for welfare services.

The main issues addressed in the late 1980s and early 1990s concerning financing care for older people were: paying for pensions, health and social care, and developing the mixed economy of care.

In most industrial countries the ratio of over-65s to younger adults is projected to rise substantially, as shown in Table 2.2. This is of particular concern in Germany. Funding state pensions for this rising proportion of pensioners would entail large increases in contribution rates, reducing pension levels, or other solutions such as raising statutory retirement age or privatising pensions. The German pension reform act

Table 2.2 *Projected increase in ratio of over 65 age group to 15–64 age group, 1990–2025*

	France	Germany[a]	Italy	Netherlands	United Kingdom	United States
1990	20.9	22.1	20.7	18.4	23.5	19.1
2010	23.8	31.2	28.3	22.3	23.7	20.0
2025	33.5	39.0	35.6	33.7	30.7	31.7

[a] former FRG.
Source: United Nations, 1991.

1989 (*Rentenreformgesetz*), to be implemented from 1992–2006, aimed to reduce the dependence ratio by gradually raising pension age and levelling out increases. In Italy there were proposals in the 1980s to introduce private pensions insurance and reduce reliance on the state scheme. The pension reform approved in 1992 attempted to produce a more equitable system and reduce generous pensions for civil servants by gradually increasing the number of years of contributions for civil servants to 35 (Florea et al., 1993; Saraceno and Negri, 1994). In the US privatisation was encouraged, for example by tax incentives for individual retirement accounts (IRAs), and in 1988 incentives were given in the UK for people to take up personal private pensions and opt out of SERPS. However, in spite of the predominance of cost containment measures, countries such as France, Germany and Italy also widened their pension coverage (Walker, 1993).

The financing of long-term social care for increasing numbers of older people with chronic health problems or disabilities posed difficulties in most countries where existing systems did not cover this risk (Laing, 1993). It was a topic of much discussion and research in the 1980s in the US where there is no federal long-term care policy or funding system. The welfare state services established in Western Europe in the post 1945 decades were largely based on the medical model, providing acute care, insuring workers against short-term interruptions to work, rather than catering for long-term disability or large numbers of people with weak attachments to labour markets.

The failure of mainstream systems to cover such groups meant increasing pressure on the budgets of safety net social assistance schemes. Insurance for long-term care was therefore discussed, particularly in countries with health insurance systems such as Germany, as a way of removing large groups of dependent people from social assistance and reducing public expenditure on such benefits. Long-term care insurance in Germany to be implemented in 1995–6 will integrate care insurance with sickness insurance under the same funds (Alber, 1993: 122). In the Netherlands there was an important debate about care insurance following the Dekker report (1987), but many of the proposals were not implemented. Another approach to resolving the difficulties of funding and providing services for older people in all six countries is to promote welfare pluralism.

Privatisation of previously state-provided services by developing the use of private markets, the voluntary non-profit and informal sectors became a preferred policy option in the provision of health and social care services in the 1980s. Private markets in health care were introduced or encouraged in countries with national health services such as Italy and the UK. Thus market criteria were introduced and social care services reviewed with the aim of increasing cost effectiveness. For example the UK Griffiths review of community care was commissioned to look at 'the way in which public funds are used to support community care policy and to advise on options for action that would improve the use of these funds' (Griffiths, 1988: iii). Similarly the Dekker review in the Netherlands was 'to advise on "strategies for volume and costs containment against the background of an ageing population"' (Baldock and Evers, 1992: 295).

Reviews and reforms of community care in the late 1980s and early 1990s were thus largely a question not of providing new forms of care but, as Baldock and Evers (1992: 304) point out 'new ways of financing and organising the traditional constituents of care'. In Italy, for example, statutory provision of personal social services was reduced and increased use was made of non-profit organisations, self-help groups and volunteers (Ascoli, 1988). One of the six key objectives of the British reforms outlined in *Caring for people* was 'To promote the development of a flourishing independent sector alongside good quality public services' (HMSO, 1989a: 5). The state would be less involved in direct service provision, more concerned with enabling, coordinating and regulating provision by other sectors.

Welfare finance policies: influences and principles

Economic influences were clearly predominant in the decades following the 1973 oil crisis and the end of high economic growth rates which had allowed the expansion of welfare states. From the mid 1970s welfare finance and provision policies were dominated by the need to control public expenditure and reduce public deficits. Older people's welfare services were very relevant in this context since pensions and health care, of which older people are high users, were among the largest items of public expenditure, thus contributing significantly to public deficits. Another major policy concern, identified in a cross-national study of long-term care (Doty, 1988: 145) and influencing community care reforms in many countries, was the high cost of institutional care.

These cost concerns were exacerbated by fears of a demographic crisis as the proportion of over-65s in the population was projected to rise rapidly, as shown in Table 2.3. The projected increase in the oldest age groups, those most likely to need care, was seen as a particular problem. Although increasing numbers of pensioners clearly affect total pensions expenditure, however, OECD analyses show that health care cost increases were significantly related to per capita GDP, but that population ageing had little effect on health expenditure increases in 15 countries between 1960 and 1984 (OECD, 1987).

Economic recession and demographic factors influenced attempts by governments to control the level of welfare expenditure and to develop different forms and methods of funding. Such policy developments were further influenced by political and ideological factors determining the theoretical and philosophical bases of funding and service provision policies. The dominant influence in the late 1970s and 1980s was that of the New Right, although other political perspectives were important to varying degrees in different countries, for example the centre left in relation to pensions and health care reforms in Italy in the 1970s, and the socialist presidency of Mitterrand in France in the early 1980s.

The New Right, or neo-liberals, for example in Germany, the UK and the US, aimed to reduce the role of government in welfare spending and

Table 2.3 *Projected increase in percentage of over 65s in populations,*
1990–2025

	France	Germany[a]	Italy	Netherlands	United Kingdom	United States
1990	13.8	15.4	14.3	12.7	15.4	12.6
2010	15.7	20.4	18.7	15.2	15.7	13.6
2025	20.8	24.1	22.8	21.3	19.4	19.8

[a] former FRG.
Source: United Nations, 1991.

provision and promote individual responsibility and the distribution of welfare resources through market forces. These goals were pursued, by parties of the New Right and others who shared these views, by attempting to contain public expenditure and by shifting responsibilities to non-state sectors in the mixed economy of welfare. In the process economic and market criteria were introduced to areas previously guided by social criteria (Baldock and Evers, 1992: 292). The pervasive influence of such ideological perspectives has led to widespread acceptance in Western Europe and North America of the policies and practices of welfare pluralism (Evers, 1993).

One of the main patterns of change in welfare systems identified by Baldock and Evers (1992: 291) is the move from 'separate to integrated social and economic criteria'. This pattern entails changing emphases in the principles on which funding policies are based. Post-1945 welfare state services tended to operate under social principles such as equity, equality and vertical redistribution of resources. Individual need was addressed without much prior attention to costs; rationing devices used were implicit. In the 1970s and 1980s funding policy moved much more towards economic principles and concern with costs to society. Thus in the reformed systems of the 1990s the underlying economic principle is cost efficiency. Cost limits are imposed, rationing devices explicit, and efficiency sought through market principles of competition and choice. Social principles such as equity and minimum standards may only be ensured through state regulation of the systems (Baldock and Evers, 1992).

As part of the cost control imperative most West European and North American countries are implementing community care systems aiming to reduce reliance on costly institutional care by operating the principle of substitution of less institutional, lower cost forms of care. This implies shifting funds from institutional and acute forms of provision to domiciliary and community services for people with chronic illnesses and disabilities.

The introduction of care insurance reflects a trend towards the principle of individual and family responsibility rather than dependence on state provision. For example, Griffiths (1988) expects individuals in future to plan provision for their own community care needs. In countries such as France, Germany and Italy, under the principle of subsidiarity children are legally obliged, in some cases, to contribute financially (after income assessment) for the care of parents who depend on means-tested social assistance, for example to pay for long-term care (Glendinning and McLaughlin, 1993).

The new care insurance system in Germany is designed to take people needing care out of the assistance system into provision through insurance (Chamberlayne, 1991/92). Reinforcement of the principle of individual responsibility, as in Germany through such care insurance, increases emphasis on the insurance/assistance divide and dual welfare provision. Those who are able to insure themselves or have family support will receive the mainstream services to which they are entitled, whereas those unable to provide for themselves will still have to resort to increasingly residual, stigmatised services funded through state social assistance systems.

Funding of main components of community care

As social security programmes are inevitably complex and constantly changing, extensive coverage of technical details is not attempted in the basic outline of the main systems below. There are also many related benefits or minor schemes, such as allowances for housing and heating costs, subsidised food and meals, which are covered in the relevant chapters. The main income maintenance systems for those over pensionable age, that is state, occupational and private pensions, and social assistance, in the different types of welfare/pension regime are examined first. These systems are based on the assumption that married women's pensions are dependent on their husbands' contributions; the implications for women of such systems are discussed later in the chapter. For unemployed disabled people under pensionable age disability or invalidity benefits were increasingly used in most West European countries in the 1980s and 1990s. The growth in early retirement and/or redundancy since the 1970s also affected social security systems and the incomes in later life of the individuals concerned. In the second part of this section, the funding of health and social care is considered, covering hospital and ambulatory (non-hospital) health care, and financing through benefits and services of long-term and social care in institutions or in people's own homes.

The overall level of support from the combined effects of these benefits and services is assessed in the final section of the chapter. Outcomes of the funding systems are determined not simply by the level of and access to pensions but also by the other free or subsidised benefits and services available, the proportion of people receiving more than the minimum, and the benefit derived from earnings-related pensions by particular groups.

Old age and retirement pensions and social assistance

The *French* social security system is based on the principle of solidarity. The main system, which is compulsory and covers about 70 per cent of employees, comprises a general scheme (*régime général*) and complementary schemes (*régimes complémentaires*); special social security systems cover public employees, self-employed people and other groups (OECD, 1988b). There is a guaranteed minimum income for over 60s (*minimum vieillesse*): the national solidarity fund (*Fonds National de Solidarité*, FNS) supplements incomes from other pensions and benefits up to a minimum level. Voluntary private supplementary schemes play a minor part in French pension provision.

Pension systems are funded by current earnings-related contributions from employees and employers. The government largely subsidises the minimum income, the public employees' system and other special schemes (OECD, 1988b). The systems are administered through regional and local branches of social insurance funds (*caisses*). Full old age pension is paid at age 60 for those with 37.5 years' contributions, reduced proportionately for shorter contribution records, and calculated from average earnings in the best ten years. This provides a total pension from general and complementary schemes of around 70 per cent of average earnings; widow(er)s' pensions comprise 52 per cent of the deceased pensioner's entitlement. Pensions are adjusted twice a year in line with national average wages (OECD, 1988b). Pension funding reform has been under discussion for a decade (Walker, 1993).

Since most over-60s receive an old age or survivor's pension or *minimum vieillesse*, the social assistance system plays a minor role. People aged over 65, or over 60 if unable to work, are entitled to apply for means-tested social assistance (*aide sociale*) administered by the *département* and the commune's social welfare office (*Centre Communal d'Action Sociale*, CCAS), which provides help in cash and services; under the '*obligation alimentaire*' families are in some cases responsible for contributing towards some categories of assistance to their older relatives (Glendinning and McLaughlin, 1993: 77–8).

Unlike the French two-tier system, *German* statutory earnings-related pensions insurance is integrated into one tier. The general scheme covers all wage and salary earners and there are separate funds for miners, farmers and self-employed people, and a non-contributory scheme for civil servants. People not compulsorily covered may pay voluntarily into the social insurance system. The scheme is being introduced gradually in the new states, with the aim of equalising eastern and western pensions by 1997. The compulsory pensions system is regulated by federal and state agencies. Additional voluntary occupational pension schemes play a small but increasing role, mainly for full-time private sector employees (Walker, 1993).

Current earnings-related contributions from employees and employers fund the statutory scheme, with annual state subsidies particularly for miners' and farmers' funds, and large subsidies to implement the system in the new states where pensions under the GDR were funded from general revenues. Private occupational pensions are financed by contributions from employers who receive tax concessions (Walker, 1993). Although statutory pension age is 65, there are provisions for earlier retirement for people with 35 years' contributions, unemployed and disabled people; these provisions will be phased out by 2006 under the 1989 pension reform, leaving an actual pension age of 65 with provision for partial early retirement. The two part pension formula, which provides for a high earnings replacement level, is based on individual average lifetime earnings and related to current gross wages; the formula will be modified under the pension reform. Widow(er)s' pensions amount to 60 per cent of the insured person's pension. Annual pension increases are mainly related to wages (OECD, 1988b).

Since the statutory insurance system covers most of the population, as workers or dependants, social assistance (*Sozialhilfe*) is intended to be a means-tested system of last resort providing financial benefits and services for those with inadequate insurance cover or resources. Children are liable to maintain parents who have recourse to social assistance; children's incomes are assessed according to regulations.

The *Italian* state earnings-related pensions system has a compulsory insurance scheme for all private sector employees and separate schemes for civil servants, self-employed people and professional groups. For the over-65s on low incomes with no other source of benefits there are means-tested social pensions (OECD, 1988b.) Most pensions are administered through the National Institute for Social Insurance (INPS). Private supplementary pensions have played a minor role but are being expanded mainly by private sector employers (Walker, 1993).

Statutory pensions are funded by earnings-related contributions from employees and employers, and flat rate annual contributions from self-employed people. The state funds social pensions, subsidises pensions for self-employed people, and partly supplements insurance pensions up to a minimum level, higher than social pensions, for those with inadequate contributions. The statutory pension age, which is being revised, is 60 for men and 55 for women (Eurostat, 1993). The pension is calculated from the final five years' earnings and replaces up to 80 per cent of previous earnings. Pensions are indexed to the cost of living and minimum wage and adjusted annually. There are proposals for restricting this generous scheme by gradually increasing pension age to 65 for men and women and reducing early retirement provisions (Walker, 1993). Under the 1992 pension reforms the level of pension will be calculated on earnings during the whole working life (Saraceno and Negri, 1994).

The Italian social insurance system, like those in France and Germany, is intended to provide wide coverage for income maintenance in old age, while the social assistance scheme is to play a minor role. Means-tested social assistance, funded by general revenues, is the responsibility of the commune, working through a regional and central government legislative framework (Ferrera, 1989a).

The pension system in the *Netherlands*, unlike those of the previous three countries, provides compulsory universal basic flat rate old age and survivors' pensions through national insurance, contributions for which are collected through the income tax system. Civil servants have a special system which supplements basic pension according to earnings and years of service. Over 80 per cent of employees in the private sector are covered by occupational schemes which provide earnings-related supplementary pensions. Some of these schemes are voluntary, others compulsory; they cover whole industries or separate enterprises or professional groups such as doctors (Roebroek, 1989).

The statutory pensions scheme, under the General Old Age Pensions Act (AOW) (1957), is funded by earnings-related contributions from employees only, with state funding for deficits. Employers' and employees' contributions finance occupational schemes, with some state subsidy. The state old age pension is paid from age 65 and adjusted twice a year in line with the net minimum wage; the future continuation of this uprating became the subject of political debate in the early 1990s. Married men and women are each separately entitled to a pension of 50 per cent of net minimum wage, whereas single pensioners and widows receive 70 per cent of this minimum wage. The system is implemented through 22 labour councils, overseen by the Social Insurance Bank (Roebroek, 1989).

As the flat rate universal pension is set at a higher rate than social assistance (*sociale bijstand*), the over-65s should not normally need to apply to this source for income maintenance. However, those under 65 who are not eligible for disability or other benefits may apply through the municipal social services department for means-tested assistance under the Social Assistance Act (ABW) (1963), which is funded from general revenues, 90 per cent from central government and 10 per cent from municipal government (Roebroek, 1989).

The *United Kingdom*'s national insurance (NI) retirement system is residual in that it provides a minimal pension, but the flat-rate basic pension is universal for all who qualify through their contribution record. The UK's compulsory state pension is two-tier; SERPS provides a small earnings-related supplement to the basic pension. There is provision for contracting out of SERPS into an occupational or personal private pension scheme. The state scheme was designed to provide a basic pension, allowing people to supplement their retirement income from private pensions. The private occupational pension sector is the largest in Europe (Ginn and Arber, 1992), and there is a growing market in personal pension plans, encouraged by government incentives.

The NI pension is funded by current earnings-related contributions from employees and employers and by state subsidies. Retirement pension is paid at 65 for men and 60 for women; the pension age is to be equalised at 65 for men and women. The amount of pension received is based on contribution records. The SERPS scheme is not yet mature. When introduced in 1978 it was to be based on the best 20 years' earnings and replace up to 25 per cent of earnings; under the Social Security Act 1986 the basis will be modified to lifetime earnings and replacement of 20 per cent of earnings. Private occupational pensions are funded by employers' and employees' contributions; there are income tax allowances for pension contributions.

NI retirement pension is below the level of social assistance (income support, IS). Thus people who mainly depend on NI pension, or do not qualify for full NI pension, have to apply for means-tested IS to bring their income up to a set level, which consists of a basic weekly allowance plus a premium for pensioners and higher premiums at ages 75 and 80. IS is a national non-contributory benefit, funded from general revenues.

In the 'residual' pension regime of the *United States* there is a compulsory federal social security system providing earnings-related insurance benefits for retired people, survivors and disabled people under the Social Security Act (1935) (Old Age, Survivors and Disability Insurance, OASDI). Supplementary company pensions are widely used to increase retirement income and individual retirement accounts (IRAs) are also used by higher income groups, encouraged by tax incentives. There is thus state pension insurance for all workers and their dependants, but as the pension level is fairly low, the private sector, through private occupational pensions and individual investments, plays a larger role than in other types of welfare regime (Esping-Andersen, 1990).

The social security system is funded by earnings-related contributions from employers, employees and self-employed people. People with incomes above set levels pay tax on up to 50 per cent of their social security benefits; these taxes contribute to financing the social security programme. Private pensions are funded by employers and in some schemes by contributions from employees. Retirement benefit, based on contributions paid, is received at 65. The pension formula provides for about 41 per cent of pre-retirement earnings for people on average lifetime earnings, 59 per cent and 27 per cent respectively for people on minimum and maximum earnings. Benefits receive an annual cost of living adjustment (OECD, 1988b). The statutory pension age is to be increased in stages to 67 by 2027 and benefits for early retirement will also be reduced (Petersen, 1991).

The federal social security system also provides a means-tested supplemental security income (SSI) for people who are over 65, or disabled or blind and unable to earn a living. SSI supplements other income and benefits up to a set level, is non-contributory, funded from general revenues and administered through local social security offices. Individual states may further supplement the person's income.

The amount of statutory pension received by individuals in all the above countries except the Netherlands is determined by their contribution records, as is the case with all the supplementary pension schemes. As discussed further below, this means that women are more likely to depend on husbands' contributions than to receive pensions in their own right, and are less likely than men to benefit from the generous earnings-related systems of France, Germany and Italy.

Health and social care

To set the context for detailed discussion of the care systems in subsequent chapters, major features of basic health and social care funding systems are summarised. The extent to which there is division between medical and social funding is a crucial issue affecting people whose needs span both types of care.

France's health system is based on the social insurance model with compulsory health insurance through social security, funded by contributions from employers and employees. For many services there is cost-sharing by patients who pay for treatment, prescriptions or consultation with general or specialist practitioners, then are reimbursed a proportion of the costs by social security (OECD, 1987). Means-tested assistance (*aide médicale*) through the social assistance system meets the costs of low income people unable to pay medical expenses. Costs of expensive or long-stay inpatient hospital care are met directly by social security; other patients pay a daily contribution for catering costs; the fund meets the balance of the costs.

Home nursing services are financed by social security or through medical aid. Home help for the over-65s, or over-60s if unable to work, with resources below a set limit is funded for a limited number of hours per month through the social assistance system; those on higher incomes may apply to social security and their supplementary pension funds for assistance with home help costs. The user pays part of the costs. In residential settings with medical care sections (see chapter 3) care costs at a set daily rate are met by health insurance, while board costs are paid from the individual's pensions and benefits, or through social assistance, subject to assessment (Henrard and Brocas, 1990). A proposed dependence insurance allowance to meet care costs across the medical/social divide is under discussion (Boulard, 1991; Glendinning and McLaughlin, 1993: 80–1).

Germany also has the social insurance model. Insurance is compulsory for everyone earning below a fairly high limit; about 90 per cent of the population is covered through a sickness insurance fund, financed by employers' and employees' contributions. Those with high earnings opt for private insurance, whereas medical fees of uninsured people without resources are met by social assistance. General and specialist practitioners, as independent contractors providing ambulatory care (outside hospital), are reimbursed directly for items of service by the regional association of health insurance doctors on behalf of insurance funds. There are small charges to patients, for example for prescriptions or dental treatment. Hospitals, mainly in the public sector, receive finance from insurance funds for doctors' salaries and other costs; inpatients pay a small daily contribution.

Specialised home nursing is funded by sickness insurance. The sharp divide between medical and social services means that different categories of basic nursing and home help are financed through the insurance and assistance systems for varying periods depending on strict criteria (see chapter 4) (Dieck and Garms-Homolová, 1991). Under the principle of subsidiarity, funding from health insurance must be sought first. Residential home accommodation and care costs are paid by the resident with help from social assistance if necessary; children's incomes are assessed for financial contributions. The heavy burden on municipalities' social assistance budgets will be partly relieved by compulsory care insurance introduced in 1995–6, when care cost elements will be met by insurance (Evers and Olk, 1991: 90).

Italy changed from the social insurance model when the national health service was established in 1978 to provide, in principle, universal coverage for residents. The service is funded mainly by general taxation and employers' contributions, with small contributions from employees. Hospital care is provided free and hospital doctors are salaried. Services from independent general practitioners are also free of charge; GPs receive capitation fees and special allocations. There is a small charge ('ticket') for specialist or diagnostic services from public or private clinics and charges for prescriptions. People on low incomes are exempt from charges (Ferrera, 1989a). Health service charges were increased and criteria tightened by the Finance Act 1992. The health reforms to be implemented in 1995 introduce more formal systems for linking the public sector with the private and voluntary sectors which had grown in the 1980s to meet gaps in the public service. The reforms also enable for-profit activities in public hospitals and an internal market in the health service (Saraceno and Negri, 1994).

Local health units, introduced with the national health service, were in theory responsible for all services including hospitals, home nursing and domiciliary care. Social services provided by the communes were intended to be coordinated with the local health units' services. Since 1985 community and home help services have been excluded from national health financing, are funded by local agencies, and are means-tested (Ascoli, 1988). Care in residential and nursing homes, however, is subsidised by the health service, with contributions from residents or from social assistance for those on low incomes (Alber, 1993). Reforms to local government under Law 142, 1990 are likely to exacerbate the division between health and social services (Saraceno and Negri, 1994: 24).

The health insurance system in the *Netherlands* has several components. Social insurance funded by earnings-related contributions from employers and employees is compulsory for those with incomes below a set level and people on certain benefits (about 70 per cent of the population). Higher earners are insured voluntarily through private insurance. Under the Exceptional Medical Expenses Act (1968) (AWBZ) all residents are insured for long-term care or treatment; funding is mainly through earnings-related contributions from employees. Sickness insurance funds, which administer social insurance, pay for acute hospital care and part of ambulatory care. There are small charges to patients for specialist consultations. Those insured privately pay for services and are reimbursed by insurance companies. Long-stay care in hospitals is funded through AWBZ.

Home nursing and home help are both paid for by AWBZ and users' contributions. Before 1989 home help was financed by central government. AWBZ may also pay for a package of intensive long-term domiciliary care for three months. The costs of nursing home care are met through AWBZ and means-tested contributions from residents' incomes. For residential home care the municipality meets the costs and is reimbursed by residents from their own assets above a limit, or through means-tested assistance funded by central government. The Welschen report recommended merging the separate funding systems for nursing and residential homes under the AWBZ system (*Commissie Modernisering Ouderenzorg*, 1994).

The *United Kingdom* has a national health service (NHS), funded mainly from general taxation, providing comprehensive universal coverage free at the point of use, except where charges are made, for example for dental costs. Pensioners are exempt from prescription charges. There is also increasing use of private health insurance, often funded by employers for professional and managerial staff, to purchase care in the private market. Tax concessions for purchase of private health insurance by the over-60s were introduced in 1990. Under the 1990 NHS reforms the functions of purchasing and providing health care, previously undertaken by district health authorities, were separated. Health authorities and large general practices holding budgets purchase care on a contractual basis from NHS and private providers.

Long-stay hospital care and home nursing provided by the NHS are free to the user, whereas there are means-tested charges for residential care, home care and other social care services purchased by local social services authorities from public and independent sector providers. Since the community care reforms implemented in 1993, social services authorities are responsible for assessing individuals' care needs and arranging purchase of care which may include residential or nursing home care. People living in care homes before April 1993 could claim means-tested income support for help with fees without assessment of care needs; this support is protected for those residents.

The *United States'* health system uses the private insurance model, with insurance purchased through individual and/or employers' contributions (OECD, 1987). There is, however, a federal system of health insurance, Medicare, for the over-65s and some people with disabilities, funded through social security contributions and user payments.

Medicare Part A (hospital insurance) covers limited periods of hospital, nursing home and home health care; Part B (medical insurance) partly covers costs of doctors' fees and other medical services. There are substantial patient charges for Medicare services. Medicare does not cover long-term nursing home care, nor most prescriptions or domiciliary services. Supplementary private insurance is available to cover some Medicare charges and gaps, but not long-term care. Another option is to join a health maintenance organisation (HMO) and pay a monthly premium for costs not paid through Medicare. For people with very low assets and incomes Medicaid, a joint federal/state funded programme, finances hospital and nursing home care and doctors' services; other services are optional, depending on state policy.

With federal permission the state can waive Medicaid requirements and provide community-based services such as personal care and home help. Community care services not covered by Medicare or Medicaid are financed by various federal sources, or provided by state funded programmes designed to prevent nursing home admission. The Veterans Administration (VA) also provides health care and benefits for eligible veterans. Since it is difficult to finance non-medical community care, most long-term care is provided in nursing homes funded by residents or by Medicaid once their incomes and assets have been 'spent down' below the eligibility limits.

In most of the six countries there is thus a divide between the medical, funded by social insurance or national health service, and the social, funded by social assistance or local authorities. The preceding overview of basic features of financing systems for income maintenance, health and social care, is intended to aid understanding of specific policies and services examined in more detail in subsequent chapters. Major implications of these funding systems and their outcomes are discussed below.

Outcomes of current funding systems

As previous cross-national comparisons of social welfare services for older people have emphasised, the scarcity of available systematic research evidence or statistics is clearly an obstacle to the formulation of sound conclusions on the outcomes of welfare services. Discussion of the implications of funding systems can therefore only be exploratory. In attempting to identify the main outcomes of the funding systems in the six countries, the impact of funding policies for different countries, geographical areas and groups of older people is first considered; differential access to benefits and services is then examined. The implications of current welfare systems for the rights and responsibilities of older people and their carers and the extent of choice afforded them are discussed next. Finally, the outcomes resulting from incentives within the systems are examined. The discussion focuses mainly on pensions and benefits and the social insurance/assistance divide, with some reference to health and social care and the medical/social divide, which are explored in greater detail in chapters 4 and 5.

Impact of funding policies

In comparing welfare systems the level of spending on social welfare is widely used as a simple indicator which clearly has some impact on overall outcomes of services, although there are many other influences. The level of expenditure results partly from political decisions and ideological perspectives. France's comparatively high expenditure on pensions and benefits for older people, for example, reflects government policy in the 1980s to increase the incomes of the whole older population (Walker, 1993: 27).

As shown in Table 1.2 in chapter 1, countries with 'liberal' welfare regimes such as the US and UK spend considerably less on social welfare as a proportion of their gross domestic product (GDP) than 'conservative–corporatist' or 'social democratic' regimes. Yet even within such broad categories there are anomalies. In the US, for instance, public expenditure for old age as a proportion of GDP is considerably lower than in the other countries, as shown in Table 2.4. Total spending on health as a proportion of GDP, however, is much higher than in other countries, as shown in Table 2.1.

One measure of the outcomes of pensions funding is the level of earnings replacement provided by pensions. According to estimates by Walker (1993), in the five European countries the net replacement ratios of basic and compulsory supplementary pensions in 1989 for a married man with full contributions (35–45 years) were: 92 per cent in Italy, 83 per cent in France, 82 per cent in the Netherlands, 69 per cent in Germany and 64 per cent in the UK. Compulsory social security pensions in the US replaced in 1983 an estimated 40 per cent of average lifetime earnings, 50 per cent of low earnings and 23 per cent of high earnings (Ginsburg, 1992: 106). Another outcome indicator for pensions systems is the extent to which poverty persists amongst older people, particularly those not eligible for insurance benefits.

Table 2.4   *Public expenditure on social protection for old age as a percentage of GDP, 1990[a]*

	France	Germany[b]	Italy	Netherlands	United Kingdom	United States
1980	10.41	11.08	10.79	8.69	9.17	5.75
1985	12.32	10.61	13.53	8.90	9.96	6.02
1990	11.70	9.90	14.85	9.92	9.72	5.82

[a] includes all old age and survivors benefits, all compulsory supplementary, occupational and civil servants pensions (Europe), occupational civil servants pensions (United States).
[b] former FRG.
Source: OECD, 1994a.

In the US, for example, 12.4 per cent of all over-65s were living at or below the official poverty level in 1986; those in poverty were more likely to be women (15.2 per cent in poverty) and black (31 per cent) or hispanic (22.5 per cent) (Arber and Ginn, 1991: 80). There are also differences between countries in the level of social assistance for those inadequately covered by pensions. In 1991 the Netherlands provided the highest guaranteed basic monthly income for a single person in the five European countries: £367, compared with £227 in France, £172 in the UK, £165 in Germany and £142 in Italy (Walker, 1992a: 172). The rate in Germany varies according to state policy, which is also the case in the US where individual states may supplement the basic SSI rate.

Thus between and within countries there are differences in the financial resources available for older people. Macro level data on overall pensions and benefits funding for 'standard' recipients, however, conceal variations in the impact of these services for different groups in heterogeneous older populations. The above discussion identifies, first, relating to pensions and benefits, the crucial division between social insurance and social assistance; and, second, the concept of dual welfare related to the dual economy of full-time secure employment and less secure, lower status, often part-time work (Sainsbury, 1993).

Within the insurance/assistance divide itself, however, further sub-groups of older people may be distinguished, for whom the systems have different levels of benefit, as illustrated in Table 2.5.

Group 1 includes those who have high levels of benefits in the pensions insurance systems. Within compulsory insurance schemes, especially in 'conservative–corporatist' systems designed to preserve status relations, those with full contribution records and high earnings gain considerably

Table 2.5 *Benefits from social insurance and social assistance*

	Insurance	Assistance
Benefits	*Group 1* Lifetime contributions in compulsory scheme	*Group 3* Claims and receives full entitlement and related benefits
High	Voluntary supplementary occupational or private pension	
	Group 2 Short contribution record	*Group 4* Does not receive full entitlement
Low	Member of low status scheme Only entitled to minimum	Not eligible Does not claim entitlement

more from the system than others. Another group with high levels of benefit from insurance systems are those who contribute voluntarily to supplementary high status occupational pension schemes, as in the UK and US where state pensions are minimal.

Group 2 comprises those who have low levels of benefits from pensions insurance. For example, Alber (1986: 61) reports on the gap in the German workers' scheme between standard pension (for average earnings and 40 years contributions) and the average pension which 'has never risen far above the standard rate of regular social assistance benefit'. Those who benefit least from contributing to insurance schemes, then, are people in less secure work and/or with shorter contributions records, contributors to low status schemes with poor benefits, and people whose contributions entitle them to a minimum pension only, or whose low pensions are supplemented by social assistance. In Italy, for example, the majority of pensioners have only the minimum or social pension (Ferrera, 1989a).

On the social assistance side of the divide, *group 3*, those who benefit most from assistance, consists of people who are living *at* social assistance level, claiming and receiving their full entitlement and related benefits or discretionary additions. *Group 4*, those living *below* social assistance level and benefiting least of all, includes people who for reasons such as restricting regulations or administrative errors do not receive the full entitlement, those who are not eligible for assistance because they do not meet nationality, immigration or residence conditions, and people who do not claim the assistance to which they are entitled, for reasons such as lack of information, stigma or deterrent administration procedures.

Access to pensions and benefits systems

Older people's access to pensions and benefits and their position in the four insurance/assistance groups (Table 2.5) will depend on the pensions system of their country, their socio-economic status and position in the labour market before retirement, their class, gender, 'race' and age, and the interaction between all these factors (Walker, 1981; 1993).

Retired professional and managerial workers are likely to be in group 1 under any system, since they are treated very favourably by both earnings-related social insurance and voluntary occupational pensions systems, which maintain class inequalities, for example between the professionals' and workers' schemes in Germany. Former manual workers and secondary labour market workers benefit less from their insurance contributions and are likely to be in group 2. Unskilled, intermittently employed people, or marginalised groups outside the labour market, the 'underclass', are more likely to have to live on or below social assistance levels (groups 3 and 4).

Related to social class differences, there are geographical or regional differences in access to high insurance benefits, for example between the old and new states of Germany. People in the south of Italy, particularly if they worked in the black economy, have limited access to insurance systems; a higher proportion of pensioners in the south than the north receive minimum or social pensions; access to benefits such as social pensions can also depend on the patronage system operated by political parties in Italy (Ferrera, 1986). The 1990 reform of local government attempted to reduce this clientelism and give users greater rights (Saraceno and Negri, 1994: 24).

Gender inequalities in pensions systems mean that few women have access to high insurance pensions (group 1) in their own right. In most systems married women's access to pensions depends on their husbands' contributions. In social insurance systems providing earnings-related benefits women as individuals are disadvantaged first through shorter contributions records because of caring responsibilities in the home, and second through lower earnings than men, often in the secondary labour market and part-time work. In Germany, for example, 'among those beginning to draw pensions in their own right in 1989, the average woman received a state pension less than half the average man's' (Ginn and Arber, 1992: 264). Women are particularly disadvantaged by voluntary occupational pensions systems because they are less likely than men to be members of these schemes which often exclude part-time workers, and benefit less than men if they are members. For example in the UK in 1987 only 36 per cent of women employees were members, compared with 64 per cent of men (Ginn and Arber, 1992: 262). Women, as individual contributors, then, tend to receive low insurance benefits (group 2).

In the UK and US voluntary occupational pensions are crucial means of supplementing inadequate state pensions. Women, however, are also disadvantaged in these state systems. In the UK only 36 per cent of women had basic pensions in their own right in 1989; in the US only 35 per cent did so in the late 1980s (Sainsbury, 1993). In the Netherlands all women are entitled to the basic pension as individuals, regardless of contribution records. In the other five countries women, inadequately protected by pensions systems, especially if unmarried, are more likely than men to receive assistance benefits (group 3), or to fall through the net if they do not receive assistance (group 4) (Evers and Olk, 1991: 63–4; Döring et al., 1994). In the US 75 per cent of people receiving SSI on the grounds of age in 1991 were women (US DHHS, 1991).

Class and gender inequalities in pensions systems may be compounded by disadvantages of 'race'. Groups discriminated against on grounds of 'race' or ethnicity include people from former colonial countries in France, the Netherlands and the UK, southern European former 'guestworkers' in Germany, and black and hispanic people in the US. Such groups are less likely than others to have been employed in high status work and to have access to group 1 benefits, and more likely to have had insecure or marginal employment in the secondary labour market, entitling them only to low insurance benefits or to social assistance (Ginsburg, 1992). Their entitlement to means-tested social assistance may be restricted by immigration rules, as in the UK, or hindered by institutionalised racism in the procedures, or by ignorance or fear about the system. 'Racialised' groups are more likely than other older people to fall through the social assistance net and live below the poverty level (group 4).

Finally there are generational inequalities which mean that the oldest pensioners have lower insurance rights, partly because they had lower incomes. Younger retired people benefit more from earnings-related and voluntary occupational pension schemes, to which the older generations in some countries are less likely to have contributed. Further, a higher proportion of the oldest groups are women, who, as discussed above, are more likely than men to depend on social assistance. Although there is a lack of data on this topic, Walker (1993) suggests that generational inequalities are wider in the Netherlands and UK, for example, than in France.

Access to pensions and benefits for older people is thus not just a simple matter of the insurance/assistance divide, but of complex interactions between types of pensions regime and socio-economic characteristics that differentiate between groups.

Rights, responsibilities and choice

Inequalities in current pensions systems confer greater rights on advantaged groups who have earned high insurance pensions through contributions to social or occupational insurance schemes. These systems are based on the responsibility of male breadwinners to contribute for their wives, and the assumption that married women are dependent, with few pension rights as individuals. For the increasing numbers of disadvantaged older people who do not fit this model, in countries such as the US and UK the state is responsible for providing safety net social assistance. However, in countries where the principle of subsidiarity applies, such as France and Germany, children have prior responsibility, in some cases, to provide for parents with inadequate means.

Changes taking place in the systems, particularly in the balance of the welfare mix, are likely to affect the rights and responsibilities of older people and increase inequalities in outcomes between groups. The promotion of increased use of private pensions in the UK, US or Italy, for example, will benefit the higher socio-economic groups, particularly white males, who can afford to exercise this choice, while curtailing rights of the more disadvantaged pensioners to decreasing state pensions. This is the case in the UK, for example, where the value of the state pension is continually being eroded; women's rights in SERPS were reduced by the 1988 changes, and private personal pensions are being promoted. The encouragement of private health insurance and the increased use of private and informal sectors for care provision, while increasing choice for the higher socio-economic classes, will similarly erode disadvantaged groups' rights to state-provided care, and increase the responsibilities of informal carers, mainly women.

In insurance systems women are increasingly being treated as individuals rather than dependants, but, as Ginn and Arber (1992) point out, this does not in itself ensure them the same opportunities as men to earn high insurance rights, because differential earnings potentials and caring responsibilities persist. There is a more general trend, influenced by New Right ideology, to place increasing responsibility on individuals to insure themselves against future risks, including provision for pensions, health care and long-term care. This again will increase inequalities between those who can afford to do this, and those who will have to rely on increasingly residualised state social assistance systems.

Outcomes of incentives in the funding systems

One final aspect of financing systems to be recognised is the extent to which there are incentives in these systems which affect the outcomes. For example there may be incentives which influence the use of particular funding methods or service settings or providers. Such incentives may be overt government policy, such as tax incentives in France, the UK and the US to take up private pensions which benefit wealthy people most. Implicit in policies such as family obligations in France, Germany and Italy to contribute towards parents' social assistance for residential care is the incentive for families to care for parents in their own homes.

Other incentives, however, may have unintended outcomes which conflict with stated government policies. In the UK in the 1980s 'perverse incentives' in the social security system led to rapid increase in private residential care funded through social assistance, in direct opposition to the government's policy of caring for people in their own homes (Griffiths, 1988). Similarly where medical services are free of charge to the user, or where it is easier to obtain services through medical funding or for institutional care, there are incentives to use such services rather than more appropriate social care. These perverse incentives are particularly prevalent in very fragmented systems such as those in France, where health insurance and social welfare agencies try to shift the costs of care on to each other's budgets (Jamieson, 1989; Henrard and Brocas, 1990). The distribution of services, discussed in subsequent chapters, is affected by such intended and unintended incentives in the funding systems.

Summary

Financing of pensions and benefits, health and social care varies in the six countries according to types of welfare regime and of pensions and health systems, influenced by demographic, economic, political, ideological and cultural factors. From the limited evidence available it appears that older women and men generally benefit most in the 'social democratic' regime of the Netherlands, where entitlement to pensions is based on residence and the whole population is insured for long-term care (Döring et al., 1994). In France, Germany and Italy, under 'conservative–corporatist' systems, benefits may be more related to socio-economic status and people's position in the social insurance/ assistance divide. France and Italy, however, have minimum pensions. The 'liberal' systems of the US and UK provide fairly minimal entitlements to pensions and health care for older people, although in the UK there is still universal access to most health services through the NHS.

Within the broad types of funding system, a political economy perspective on ageing shows differences in access to pensions and care between groups according to class, gender, 'race' and age (Walker, 1981). Lifetime inequalities continued into older age influence whether people receive high or low benefits either through entitlement to insurance or from social assistance. Differential access to pensions and benefits also affects people's access to long-term or social care, especially in countries with a strong emphasis on the medical/social divide in care services.

In all the systems, financing long-term care for dependent older people poses difficulties. The main approaches to this issue are to reduce care in institutional settings, to increase use of non-state sectors of provision and to reform health and social care funding systems. These changing patterns of financing and providing services, and in particular increasing privatisation which allows wealthier people more choice but restricts choices of those with limited resources, seem likely to increase inequalities between groups of older people. Trends and incentives in financing systems also influence the appropriateness of outcomes of services for dependent older people and their carers.

3

Accommodation for Older People

Older people's housing arrangements constitute a second key component of community care. Housing circumstances and options are often related to the first key component, access to financial resources, discussed in chapter 2. Needs for community care, defined as care for people who live in their own homes, depend to some extent on the nature of those homes and the composition of people's households. Their 'homes', the settings in which older people live, whether alone or with others, and where they spend much of their time, mainly consist of 'ordinary' housing, but also include the whole spectrum of 'specialised' purpose built, adapted or sheltered housing, residential or nursing homes, or other forms of group living. Suitable housing of an appropriate size, in good repair, accessible, warm and affordable, will contribute significantly to people's ability to live independently, whereas unsuitable housing may increase needs for support. People's living arrangements, such as with whom they live, or the proximity of family or friends, will also affect whether, how and by whom care is offered if needed.

In this chapter the policies and principles affecting older people's housing circumstances are explored first. The range of housing support and options available for older people and the systems of providing and financing such services are then examined. Third, differences in access to housing choices and in outcomes of these policies and systems for the various groups of older people are identified and discussed.

Background to current housing policies

One paradox in social policies concerning older people is that most policy discussion on where older people live has been focused on institutional settings, although only a small minority of people aged over 65 live in institutions such as residential homes. Social policymakers and analysts in West Europe and North America have until recently neglected to address needs for the 'ordinary' housing in which most older people live, perhaps because housing has not been perceived as part of health and social care. Emphasis has thus been placed on 'specialised' sheltered or residential accommodation meeting both housing and care needs.

Development of housing policies

General housing policies were formulated after 1945 in the context of post-war reconstruction in Europe and the continued development of welfare states in western societies. West European governments encouraged large scale building programmes through subsidies on 'bricks and mortar' and increased social rented housing (state-subsidised rented housing) to meet high levels of housing need arising from war damage, increasing birth rates and immigration (Emms, 1990). In the UK local authorities were directly responsible for both building and managing social housing, whereas in other European countries other agencies took on these functions with financial subsidies from the state. Housing policies in the US conformed to the 'liberal' model of welfare, with state help for those on low incomes in housing need (Heidenheimer et al., 1983: 93).

In the 1970s the policy focus shifted from new building to rehabilitation of existing housing stock. Different types of housing need emerged as the housing built during the post-war period for families with children proved unsuitable for increasing numbers of small households, single people, older people and those with physical and mental disabilities (Kleinman, 1992: 46). From the late 1970s there was a change in emphasis from subsidising buildings to subsidising individuals through means-tested housing allowances and tax allowances.

Trends in housing policy in the 1980s and 1990s followed those in other areas of social policy. In developing the mixed economy of welfare, governments aimed to reduce state expenditure and the state's direct role in housing. Housing costs to individuals rose and the role of markets was encouraged. An increase in owner occupation was promoted by most West European governments. Social housing agencies, for example non-profit housing associations in Germany and the UK, had to become more market oriented (Kleinman, 1992), although UK housing associations still received central government subsidies. Such policy trends led to the residualisation of social housing across West Europe (Emms, 1990).

In the decades since the second world war countries varied in the amount and type of government intervention through housing provision, regulation and subsidisation, and in the role of the public and private sectors in housing. Yet in spite of these differences, Kleinman (1992: 48) holds that the levels of state intervention were similar in West European countries and suggests that 'these similarities come into sharper focus if one were to make the comparison between almost any Western European country . . . and the United States, with its tiny residualised public sector'. For the countries in this study the main distinction in housing policy is between the 'liberal' welfare regime of the United States and any of the West European countries' welfare regimes.

In West Europe, then, broadly similar housing policies from 1945 concentrated on building for families with children. Not unnaturally at the time, these policies paid little attention to the needs of older people, which are basically for small, physically accessible and convenient housing units. For older people unable to provide suitable housing for themselves when their existing housing conditions proved unsatisfactory, the main policy response from the 1960s onwards was to rehouse them in specialised types of housing such as sheltered accommodation, service flats or institutional care. In the US there was a similar lack of attention to housing in relation to care needs of older people, reflecting the residualised housing policy and leading to widespread use of nursing homes as the main form of long-term care (Estes and Lee, 1985).

Sheltered housing in the UK and similar forms of provision in other European countries tended to be seen as a panacea for meeting the housing and social needs of a broad group of older people who needed some social support such as the availability of a warden. The purposes and form of such provision and its categorisation as a housing, social or institutional service, however, vary within and between countries, making cross-national comparison difficult.

In both Europe and the US in the post-1945 period stated policies on care for older people were mainly on institutional care. In Britain the 1948 National Assistance Act focused on residential care, placing a duty on local authorities to provide such accommodation with services where it was otherwise unavailable. Yet it failed to legislate for community care, although Means (1990) argues that actual policy was for older people to remain in their own homes. A post war shortage of housing was one reason for the encouragement of institutional care for older people in the Netherlands, which led to a higher rate of institutionalisation than in most European countries. In the US the introduction of Medicaid in 1965 produced a rapid increase in private nursing homes which reflected a major shift from social care in residential homes and mental hospitals rather than a rise in institutionalisation as such (Doty, 1988: 146).

From the 1970s institutional care was increasingly viewed negatively because of the harmful effects of institutionalisation highlighted by writers such as Goffman (1961) and Townsend (1962); because it was considered that too many people were unnecessarily living in institutions; and because institutional care was perceived as too expensive. Governments set goals of reducing the proportion of older people in residential or nursing home care, for example in the Netherlands (Alber, 1993), or in long stay hospital care, for instance in the UK's 1962 Hospital Plan. In 1975 France adopted a policy of replacing antiquated 'hospices' with medico-social long or medium stay units or homes for elderly people (Doty and Mizrahi, 1989). Among the six countries studied, the exception is Italy, which has a low rate of institutionalisation of older people and is expanding residential care (Florea et al., 1993: 54).

It was recognised from around the late 1970s that housing needs of dependent older people were not always appropriately met by standard solutions such as sheltered or residential accommodation, and that more varied forms of provision for special needs and disabilities were necessary. Ways of helping people to stay in their existing accommodation were promoted. These included adaptations and improvements to their housing, sometimes financed by using the equity in owner occupied homes, and intensive social support such as domiciliary welfare services and alarm systems (Tinker, 1992). Housing became recognised as an essential component of community care, for example in the British policy paper *Caring for people* (HMSO, 1989a: 9, 25). The role of institutions expanded but became more community-based. Care homes began to provide resources and services to the local community, such as day care and respite care. In France and Germany there was a move towards decentralisation, providing smaller units more integrated into the community (Alber, 1993: 124).

As part of the aim to shift away from standardised solutions to more individualised provision, there was a move in the late 1980s and 1990s, in countries such as the Netherlands and the UK, towards treating housing and care needs as separate, as advocated in the Wagner report (National Institute for Social Work [NISW], 1988). The emphasis changed to providing care to people in their homes, whether these homes consisted of ordinary housing, specialised, sheltered or institutional provision. This may entail providing intensive domiciliary support, increasing the care components of sheltered housing, or providing more flexible packages of care in institutions, allowing individuals more choice. These policies also depend on close collaboration or integration between the housing and care services, on developing adequate domiciliary care and suitable housing, and on allowing people effective choice between staying put or moving (Oldman, 1990; NISW, 1988; Potter and Zill, 1992).

In general policymakers have taken a piecemeal approach to housing for older people in both West Europe and North America. Community care policies that aim to reduce institutionalisation, substitute less expensive forms of care and meet individual needs more flexibly, depend on a closer integration with housing policies. From the 1970s housing policy tended to focus on the special needs of the general population and of older people; social housing became residualised as its function was increasingly to meet such special needs as well as those of low income people with no other access to housing. Older people's housing options are thus limited unless they are able to provide for themselves in the private market.

Housing policies: influences and principles

Housing circumstances and options for older people are affected by trends in housing policy and in policy on care for dependent people; policies in these areas are rarely well integrated, but often impinge on each other, sometimes to the detriment of older people. These policies are influenced by economic, social and political factors and the principles and assumptions on which the policies are based.

The importance of economic influences since the 1970s has already been emphasised in relation to funding of services and benefits. Governments' concern to control public expenditure and reduce public deficits affected policies on both housing and care. Although governments had difficulty implementing cost containment policies in health care, housing was one policy area where public expenditure was effectively reduced, for example in the UK from 3.3 per cent of GDP in 1973–4 to 1.6 per cent of GDP in 1988–9 (Hills and Mullings, 1991: 147). In the field of caring for dependent people the high cost of institutional care led to policies of deinstitutionalisation and substitution of ostensibly less expensive forms of care (Tunissen and Knapen, 1991; Baldock and Evers, 1992; Coolen, 1993).

Such community care policies increased needs for other types of housing at a time when general housing demand was also rising as a result of increasing prosperity of the majority in western populations as well as for demographic reasons. A rise in the number of households was the most important demographic factor affecting housing demand. This increase was largely due to the formation of smaller households through divorce, lone parenthood or widowhood, or by single people choosing to live alone. The numbers of older people living alone, the majority of whom are widows, will continue to rise as the proportion in the oldest age groups grows. Such demographic factors crucially affect the type of housing needed, particularly small accessible units.

Political ideologies also influence government intervention in housing; the basic relationship between the state, market and family depends on the post-1945 welfare regime types identified in chapters 1 and 2, and subsequent developments and changes in the welfare mix brought about by the main ideological influences of the 1980s and 1990s. The influence of the New Right is found in both housing and care policies. In housing, western governments have reduced the role of the state, particularly in direct provision or subsidy of buildings, and promoted individual responsibility of households to provide their own accommodation, with financial subsidies for its purchase or rent. Policy on care for dependent people has also emphasised individual and family responsibility and a reduced role for the state. Such policies are also influenced by cultural beliefs and values about the role of the family and attitudes to the use of institutional care. Since the 1970s there has been a move towards the predominance of economic principles in housing and care policies. The principle of cost efficiency has been applied to housing services, with marketisation and the introduction of business management criteria. In the field of long-term care, cost efficiency principles underly the shift towards seeking cheaper and less formal solutions than institutional care.

Stated policies on older people's accommodation also include humanitarian principles such as helping people to remain independent in their own homes and avoiding unnecessary long-term institutional care in hospitals or homes (Jamieson, 1989). The principle of social integration is advanced in helping older people to continue to live in their community, especially in France, with policies based on the ideal of an independent active 'third age'. Social integration is also used to justify moving older people into grouped housing such as sheltered or congregate housing or residential homes, where it is often assumed that the presence of other older people will relieve loneliness. There has been a long debate on this issue with evidence for and against the social benefits of ostensibly integrated yet more widely segregated settings (see Rosow, 1967; Butler, 1986). A large scale study of sheltered housing in Britain found that the main benefits for tenants were in terms of housing conditions rather than social contacts (Butler et al., 1983).

The move towards more individualised care reflects a growing recognition of the principle that older people's choices should be respected, including whether or not they prefer to live among their own age group. Policy statements promoting the principle of individual choice tend to assume that older people prefer to stay in their own homes rather than move to specialised or residential accommodation. Research evidence from the US and West Europe supports this assumption (Butler, 1986). Oldman (1990), however, stresses that some older people would still prefer to move rather than stay in unsatisfactory conditions.

The extent to which people are able to make a positive choice of residential care will depend partly on assumptions made by policy-makers and the general population about such care. Community care policies have been based on negative assumptions about institutional care, for example that 'typical institutional life curtails the freedom and independence of the individual' (Jamieson, 1989: 448). In Britain residential care is stigmatised as a last resort (Foster, 1991: 108). Policymakers have an interest in maintaining such perceptions to ensure that family carers continue to care for older people at home and feel guilty if they are admitted to institutional care (Jamieson, 1989).

Community care policies rely crucially on the assumption that informal carers, usually female relatives, will be available and willing to provide unpaid care, and that dependent older people will accept such care. These policies are based on the ideology of familism, that it is the role of the family to care for dependent members (Dalley, 1988). Feminist critiques of social policy, especially in the UK, have focused on the sexist assumptions of such policies and on their implications for women (see, for example, Finch and Groves, 1983; Finch, 1984). Although expectations about family care are widespread in West Europe and North America, they are particularly strong in South European countries, including southern Italy, and countries with a 'conservative–corporatist' welfare regime type which apply the principle of subsidiarity, explicitly giving primary responsibility to families to care for dependants. In countries with 'social democratic' regimes such as the Netherlands, however, there are fewer explicit requirements of family care; the level of institutionalisation is higher, residential care is of a higher quality, and is less stigmatised and more acceptable to older people and families than in other countries.

Residential care is not necessarily an unattractive option, if provided to high quality standards and promoting residents' independence (Foster, 1991). As the Wagner report (NISW, 1988) advocates, it should be a positive choice, part of a range of community care options, based on the same humanitarian principles as stated for community care policies in general in the 1990s, with an emphasis on individual needs and preferences.

Housing options and living arrangements

This section begins by identifying the different types of housing available and the options older people have for 'staying put' or moving if their existing housing is no longer suitable. The current housing circumstances of older people in the countries studied are then examined. Turning to aspects of service provision, for each country the sectors of the welfare mix responsible for different services are identified, funding services and financial benefits available for housing are outlined, and administrative procedures for assessment and service allocation are identified.

Types of housing and options for 'staying put' or moving

Types of housing for older people have traditionally been viewed as a spectrum or continuum, meeting mainly housing objectives at one end and mainly social welfare objectives at the other (Butler, 1986). The types range from ordinary housing to long stay hospital care. Although this is a useful way of setting out housing types and their purposes, it may be seen as being based on a model of ageing as a period of continual decline and increasing dependence. In this 'downhill all the way' model (Wilson, 1991: 43), people's social worth and independence decrease in stages corresponding to their need for domiciliary services, then residential care, then hospital care.

Recent trends, however, have moved away from standard solutions to more flexible approaches geared to individual need. Community care systems in the 1990s, following these trends, could ideally be based on a more accurate model of older people's lives, that they remain fairly independent with occasional episodes of dependence followed by rehabilitation, until their final illness (Wilson, 1991: 44–5). Services based on this model would not differentiate so clearly between 'ordinary' and 'specialised housing', but allow for more flexible use of all types of housing or residential care provision, so that progression was not always towards greater dependence. This flexibility is borne in mind when setting out the different housing options below.

Ordinary housing, without services or special facilities, consists either of small ground floor units intended for older or single people, or of housing for the general population. Such housing may become unsuitable through need for repairs or improvements, or because the older person has disabilities. Ways of helping people who prefer to remain in their housing include adaptations, such as widened doorways or ground floor bathrooms, or the provision through home alarm services of emergency cover as offered in some sheltered housing. For owner occupiers there are services which give advice and practical help with arranging repairs and raising finance for them, for example 'care and repair' services in the UK. If needs are mainly for care, intensive home care services may be provided (Tinker, 1992).

The main type of option for moving is into grouped housing for older people, for example service flats, sheltered housing, or congregate housing, with some form of support. In some cases such housing is specially designed for people with disabilities. For example in the UK 'wheelchair' housing is purpose built to standards suitable for wheelchair users and 'mobility' housing has level access and design features suitable for people with disabilities. Sheltered housing in the UK takes various forms but all are intended only for elderly people and have some type of alarm system (Oldman, 1990: 24); they often have communal facilities such as a sitting room and laundry. In France sheltered housing (*logement foyer*) is mainly a social provision offering housing with communal areas and services such as restaurant, laundry, domestic and care services. Congregate housing in the USA also offers meals and communal facilities such as a library or hairdresser (Butler, 1986: 144).

Grouped housing of this type, usually intended for fairly independent people, may itself become unsuitable for residents who become more dependent. To avoid 'downward progression' to institutional care, such settings are increasingly made more specialised to allow frailer people to remain there. For example 'very sheltered housing' in the UK provides 24 hour cover and extra facilities (Tinker, 1989). Nursing facilities may be added to congregate housing provision in the USA (Butler, 1986: 144) and a 'medical care section' may be included in sheltered housing in

France. By increasing the care elements of such housing to avoid institutional care, the institutional character of the housing may be increased, again blurring the distinctions between types of housing.

Institutional long-term care is the other main type of moving option, with a traditional distinction between residential homes, nursing homes and hospitals, for different levels of dependence, although it is often funding sources that determine the category of institution used. Definitions also vary across countries, making comparison difficult. Residential homes for older people generally provide accommodation, meals, domestic services and some personal care, whereas nursing homes and hospitals are more medically oriented. In practice, however, in the 1990s people who are admitted to such homes are already in need of fairly high levels of care. Again distinctions are becoming blurred as homes for elderly people are medicalised, for example in France by adding a medical care section, as a way of reducing use of long-term hospital care. Further, the use of homes for purposes other than standard packages of long-term care is developing, so that there is increasing flexibility in institutional care, and services such as short-term respite care are developed.

The need for flexibility and movement between types of housing has also led to innovative forms of provision combining different types, such as sheltered housing, nursing homes and communal facilities, on the same site so that people do not have to move as their needs change. In the US this approach is highly developed in the 'continuing care retirement community' (CCRC), a small village with a range of housing, residential and support services, nursing home and leisure facilities. Wealthier older people buy into the CCRC early in retirement, pay monthly service fees and are assured of any nursing home care they need in later life (von Mering and Neff, 1993).

On a much smaller scale, other innovative forms of living arrangement include various types of group living in small homes or hostels with a resident housekeeper, or home sharing. Family placement or adult fostering arrangements allow older people to live in the family home of non-relatives. This system is increasingly used in France to avoid admission to residential care. For older people who have families a 'granny flat' within or next to the main family home allows independence with access to family care. Other approaches integrate older and younger people in the same housing project, such as that in Toulouse where there is housing with services for older people within more general housing (Potter and Zill, 1992: 127).

Housing circumstances of older people

Although few comparative statistics are available, information from various sources indicates the different proportions of older people living alone or with others, in various types of setting, in owner occupied or rented housing, often in poorer housing conditions than younger people.

The proportion of older people living alone increases with age; those living alone are more likely to be women than men, especially in the older age groups. Table 3.1 shows the proportion of over-65s living alone in the six countries studied, ranging from 22 per cent (over 60) in Italy to 39 per cent in Germany. Among the over-75s the proportion living alone is higher; for example 63 per cent of women and 23 per cent of men aged over 75 lived alone in Germany in 1987 (*Bundesministerium für Familie und Senioren*, 1990: 119). Older people living with others are most likely to live with a spouse; for example in the US in 1991 54 per cent of over-65s lived with a spouse (74 per cent of men and 40 per cent of women), 13 per cent with other relatives and 2 per cent with non-relatives (US Bureau of the Census, 1992). In the European countries older people in Italy were more likely than those elsewhere to live with children; in Italy 35 per cent of over-60s lived with a child, compared with 16 per cent of over-65s in Britain and 11 per cent of over-65s in the Netherlands (Grundy and Harrop, 1992: 33). This reflects cultural differences between South Europe where co-residence with children is more accepted, and North Europe where most older people prefer to live near rather than with children, and have frequent contact with them (Walker, 1993).

In all six countries at least 90 per cent of over-65s live in ordinary housing. As definitions of residential care vary, in some cases including sheltered housing, data are not always comparable and there is often inconsistency between different sources. Table 3.2 shows the proportion of over-65s in residential and nursing home care, with the highest proportion in the Netherlands and the lowest in Italy. The proportion of older people in residential care increases with age.

Where sheltered housing is classified separately it is estimated that there are places for 2.6 per cent of over-65s in the Netherlands, 5 per cent in the UK (Alber, 1993), 2 per cent in Germany (Butler, 1986), and that 1.2 per cent in the US live in supportive housing (van Nostrand et al., 1993).

Among older people living in ordinary housing, the proportion in different housing tenures varies between countries; again comparison is

Table 3.1   *Proportion of over 65 age group living alone*

	France (1982)[1]	Germany[a] (1982)[1]	Italy (1988)[2]	Netherlands (1992)[3]	United Kingdom[b] (1991)[4]	United States (1991)[5]
% over 65						
total	32	39	29	36	37	31
male	16	16	11	17	23	16
female	43	53	42	50	47	42

[a] former FRG.
[b] Great Britain.
Source: [1] Wall, 1989: 129.
             [2] Florea et al., 1993: 72.
             [3] Centraal Bureau voor de Statistiek, 1993: 35.
             [4] Office of Population Censuses and Surveys, 1993: 19.
             [5] US Bureau of the Census, 1992.

Table 3.2   *Places in residential and nursing home care per 100 people aged 65 and over*

	France	Germany[a]	Italy	Netherlands	United Kingdom	United States
Places in						
Residential care	5.1	5.4	2.3	9.7	5.0	0.9
Nursing home						
care	2.4[b]	2.3	–	2.6	–	4.6

[a] former FRG.
[b] includes long stay beds in hospitals.
Sources: Alber, 1993.
              Van Nostrand et al., 1993: 110.

difficult because definitions of tenure type vary. In the US 77 per cent of older households owned their homes in 1992 (AARP, 1993). Potter and Zill (1992: 114) estimate that of the over-65s in the European countries 75 per cent are owner occupiers in France, 74 per cent in Italy, 63 per cent in Great Britain, 60 per cent in Germany and 40 per cent in the Netherlands. In countries with lower rates of owner occupation, social rented housing is more important (Potter and Zill, 1992: 115).

Whether older people's housing is owned or rented, surveys in the US and West Europe show that they tend to live in poorer housing conditions than younger ones (Butler, 1986: 139). They are more likely to live in old properties and be unable to afford repairs and heating costs, and more likely to live in inner city areas, or rural areas where housing lacks amenities. In poor housing fuel costs tend to be higher, adding to difficulties older people experience in keeping warm in winter. Housing conditions in West Europe are generally worse the older the age group (Walker, 1993).

Provision of housing services for older people

The provision and funding (see also chapter 2) of the main types of housing service by different sectors of the mixed economy of welfare are outlined below for each country.

In *France* ordinary housing for people on low incomes is provided through *Habitation à Loyer Modéré* (HLM) organisations, 44 per cent of which are sponsored by local authorities, the others being non-profit companies (Emms, 1990). HLM housing is allocated to people with an income below a fixed limit. Older people may be entitled to housing allowance (*allocation de logement*, AL) which is means tested and linked to social security. The personal housing benefit (*aide personalisée au logement*, APL), introduced from 1978 for people in subsidised housing, is gradually replacing AL (Emms, 1990). Housing benefits are administered through the local family allowance office (*Caisse d'allocations familiales*, CAF). Grants for home improvements, undertaken by non-profit associations, are also available for people on low incomes.

In residential institutions for elderly people, 60 per cent of places are provided by the public sector, evenly distributed between those located in hospitals, homes for elderly people and sheltered housing; 28 per cent are in private homes for elderly people and 9 per cent in private sheltered housing (Guillemard and Argoud, 1992). The private provision is mainly by non-profit associations. Where institutions are medicalised with a medical care section (*section de cure médicale*, SCM) health insurance pays for the costs of care; the state has a role in recognising SCMs and regulating standards. Before a person is admitted to a SCM the level of dependence is assessed by a health insurance doctor. At the end of 1990 over one-third of institutions had a SCM, including 50 per cent of homes for older people and 8 per cent of sheltered housing (Guillemard and Argoud, 1992).

In *Germany* two-thirds of social rented housing is provided by non-profit housing associations (*Gemeinnutzige Wohnungsunternehmen*) and one-third is provided by the private sector (Tomann, 1990). Social housing is designated for applicants with incomes below a set limit. The states (*Länder*) are responsible for subsidies for building and improvement of social housing; local authorities can pay for small adaptations to older people's housing. People with low incomes are entitled to claim housing benefit (*Wohngeld*). The means-tested benefit is linked to social assistance and administered through the local social assistance office. For people receiving social assistance 'adequate housing and heating' costs are fully covered (Walker, 1992a: 173). Housing benefit is mainly received by tenants and is intended to ensure that housing costs are kept below about 20 per cent of household income (Emms, 1990).

Sheltered housing (*Altenwohnheime*), residential homes (*Altenheime*), nursing homes (*Pflegeheime*) and facilities combining these types are mainly provided by non-profit welfare organisations, subsidised by the state and local government to varying levels. Of all residential places, 65 per cent are in the non-profit sector, 19 per cent provided by the public sector and 17 per cent by the commercial sector (Alber, 1992). Minimum standards in homes are regulated and inspected under the Federal Residential Homes Act 1974, which also requires that each resident has a contract with the home and that each home has a homes council. The regulations were strengthened in 1990. Since residential care is not covered by health insurance, admission largely depends on whether the person is able to afford the fees, or is eligible or willing to apply for social assistance.

The provision of housing services and residential care in *Italy* varies between regions and data are often unavailable at national level. Since a high proportion of older people in Italy own their homes, nearly 79 per cent of the over-70s, the proportion in rented housing is low (Florea et al., 1993). However, with increasing rents since the 1980s older people have difficulty affording rents. A social fund set up in 1978 to provide rent allowances for low income families proved inadequate; there was pressure from trade unions in the early 1990s to initiate a fund to cover rent for those below minimum pension level. There is a public building programme for housing for certain categories of people on low incomes, including elderly people, administered through the regions. There is also a small fund for home improvements for older people (Florea et al., 1993).

Specialised residential health facilities for health care and rehabilitation of dependent elderly people are planned to increase substantially during the 1990s. Residential accommodation such as nursing homes, homes for older people (*case di riposo*) and sheltered housing (*strutture protetti*) are provided mainly by the private sector (68 per cent) (Florea et al., 1993). The level of provision is higher in the north than the south. As indicated by waiting lists, the number of places does not meet demand. An experimental family placement service (*anziano in famiglia*) in Milan provides cash benefits to relatives or neighbours who care in their own homes for elderly people on waiting lists for residential care (Nijkamp et al., 1991).

Social rented housing in the *Netherlands* comprises over two-fifths of housing and is mainly provided by housing associations (*Woningcorporaties*) which are non-profit associations approved by central government. Municipalities also own some subsidised housing and 'in effect control and steer social housing activity within their areas' and provide a 'channel for all central government subsidies and grants for social housing' (Emms, 1990: 200). Central government subsidies are provided to local authorities for renovation of older properties in large towns (Baars et al., 1992). There is a housing benefit system providing means-tested benefit for people on low incomes. This is to contribute to rent for individual accommodation, which includes sheltered housing and support homes (*aanleunwoningen*) where people live independently, usually linked by alarm to nearby residential homes.

The vast majority of provision of sheltered housing, residential and nursing homes (traditionally divided into somatic and psychogeriatric homes) is in the private non-profit sector. The public sector rarely provides institutions directly and the for-profit sector has only a small involvement in service flats and sheltered housing (Baars et al., 1992). Local multi-disciplinary committees, including doctors, nurses and social workers, assess all applications for residential and nursing home care; if people are considered in need of care, they are allocated a place when available. The proportion of older people in institutional care is being reduced under the policy of 'substitution' (Tunissen and Knapen, 1991).

In the *United Kingdom* social rented housing is provided in the public sector by local authorities and in the non-profit sector by housing associations. Of the 70–9 age group, one-third are local authority tenants, 5 per cent housing authority tenants and 9 per cent rent privately (Walker, 1992b: 67). Sheltered housing and various types of very sheltered housing are mainly provided by the public sector (66 per cent), whereas 26 per cent is provided by housing associations and 8 per cent in the private sector (Walker, 1992b: 21). Housing benefit for payment of housing costs, including some parts of sheltered housing service charges, is linked to the social assistance (income support) system. Housing benefit is means-tested and administered by the local authority. Means-tested disabled facilities grants are also available through the local authority for adaptations to housing for disabled people. These, however, have very limited budgets.

The balance between sectors in the provision of residential and nursing homes changed in the 1980s as a result of incentives for care in private homes through the social security system. There was a dramatic increase, 130 per cent from 1979–90, in the number of places in private homes. By 1990 51 per cent of places were in the private sector, 37 per cent in the public sector and 12 per cent in the voluntary (non-profit) sector (Walker, 1992b: 44). Since April 1993 people applying for state financial support for residential and nursing home care have their need for care assessed by the local social services authority, in cooperation with health and housing authorities; their income is also assessed for contribution to the local authority's costs under a national charging system. A residential allowance is paid through income support for people with low income and assets in independent (private or non-profit) homes (Meredith, 1993: 129–31).

In the *United States* about one-quarter of older people rent their homes in the public or private sector. There are rent subsidies for people on low incomes through the lower income housing assistance programme; people who receive subsidies have to contribute up to 30 per cent of their family income to rent. There are also direct federal loans for building, rehabilitation and management of housing for rent by older people. Public subsidies are available for congregate housing with meals and other services provided by non-profit organisations or cooperatives. Under the Older Americans Act (1965) some funding is available for repairs, renovations and adaptations to housing for older and disabled people. The federal low income energy assistance programme provides assistance with fuel bills and insulation.

The main role in the residential care sector is played by nursing homes. Board and care homes do not qualify for medical funding and are less strictly regulated by state governments, which fund a large part of nursing home care through Medicaid and have a major influence in regulating nursing home provision. Nursing homes are certified for Medicare and Medicaid purposes in three categories: skilled nursing facility under Medicare; skilled nursing facility under Medicaid; and intermediate care facility under Medicaid; about 75 per cent are certified. Most nursing homes (75 per cent) are provided in the for-profit sector, 20 per cent in the non-profit sector and 5 per cent in the public sector at federal, state or local level (Keenan, 1989: 82–3). The Veterans Administration (VA) also provides nursing home facilities for veterans. For most people ability to pay is the main criterion for nursing home admission, unless their income and assets are low enough for eligibility through Medicaid.

Outcomes of housing policies and systems

The piecemeal approach to policies on where older people live in West Europe and North America is illustrated above. There is little integration between housing and social care policies and systems. One would expect, therefore, that outcomes would vary considerably between geographical areas and for people of different class, gender, 'race' and age. The implications of policies and systems, differences in access and outcomes, and issues of rights and choice are explored below. As emphasised in chapter 2, there are few comparative statistics or systematic studies to provide evidence for sound conclusions on these issues.

Implications of policies for accommodation of different groups of older people and carers

Older people's housing needs vary widely, first according to their personal and housing circumstances and preferences, and second according to any disabilities and/or care needs they may have. The appropriateness of their present housing situation to meet these needs depends on a combination of factors such as their financial status, government policies on housing and institutional care, policy implementation and resources at local level, the availability of informal and formal care, and access to services.

Countries differ in the level of public funding for housing and care services and in policies on types of provision. The countries studied, however, follow similar trends both in reducing public expenditure on housing and institutional care, and in focusing financial support for housing on individuals through benefits for housing costs. Older people's housing conditions also vary between countries, with generally poorer conditions reported in Southern than Northern Europe (Walker, 1993).

Important differences are also found in older people's housing situations between geographical areas within countries. First, as a result of factors such as migration the geographical distribution of older people themselves, and therefore of housing and care needs, is often uneven (Butler, 1986). They tend to be concentrated, for example, in rural areas of France, inner urban districts of northern Europe, retirement areas such as the south coast of England, or in particular US states, for example California, New York and Florida (AARP, 1993).

Second, the distribution of housing and care services varies within countries. Policy on level of provision is usually made at a local rather than central government level, although resources may be controlled by central government, as in the UK. There are thus differences between regions, states and local authorities, in spending on social housing subsidies, renovations and adaptations, 'care and repair' projects and social care services. The distribution of specialised and residential accommodation also tends to be uneven, particularly where provided by the for-profit sector which concentrates supply on more affluent areas, for example in the UK (Mackintosh et al., 1990: 121). In the US there is wide variation between states in the supply of nursing home beds (Jazwiecki, 1989: 311). Cross national comparative data on supply in relation to need are not, however, available for the countries studied.

From a political economy perspective, socio-economic class, linked to income and assets, both in earlier life and present circumstances, is a major factor determining access to and choice in appropriate housing in older age. As Mackintosh and colleagues (1990: 144) point out: 'A life of poverty and poor housing will be the main cause of housing problems in later life for many.' As a result of public expenditure reductions in the 1980s leading to lower subsidies, fewer suitable housing units being available, and increased rents in public and private sectors, the affordability of housing has become an issue (Oldman, 1990).

Housing inequalities are also claimed to have increased in the 1980s with greater segregation between better off owner occupiers and poorer people in residualised social housing (Means, 1990: 280; Kleinman, 1992: 54). Housing tenure is an important determinant of housing options in later life, since owner occupiers, usually in the higher socio-economic groups, have advantages over tenants who tend to be less wealthy. Owner occupiers are more likely to be able to move using the sale of their house to finance the purchase or rental of smaller or specialised housing, whereas tenants' options to move to a different tenure or more suitable housing are more limited (Oldman, 1990). Owner occupiers are also more likely to be able to afford 'staying put' options such as adaptations or to have access to 'care and repair' or equity release schemes. There are, however, differences within tenures; owner occupiers may have low incomes, whereas some wealthy older people prefer to rent housing, particularly in countries where renting is the norm.

Social class, income and tenure also affect older people's access to specialised housing and long-term institutional care. Since state support was reduced in the 1980s, such provision is more likely to be targeted to the most dependent people and those on lowest incomes, who will gain access to services if they apply through the relevant assessment systems and meet the criteria. Older people with most financial resources will also have access to the private for-profit sector in sheltered housing or residential care. Those on middle incomes, however, the 'not rich, not poor' are likely to have more difficulty gaining access to any of the options for moving or staying put, if they are not entitled to state support or social housing, but can neither afford private sheltered or residential accommodation, nor repairs or adaptations to their existing housing (Bull and Poole, 1989; Means, 1990; Oldman, 1990).

Turning to the effects of gender, women are more likely than men to have changing housing needs in later life. Most older married women gained access to housing through their husband as owner or tenant. In older age, particularly in widowhood, the family home may no longer be suitable if too large and difficult to heat and repair. Older women are more likely than older men to live alone and to have disabilities and health problems; they thus need small units of housing, accessible and adapted for disabilities, and situated close to shops and services to help maintain independence.

Women are, however, less likely than men to be able to meet their housing needs in later life. As women's access to income and wealth is generally lower than men's (see chapter 2), most women will not have the financial resources crucial to providing suitable housing for their old age. Whether they are owners or tenants they are likely to have more difficulties in moving or staying put satisfactorily. Women home owners are likely to have difficulties with affording or carrying out repairs, adaptations and improvements, especially when widowed with no experience of these matters (Arber and Ginn, 1991). Moving options are limited if they cannot afford private purchase and cannot gain access to limited public sector specialised housing or to housing close to a family caregiver, such as a daughter. Women are thus more likely than men to have to stay in unsuitable owner occupied housing or residualised social housing, or to enter residential or nursing home care supported by social assistance. There is a much higher proportion of women than men in institutional care in West Europe and North America, partly because women live longer than men. For example: 'Across all ages, elderly women in Britain have an 85 per cent higher chance than elderly men of residing in communal establishments', and in the US there is a 72 per cent higher chance of women aged over 85 living in nursing homes (Arber and Ginn, 1991: 115–16).

In West European countries populations from black and ethnic minority communities are ageing; similarly in the US 'all of the ethnic minority group elderly populations are expected to double by the year 2000 or shortly thereafter' (Valle, 1989: 345). The special housing needs of people from minority ethnic communities have rarely been recognised or addressed (Tinker, 1992: 134), although some provision is made through special projects rather than mainstream services. However, the increasing numbers of minority ethnic elders will have similar needs for suitable housing to the rest of the older population, with the additional requirement for provision that is culturally appropriate and does not isolate them from their ethnic group (Carlin, 1994).

As shown in chapter 2, older people from minority ethnic groups are more likely than the majority population to have low incomes. They are also more likely to be concentrated in residualised social housing, in the worst housing in inner cities or peripheral estates, as a result of lower incomes, discrimination in housing allocation practice and the increased segregation of housing as a result of 1980s policies (Emms, 1990; Kleinman, 1992). Whether tenants of poor housing or owner occupiers, their resources and options for improving their housing situation are likely to be limited. Residential settings, for example in the UK and US, have in the past rarely provided solutions that were appropriate to cultural needs and such long-term care services tend to be underused by minority ethnic elders (Norman, 1985; Valle, 1989: 344). For people in the oldest age groups, the disadvantageous effects on their housing situation of social class, gender and 'race' may be compounded at a time when housing needs are greatest. The oldest age groups, mainly women, are most likely to have low incomes and to have exhausted any savings they had, thus lacking the financial resources to provide suitable housing for themselves.

Rights, responsibilities and choice

Accommodation for older people is an area of provision where there are few entitlements in the countries studied. Increasingly the responsibility rests mainly with the household to provide its own accommodation, with means-tested financial assistance towards costs. Assistance with provision of housing, improvements and adaptations, emergency alarm and other support services is usually at the discretion of the local authority, housing agency or welfare organisation concerned. For institutional care provided on a medical basis there are rights under health insurance or national health systems, but where long-term social care is required with support from public funds, access may depend on assessment of need and on financial assessment for contribution to costs, as in the UK. Needs for residential care in the Netherlands must be assessed; a 'positive' assessment, however, does not give immediate access to a place in a home, which depends on availability.

Contracts, inspection systems and complaints procedures help to safeguard the rights of older people in institutional care, who have more protection than those in other housing settings. In care homes in Germany, for example, residents each have a contract with the home setting out terms and conditions; there are also elected homes councils (Brooke-Ross, 1987). In 1990 legislation on residential care established firmer rules for such contracts and councils, for recourse to an ombudsman, and for the provision of flexible care (Alber, 1993: 123). Nursing homes in the US under Medicaid and Medicare programmes have patients' rights policies and each state has a nursing home ombudsman. In the UK new complaints procedures and inspection units were implemented under the 1990 NHS and Community Care Act. To measure outcomes of residential care a comparative analysis, beyond the scope of this study, could be undertaken of data obtained from monitoring such systems.

Policies resulting in the reduction of institutional care and state provision of services as well as the promotion of more flexible solutions and individual and family responsibilities have meant targeting of publicly supported institutional care to those most dependent, without family support and on low incomes. For the majority of older people with care needs who do not live in care homes, informal carers, usually female relatives, are responsible for providing most of the care. These responsibilities, however, tend to be taken on more often by working class than middle class families which have greater resources to provide for other caring solutions (Arber and Ginn, 1992). The responsibilities of family carers are discussed further in chapter 4.

The policy rhetoric of community care reforms in the 1990s, for example in the UK, suggests that greater flexibility and more individualised care solutions will promote individual choice of older people and their carers. For those who are dependent on state support in terms of finance or service provision, however, it is not clear how far such choice is available (see for example Age Concern England, 1993). Despite policy statements advocating a coordinated approach, housing services are, in practice, poorly coordinated with health and welfare services in the six countries.

The amount of choice people have in where they live in later life depends on the interaction of several variables: their present housing circumstances, need for care and access to formal and informal sources of care; the range of provision available in their local area in tenures to which they have access; their access to information on assessment and allocation procedures for such provision; incentives in the funding systems for housing and care; and their financial resources.

These financial resources are probably the most crucial in view of the increasing housing inequalities between groups as discussed above. Those with most resources, from professional and managerial backgrounds, with financial and housing assets and high benefits from social insurance and pensions (see chapter 2, table 2.5) will have most choice in improving their housing situation, whereas those on lower incomes, but who are not poor, may well have difficulties financing such options. People on the assistance side of the insurance/assistance divide are likely to be renting poorer quality housing in the public or private sector or to be unable to afford necessary repairs or adaptations if they own their homes. Those on the lowest incomes and/or whose assets have been spent on long-term institutional care are most likely to have residential care fully funded by the state if they have no other options available.

As suggested in chapter 2, the funding systems for long-term institutional care contain intended and unintended incentives which may influence people's choices of particular forms of care which are not necessarily the most appropriate for them (see, for example, Henrard and Brocas, 1990). In France and Germany the obligation of families to contribute to costs of residential care deters older people from applying for social assistance for care (Guillemard and Argoud, 1992: 98). Where long-term care is provided free of charge through health service or health insurance systems, as in France, there are incentives for older people and families to use this form of care, although governments are reducing the amount of provision available in the medical sector. In Italy community and home help services have not been covered by state funding since 1985; local authorities which would otherwise have to fund these services thus have an incentive to place older people in private residential homes paid for by the national health fund (Ascoli, 1988: 172). The lack of insurance for long-term care in the US means that older people must pay for nursing home care from their own resources until impoverished enough to qualify for Medicaid (Jazwiecki, 1989).

Detailed comparative research is needed to determine more clearly the effects of the complex interaction of variables which influence older people's housing choices in North American and West European countries.

Summary

Post-1945 housing policies were not geared to providing suitable housing for older people; specialised, sheltered and residential accommodation were developed as standard solutions to older people's housing needs. From the 1970s general housing policies moved from subsidising buildings to subsidising individuals, state provision was reduced and marketisation encouraged. Responses to older people's housing needs began to become more flexible in accord with community care policies, while institutions became more community-based. The need for closer integration of housing and care services was recognised.

Economic, demographic and political influences are reflected in the principles and assumptions on which policies are based in the 1990s. These policies advocate greater flexibility in housing options for older people. There are three main types of option: those based on ordinary housing, including ways of helping people to stay in this housing; options for moving into various types of grouped housing for independent living with some support; and institutional long-term care. Distinctions between types of provision are becoming blurred and innovative forms combine different types. Older people's housing situations vary between and within countries. Socio-economic class and financial resources are major factors determining access to housing choices in later life. Gender, 'race' and age also affect people's housing needs in older age and their ability to meet these needs.

Housing provision for older people is a field of social policy in which needs are extensive and growing, entitlements are few and, beneath the rhetoric of policy statements, the range of authentic choice is limited. Although at policy level the need to link housing and care services is recognised and the provision of flexible integrated services to meet individual needs is a policy goal, in practice such integrated services have not yet been achieved in the countries studied.

4
Domiciliary Care

Domiciliary health and welfare services such as home nursing and home help form the nucleus of community care service provision. This chapter adopts a wide definition of domiciliary care which embraces any type of care or support offered to older people in their homes, whether in ordinary or specialised settings, by formal or informal carers. The tasks or services include basic care such as help with daily living activities, mobility and self-care; medical care, nursing or therapy services; counselling, emotional support and social contacts; support for informal carers, that is family, friends and neighbours, who provide much of this care; and advice and information for older people and carers. These services cross the medical/social divide and are supplied by both health and social care systems and all sectors of the mixed economy of welfare.

The development of domiciliary care is considered first, in the context of community care trends and policies in the six countries studied, taking account of influences on these policies and the assumptions and principles on which they are based. The second part of the chapter outlines the provision, funding and organisation of domiciliary care services. The implications and outcomes of the various domiciliary care systems for older people and carers in different geographical areas are then discussed, with attention to different patterns of class, gender, 'race' and age.

Background to domiciliary care services

Development of policies on domiciliary care

Policies on domiciliary care developed slowly in the post 1945 period. As shown in chapter 3, stated policies on care for older people generally concerned institutional care. Services such as home help and home nursing existed and grew, for example in the Netherlands and UK, but were rarely the subject of explicit policies. Jamieson (1991: 278) refers to

76

the 1960s and 1970s as a period of 'growth without policies' where home care services are concerned. Domiciliary care became more focused on older people as their proportion in the population increased, entailing greater demand for services. There was no integrated approach to the overall home care needs of dependent older people as the medical services, such as home nursing, generally developed separately from social services such as home help, with different statutory frameworks and funding sources.

From around the 1970s policies on domiciliary care were formulated in response to changing attitudes to institutionalisation and positive concepts of care in the community. As policymakers favoured community care rather than institutional care for both humanitarian and organisational reasons, domiciliary services were promoted to support older people with care needs living in their own homes. However, these policies also developed in the context of cost containment imperatives in the late 1970s and 1980s. The need for domiciliary care was recognised but the services, subject to resource constraints, could not expand to meet growing demand for them. During the 'policies without growth' period of the 1980s the focus shifted to 'ways of distributing *existing resources* more effectively' (Jamieson, 1991: 279, 281). The shortfall between demand and provision was to be met by informal carers as policies emphasised family care as the norm and the role of formal services shifted to that of meeting needs where informal care was unavailable.

The stated aims of home care policies in the 1980s, then, were mainly to help older people to live independently in their own homes rather than in institutions, whether hospitals, residential or nursing homes. This conformed with the western European trend of reducing use of institutions and promoting forms of care considered to be more cost effective. The consequences of this trend were that, in theory if not in practice, institutional care was increasingly to be targeted to those considered most in need and domiciliary care to those who might otherwise be admitted to institutional care. This consideration of care needs was part of the move towards an ideal of more flexible, less standardised forms of care in care packages tailored to the individual, based on needs assessment by a care manager in consultation with other professionals as well as the older individuals and informal carers concerned.

A further trend in northern European countries was explicit recognition of the contributions and needs of informal carers, and the aim of incorporating informal care into the stated policies and procedures of community care (Baldock and Evers, 1992: 299). This in turn was one aspect of the trend to reduce the role of the state and develop the mixed economy of care, through increasing care provision by the non-governmental sectors. In the US the for-profit sector in home health agencies increased rapidly in the 1980s (Estes and Swan, 1993). The balance of the welfare mix in many countries changed as the use of the commercial and non-profit sectors increased, and markets were also opened up for cross-national service provision by non-governmental agencies.

Although general trends can be identified, policies of countries with different welfare regime types vary in the level of provision of domiciliary care services and in expectations about the roles of informal carers. 'Liberal' and 'conservative–corporatist' regimes generally place more emphasis on families' responsibility to care, and also have a lower level of provision than 'social democratic' regimes. The domiciliary care policies of the six countries studied are outlined briefly below.

France's domiciliary care policies, originating in the 1960s (Laroque, 1962), have been reiterated in successive policy documents including the Braun report (Braun and Stourm, 1988) which called for priority for domiciliary support. The strong medical/social divide is recognised in government reports as an obstacle to coordination (Boulard, 1991; Schopflin, 1991). The Boulard report considered ways of linking health and social care, of giving older people more choice in their care, and of supporting informal carers. In the Schopflin report caring for carers forms a third dimension of state policy on older age, in addition to community care and residential care (Jani-Le Bris, 1992: 38).

In *Germany* domiciliary care policy is strictly divided between nursing care under the health insurance system and social care, funded mainly through social assistance. In 1984 the social assistance law was amended to give home care priority over residential care for long-term care funding. Home help services are poorly developed because under the principle of subsidiarity, household members are required to provide such care for people needing support from social assistance. Medically oriented home nursing services are not geared to long-term care of frail older people. In the late 1980s the lack of insurance cover for risk of long-term care became a policy issue. Limited health insurance cover for such care was introduced in 1991 under the Health Service Reform Act 1988 (Dieck, 1994); compulsory care insurance is to be implemented for home care, day and respite care from 1995.

Italy has a low level of institutional care; the main form of support for frail older people is family care. The national health service, introduced from 1978, created local health care units to manage public health services; local authorities are responsible for social services. Government policy under the project for older people (*Progetto Obiettivo Anziani*) 1991–5, approved within the national health care plan, introduced guidelines on integrating health and welfare services, and measures to encourage older people to stay with their families, including an integrated home care programme from 1990 and plans for home hospitalisation services (Florea et al., 1993; Mengani and Gagliardi, 1992).

Domiciliary care services have formed part of community care policy in the *Netherlands* since the late 1960s. Policy in the 1980s focused on reducing the proportion of older people in institutions. The principle of 'substitution' of home care for institutional care and less formal for more technical services was adopted. The Dekker report (1987) emphasised a move to flexible packages of care to meet individual needs. Measures taken in the 1980s to coordinate home help and home nursing services included bringing them under the same funding source (AWBZ, see chapter 2) and cooperation between service providing agencies. Innovative forms of home care were stimulated through government incentives for substitution (Romijn and Miltenburg, 1993).

In the *United Kingdom* there was no specific legislation for domiciliary care until the 1968 Health Services and Public Health Act under which local authorities were given the power to promote the welfare of elderly people. Home help services were provided mainly by local authorities, home nursing through the national health service. Policy in the 1980s emphasised informal care as the norm. Community care reforms implemented in 1991–3 under the National Health Service and Community Care Act 1990 aimed to reduce direct provision of care by local authorities and develop the independent sectors; to develop domiciliary care, promote flexible packages of care based on assessed needs, and support informal carers.

Domiciliary services in the *United States* vary widely as there is no national long-term care policy; health and social services are fragmented, funded mainly through the Medicare and Medicaid systems, and thus very medically oriented. Medicare insurance provides for short-term home health care for people in medical need, while means-tested Medicaid can fund optional community services, depending on state policy. Under the home and community based waiver programme introduced in 1982, the state can apply to the federal government for Medicaid requirements to be waived, to allow community services such as home help and personal care to be provided. Policy discussion from the late 1980s, for example the Pepper Commission (1990), focused on ways of expanding and financing domiciliary care and on supporting informal carers, in order to meet long-term care needs more appropriately.

Domiciliary care policies: influences and principles

As emphasised in previous chapters, the overriding influences on policy trends have been economic ones. Since the economic crises of the 1970s and more recently the recession of the early 1990s, domiciliary care, like other aspects of community care, has been subject to politicians' concern with cost containment and reduction of public spending. Analysis of expenditure on health and social services shows that costs for the oldest age groups are proportionately much higher than for younger groups. For example in Germany: 'Pensioners represent only 29 per cent of all sickness insurance members, but require 41 percent of the benefit expenditure of the statutory sickness scheme' (Alber, 1992: 57). In England: 'The ratio of expenditure per head of hospital and community health services on those aged 85 and over compared with the 16–64 age group is more than 10: 1 and the personal social services expenditure ratio is more than 20: 1' (Walker, 1992b: 42).

Since the over-75s and especially the over-85s are considered more at risk of dependence on health and social care services, policymakers' concerns about high costs of this care are compounded by demographic projections showing rapid increases in these age groups. There are, however, arguments that in future high needs for health and welfare services of very old people will not be inevitable. Fries (1989), for example, maintains that improvements in health and lifestyle changes and the 'compression of morbidity' into a short period, will mean that many very old people will remain healthy and active (see also Arber and Ginn, 1992: 118–20).

Further demographic evidence showing reduction in the potential availability of family carers adds to policymakers' anxieties. The number of women aged 45–69, the traditional pool of carers, has decreased in proportion to the numbers of people aged over 70, from a ratio of more than two to one in 1960 to 1.5: 1 or lower in 1990 in the countries studied. For example in Germany from 1960 to 1990 the ratio fell from 2.6 to 1.6, and in the Netherlands from 2.2 to 1.5 (Alber, 1993). This decrease is projected to continue. Other demographic factors that affect the potential supply of carers include smaller families, increased divorce, geographical mobility and increased paid employment of women.

Turning to political and ideological factors, the New Right has influenced domiciliary care, for example in the UK and US, particularly through policies of reducing the role of the state, developing the private commercial or non-profit sectors and emphasising the responsibility of families to care. The political power of the medical profession has also contributed to the perpetuation of the medical/social divide in domiciliary care and the lack of attention to the long-term care needs of dependent people for care provided on a social rather than medical model. The lack of power of older people and family carers means that long-term home care services are not a political priority and that reduction in expenditure on such services will not attract strong protest.

The medical/social divide is also reflected in the levels of government at which decisions on domiciliary care are taken: decisions on medical services tend to be more centralised whereas those on social services are more local. The centralised services are generally subject to more control and are less variable than those governed by more local levels. For example in Italy social services policy is decided locally: 'the planning as well as the operation of social services are almost totally dependent on the (ever changing) local political leadership, and hence subject to a great deal of discontinuity and unpredictability' (Jamieson, 1991: 292). The fact that in most countries policies are made and services planned and delivered at different levels and by different administrative bodies also exacerbates difficulties in service coordination. The promotion of domiciliary care as a cost effective solution to the care needs of older people, and the principle of substitution downwards, as adopted in the Netherlands, were originally based on the assumption that domiciliary care is generally cheaper than institutional care. The accuracy of this assumption depends on various factors such as the relative costs of types of care and the costs that are included in the calculation. Another consideration is the level of care required by individuals which is less expensive to provide outside institutions. The provision of many hours of intensive domiciliary care services is unlikely to be a cheaper substitute for institutional care. It is, however, evidently less expensive for the state if the care is provided in the home by unpaid carers whose contribution is not costed. It is thus in the state's interest to promote informal care and support to help relatives, usually women, to continue to care, rather than to develop formal domiciliary care (Jamieson, 1991: 289–90).

The extent to which families are expected to provide care, however, varies between types of welfare regime. In the 'liberal' type, for example the US, state services are residual and it is implicit in the system that individuals will provide for themselves and their families. UK policy has increasingly moved towards this position. In the reformed community care system of the 1990s, families are not legally obliged to provide care but are expected to do so as a major component of the care system, with formal services to provide support and, if necessary, residential care when informal carers are not able or available to care (Finch et al., 1992).

In countries with 'conservative–corporatist' regimes the implications of the teachings of the Catholic church and the principles of subsidiarity and self-help are that families are explicitly required to provide care. In Germany, for example, there is a strict hierarchy of responsibility vested in the first place at the lowest level, the family, moving up to the community, welfare organisations and state agencies only when those at a lower level are unable to provide (Spicker, 1991).

The policies of 'social democratic' regimes generally contrast with those of 'liberal' and 'conservative–corporatist' ones in that there are fewer expectations that families will provide care. In the Netherlands there are: 'no formal obligations for family members (not in cash, neither in kind) or for other network members to contribute' (Baars et al., 1992: 51), although spouses are expected to care and professionals may request help from family members living nearby. Informal care is increasingly promoted as part of substitution policy; this has met with criticism from the women's movement (Steenvoorden, 1992).

In the former GDR, a 'bureaucratic state collectivist' regime (Deacon, 1992), where in theory the state provided comprehensive services for older people and there was no requirement for families to care, services were unevenly distributed and families did provide most of the care for dependent older people (Dieck, 1992).

In practice, as shown below, in all types of welfare state regime, informal carers provide the great majority of care; policies on support for carers and provision of domiciliary services, however, vary according to policymakers' expectations, explicit or implicit, about the role of family carers.

Provision of domiciliary care

As policy on domiciliary care developed in an uncoordinated way, the various health and social services have mainly been provided separately, until the late 1980s, with little attention to the overall care needs of the individual. The range of caring tasks and components of domiciliary care service provision, and the care needs of older people, are now reviewed. The care provided by the informal, statutory and independent sectors, and the ways in which services are organised and funded in the countries studied, are then examined.

Types of service provided to meet care needs

As suggested at the beginning of this chapter, the range of caring tasks and services offered to older people in their homes is extensive. The services can be divided according to the type of need they meet: basic care and activities of daily living (ADL); physical and mental health care; counselling, emotional support, social contacts and emergency help; support for informal carers; and information and advice for the older person and/or carer. Table 4.1 summarises the types of need covered by these categories and gives examples of the relevant services and professionals offering the care. It must be emphasised that informal carers supply most of the help with basic care, and much help in other categories such as nursing, emotional support, social contacts, information and advice. The components of formal care are similar in all the countries, although they are organised and funded in different ways.

Most older people, however, are healthy and independent and do not need any of these domiciliary care services. If they have disabilities they often adopt strategies of self-care to manage daily living activities before turning to informal or formal care (Wilson, 1994: 239–40). Those who do receive domiciliary care are likely to be unable to carry out activities of daily living without help, or to have physical or mental health problems which require professional care. Since such care needs tend to increase with age, overall needs for a population are sometimes estimated from the numbers or proportions of people in the oldest age groups and projected increases in these figures. The proportion of women in these older age groups is considered significant since women have longer life expectancy than men, as shown in Table 4.2, and are more likely than men to be widowed, to live alone and to use health and welfare services.

In the over 80 age group the proportion of women in the population is over two-thirds, as shown in Table 4.3, and their proportion continues to increase with age; for example in Germany 75 per cent of those over 85 are women (Alber, 1992: 81), and in France 84 per cent of the over-94s are women (Jani-Le Bris, 1992: 104).

Overall population needs for long-term care are usually assessed from survey evidence or dependence scales which measure, for example, people's abilities in activities of daily living (ADL). Such measures are

Table 4.1   *Domiciliary care needs and services*

Services to meet needs for	Examples of formal services
1 *basic care*	
cooking, laundry, shopping, cleaning	home help, meals service
dressing, bathing, toileting	home nurse, care assistant
mobility within the home	walking aids, ADL equipment
2 *physical and mental health care*	
footcare, therapy	
medical care, medication	general practitioner, specialist
nursing, continence, injections	home nurse, psychiatric nurse
	chiropodist, physiotherapist
3 *counselling, emotional support, contacts*	
coping with illness, disability, dying	social worker, counsellor, health
social visits, social contacts	visitor
emergency contacts	voluntary visitor, telephone service
	alarm service, mobile warden
4 *support for informal carers*	
coping with caring responsibility	social worker, carers group
practical help with caring	home help, care attendant
relief from caring	sitting service, night nurse
5 *information and advice*	
benefits and services available	professionals providing home care
	press, radio, television, leaflets
	voluntary organisations

Table 4.2   *Life expectancy at birth for men and women, 1989*

Life expectancy (years)	France	Germany[a]	Italy	Netherlands	United Kingdom	United States
males	72.5	72.6	73.5	73.7	72.8	71.8
females	80.6	79.0	80.0	79.9	78.4	78.6

[a] former FRG.
© OECD, 1993, OECD Health Data Version 1.5. Reproduced by permission of the OECD.

Table 4.3 *Percentage of women in older age groups, 1989*

% of women	France	Germany[a]	Italy	Netherlands	United Kingdom	United States[b]
in population aged 60+	59	63	58	58	58	58
in population aged 80+	70	72	67	69	70	68

[a] former FRG.
[b] figures for 1991.
Sources: Jani-Le Bris, 1993: 165.
US Bureau of the Census, 1992: 15.

rarely taken on a cross-national basis; comparison is thus difficult. The various scales used in different countries to measure performance of activities of daily living, self-care, mobility and so on, show that the majority of older people do not have difficulties, but that the need for help increases with age, particularly from about 75 years, and is higher for women than men. For example in the Netherlands 3 per cent of those aged 65–74 and 12 per cent of the over-75s have serious problems with one or more activity of daily living (Baars et al., 1992: 76). In the UK the prevalence of severe incapacity per 1,000 population rises from 47 in the 60–69 age group to 100 of those aged 70–79 and 388 of the over-80s; and 'the prevalence of very severe disability among women aged 75 and over is more than three times greater than the rate for men in the same age group' (Walker, 1992b: 42).

Such survey data are used to estimate the proportions of older people in different age groups who may need domiciliary care; these estimates use a narrow definition of need based on help with ADL, rather than covering a range of social and health care needs as shown in Table 4.1. To obtain a more accurate assessment of which groups are more likely to be dependent on care from others, including the state, account must also be taken of the resources on which people are able to draw if they have difficulties with daily living activities. Arber and Ginn (1991: 68–9) argue that material resources, health resources and caring resources ('the resource triangle') are all important factors in whether or not people retain their independence; that access to these resources is influenced by gender, class and 'race'; and that those who are disadvantaged are more likely to have to depend on others when they need care.

Domiciliary care consists of the various services identified above, which developed separately in most countries but which, in the 1980s and 1990s, were increasingly seen as potential components of care packages tailored to meet assessed individual needs. However, reformed systems based on meeting individual needs are not yet fully established; this study examines domiciliary care provision in practice in the early 1990s.

Informal domiciliary care and support for carers

The majority of care for people who are unable to manage their daily activities through self-care is provided by informal carers. In European and North American countries, irrespective of the type of welfare regime, it is estimated that informal carers undertake 75–80 per cent of care for older people. For example the family provides care in 74 per cent of cases where Italian family members need care, a combination of family and professionals provide 16 per cent, and institutions 10 per cent of care for those in need (Mengani and Gagliardi, 1992). The contribution of family carers in Germany (in both former FRG and GDR) is estimated at 80 per cent (Dieck, 1992).

There is, however, a lack of representative national or cross-national research on informal care, as found by the European Foundation study on family care of dependent older people in the early 1990s (Jani-Le Bris, 1993). For Great Britain a national study undertaken as part of the General Household Survey (GHS) 1985 provides representative data (Green, 1988), but for most European countries such research has not yet been completed; estimates rely on small scale or outdated surveys. The available evidence shows that informal carers are predominantly family members, although friends and neighbours provide some care.

Although most family carers are women, mainly wives, daughters and daughters-in-law, the role of older men as carers has tended to be neglected in literature focusing on daughters caring for parents (Arber and Gilbert, 1989). The European Foundation study found that, except in southern Europe, the majority of carers were spouses and that these were as likely to be men as women; however, among children caring for parents, women predominated (Jani-Le Bris, 1993: 53).

Analysis of the GHS data for Great Britain shows that in contrast to the assumptions about middle aged women being the main providers of care, older people provided 35 per cent of care for other elderly people, whereas middle aged women provided 28 per cent; 37 per cent of all care was provided by men (Arber and Ginn, 1990: 449–50). People aged over

75 spent on average more than 50 hours per week caring, whereas the average for carers of all ages was 20 hours for men and 22 hours for women. Women were more likely than men to be caring for someone in another household; co-resident carers spent on average 52 hours per week compared with 8.8 hours per week spent by those caring for someone in another household (Arber and Ginn, 1990: 441–2).

Surveys for other countries show similar findings: informal carers, whether daughters, spouses or others, provide an enormous volume of domiciliary care compared with the contribution of the formal sectors. However, although policy statements pay lip service to supporting family carers, the amount of help they receive is very limited and the majority do not have any services from formal agencies. In countries where the principle of subsidiarity is applied, policymakers are especially reluctant to provide help in case this leads family carers to reduce their effort. Services such as home help and nursing provided for the older person also relieve the carer, but few services are offered specifically to carers.

Domiciliary services in the Netherlands and UK are becoming more geared to taking account of carers' needs. In the Netherlands district nurses and home helps receive training in emotional support for carers; volunteers are also increasingly involved in providing help in the home and counselling for carers, particularly where terminal care is being given (Steenvoorden, 1992). In the UK some local authorities provide night sitters, and some health authorities or voluntary agencies offer night nurses to relieve carers and/or provide terminal care; care attendant schemes such as Crossroads offer care attendants to give flexible practical help in the home or provide a break for carers (Twigg, 1992).

A small amount of financial support for people with disabilities or their carers to mitigate the costs of caring is also offered in most countries (Glendinning and McLaughlin, 1993). French people aged 65 and over with 80 per cent or more disability and needing help from another person for essential daily living activities, can apply for the means-tested compensatory allowance (*allocation compensatrice*), which may be used to pay for home help or nursing or to pay a relative to care. In Germany under the 1989 pension reforms implemented in 1992 there are pension contribution credits, based on 75 per cent average wage, for those providing at least ten hours unpaid care per week. The social assistance system provides a means-tested care allowance based on level of disability. Italy introduced companion payments in 1980 for severely disabled people unable to walk or perform activities of daily living; these payments, mostly to dependent older people, are intended to help them stay in their own homes with care from family (Mengani and Gagliardi, 1992: 23).

In the Netherlands there are small tax concessions for the costs of caring and, subject to strict criteria, carers on minimum income can receive a social security supplement. People needing much help with care in their own homes in the UK can claim cash help: attendance allowances for those over 65 and disability living allowances for under 65s; carers aged 16–65 caring for at least 35 hours a week for a person receiving one of these allowances, and not working full time, can claim invalid care allowance (ICA); if the carer is receiving income support there is a small weekly addition (carer's premium) to the IS benefit. There is no federal payment for care costs in the US but the Veterans Administration provides an aid and attendance allowance, a supplement to the VA pension, for disabled veterans who need regular help from another person. Such benefits and allowances recognise the costs of caring and provide a token recompense but only meet a small proportion of the actual costs.

Organisation and funding of formal domiciliary care

The formal care delivery systems in the six countries are outlined below; basic details of funding for health and social care are given in chapter 2.

The medical/social divide in *France* is reflected in the systems of administration for domiciliary care. An elected general council in each *département* is responsible for social and medico-social services, while the central state is responsible for medical decisions. Some social services are provided by the commune through the *Centre Communal d'Action Sociale* (CCAS). Non-profit associations provide 70 per cent of domiciliary services (Robbins, 1990). There is as yet little provision by the commercial sector.

Home help services are offered by associations or CCAS to help older people stay in their own homes. After assessment by the service, applications are submitted to funding bodies (social assistance or pension funds) which decide hours of help and user's financial contribution. Domiciliary meals services, laundry services, home alarms and telephone help lines may also be provided by CCAS or associations. Social workers based in various social and medical agencies give advice and emotional support.

Home nursing services organised by the CCAS or associations provide nursing and personal care, equipment, and chiropody, physiotherapy and other services as prescribed by a doctor. The hospital at home service allows people needing continuing medical care to be nursed at home. Psychiatric services based in hospitals offer a home care service. All these medical services are funded by health insurance. Home carers provide help not covered by home help or nursing services; they are organised by associations which place workers with older people who can receive help with the costs (Guillemard and Argoud, 1992).

The strong medical/social divide in *Germany* is manifested in strict hierarchies in service provision. Under the subsidiarity principle the family has first responsibility for caring; then formal services, if necessary, are provided by non-profit welfare organisations (*freie Wohlfahrtsverbände*). As specified in the social assistance act, if a welfare organisation is willing to provide a service, the social assistance authority must support it; if not, services may be provided directly by communes or districts (Jarré, 1991). Most domiciliary services are provided by non-profit organisations; the commercial sector is growing, but does not receive state subsidies.

Welfare organisations often provide domiciliary services from community care centres (*Sozialstationen*), which are state-subsidised. Access to these services depends on eligibility for funding. Community nursing is organised in three categories: specialised nursing, basic nursing and home help. To qualify for basic nursing and home help through health insurance the person must first need specialised nursing. The nursing is only provided for four weeks. Under social assistance, however, people can have home nursing and home help without need for medical treatment if no one in the household can provide it (Dieck and Garms-Homolová, 1991: 119). Since 1991 very frail people can have 25 hours per month of community nursing funded by health insurance; a monthly cash alternative is available, and often preferred (Evers and Olk, 1991: 81). The care insurance system from April 1995 includes a similar arrangement whereby people may choose services up to a monthly limit, according to the degree of dependency, or a lower amount of cash.

Other domiciliary services offered by community care centres include meals on wheels and loan of ADL equipment. They may also employ social workers who give counselling and advice, and psychogeriatric workers. Doctors and paramedical professionals work in private practice, reimbursed by health insurance.

In *Italy* domiciliary care services are provided by statutory health and social services, social cooperatives, non-profit and religious organisations, volunteers, and commercial agencies. Health services offered by the local health unit are financed by the national health care fund, whereas public social services are organised by communes, following regional guidelines and financed through regional social funds with means-tested contributions from users. In some regions agreements are drawn up between local health units and local authorities for coordination of services; in others health care and social units administer health and social services (Florea et al., 1993).

Home care services offered by communes directly or through social cooperatives aim to help dependent older people remain in their own homes. The services and their administration vary widely according to local authority policy and are not available throughout the country (Costanzi, 1991). Staffed by nurses, home helps and social workers, they offer domestic help, nursing and personal care, help with administration and form filling, visits and social contacts, and in some places, domiciliary meals, laundry, chiropody, or telephone alarm systems. Home care services are mainly allocated to people on low incomes who live alone.

Since domiciliary care services currently provided are insufficient, the health ministry's plan for older people 1991–5 introduced a programme of integrated home care, intended to help 2 per cent of the dependent over-75s. The domiciliary service includes medical and nursing care, home help and social work. Home hospitalisation projects are also being developed to allow people to remain in their own homes rather than in long-term hospital care (Florea et al., 1993).

The government in the *Netherlands* is responsible for planning and regulation of services at national, regional and local levels, whereas service provision is by non-profit organisations, funded by state and social insurance sources. There is little involvement by the commercial sector (Baars et al., 1992). Home help is offered by home help agencies and home nursing by cross associations (*Kruisverenigingen*); these organisations are to merge at local level, as the national associations did in 1990. Both services are funded by AWBZ and user contributions.

Home help agencies provide domestic help and personal care services. There is also a system of 'alpha' help, arranged by home help agencies, whereby users pay a worker for up to 12 hours a week of basic domestic help. Home nursing services offer skilled nursing, personal care, preventive work and loan of equipment (Baars et al., 1992). As part of the substitution policy the government is promoting 24 hour home care and nursing.

Most general practitioners and physiotherapists are private practitioners. Community psychiatric nurses are organised through regional institutes (RIAGGs). Other domiciliary services are offered by associations for coordinated work for older people (*gecoödineerd ouderenwerk*), controlled by municipalities and financed through the general welfare budget; services include domiciliary meals, alarm systems, advice and information (Baars et al., 1992). The substitution policy has also led to encouragement for home care through various government funding incentives since 1984; for example, funding for residential homes to develop outreach services such as meals on wheels and alarm services, and for support for people in their own homes or in residential homes who would otherwise need admission to a nursing home. The involvement of volunteers in visiting and helping older people and providing sitting services has also increased (Steenvoorden, 1992).

Until the 1990s reforms domiciliary services in the *United Kingdom* were mainly provided and funded by the statutory sector: health care such as home nursing by the NHS and social care such as home help and meals by the local authority. The NHS is centrally funded and controlled through regional and local health authorities; since the 1980s central government has increasingly taken control over the level of expenditure by elected local authorities.

In the 1990s the purchasing and providing functions of both health and local authorities were separated. Health authorities and fundholding general practitioners purchase community nursing services such as district nurses and community psychiatric nurses from providers in their own authority or other agencies. Equipment for daily living is supplied on loan through either health or social services authorities; occupational therapists based in hospitals or local authorities assess need. Domiciliary visits are also made by NHS physiotherapists and chiropodists. Under the reformed community care system local authorities are expected to provide fewer services directly, to purchase them through contracts with commercial or non-profit agencies, and raise means-tested charges from users. The commercial sector which had little interest in domiciliary care is developing these services. The non-profit sector is mainly involved with meals services, care attendants, voluntary visitors, alarm services, help lines, advice services and, increasingly, home help. Social workers are employed by local authorities and provide counselling and support; they may also be care managers who assess needs for services and coordinate care packages.

In the *United States* domiciliary services are provided mainly through medical rather than social agencies and funding. Services are offered by private commercial or non-profit agencies; home health care is also provided for veterans by the VA. The growth of profit-making home health care agencies was encouraged by the Reagan adminstration in the 1980s; large private hospital organisations are also moving into home care provision (Estes and Swan, 1993). Home health care agencies offer nursing and therapy services, personal care, housework, meals, chore services and respite care in the home. Medicare insurance covers limited necessary skilled nursing or therapy services for housebound older people, but does not pay for home carers. Under Medicaid home and community based waiver programmes states may provide home help and personal care to people on low incomes who would otherwise need nursing home care. For people above the income limit for Medicaid who cannot afford to pay for their own home care, church organisations, volunteers or informal carers may be the only sources of help.

Services may also be financed through state and area agencies on ageing by federal funding under Title III of the Older Americans Act 1965; this covers domiciliary meals services, home health, home help and chore services, visiting and telephone contacts. The social services block grant from federal government allows some social services to be provided, depending on state policy. Other funding sources are community development block grant, county and municipal finance, and funding from voluntary contributions through charity organisations.

The provision of domiciliary care services by different agencies with various funding sources is a symptom, in most countries, of a lack of coordination between services, as agencies have an interest in retaining their own budget and identity. The Netherlands has addressed this issue by merging funding sources and agencies. Care management, information services and other initiatives designed to promote coordination between services and sectors, including informal carers, are discussed further in chapter 7.

Outcomes of domiciliary care systems

With a greater focus on care at home, a range of domiciliary care is increasingly needed to help older people with disabilities or health problems to live in their own homes. Potentially positive developments such as individually tailored 'care packages' (combinations of services) and support for carers are not yet widely established. The uncoordinated provision of care by informal and formal carers and different agencies affects outcomes of domiciliary care and older people's access to caring resources.

Implications of domiciliary care policies for different groups of older people and carers

The emphasis on cost containment since the 1970s has meant that the overall levels of domiciliary service provision have not risen in proportion to increasing demands, although the services have developed. In the UK 'the number of home helps per thousand of the population over 75 fell from 20.6 in 1975–6 to 14.5 in 1987–8' (Walker, 1992b: 48). The lack of cross-national comparative statistics on domiciliary care makes it difficult to assess the extent to which need is met, but information from all the countries studied suggests that there is underprovision. Cost containment in health care and inadequate resources for the development of domiciliary care have increased the financial and caring burdens on individual older people and carers. For example in the US reductions in Medicare and Medicaid have increased the amount that older people have to pay for their own home health care; if they cannot afford these costs, the alternatives are informal care or nursing homes.

Data on the provision of home care services in the six countries give some indication of the levels of home help and home nursing provided, but should be treated with caution as definitions and services vary, and different sources are sometimes inconsistent. The proportions of people over 65 receiving home care are highest in the Netherlands and the UK, lower in France, and lowest in Germany, Italy and the US, as shown in Table 4.4.

People living alone are most likely to receive home care in all countries; use of services increases with age. Those who have difficulties with ADL are also more likely to receive services, but services are not always appropriately targeted. In France, for example, the numbers receiving home help increased in the 1970s and 1980s but the average number of hours decreased so that many people had very little help; services were also poorly targeted and many severely disabled people did not receive help (Henrard et al., 1991; Jani-Le Bris, 1992). With policy trends towards home care rather than institutional care and the implementation of substitution policies, however, there is increased emphasis in countries such as the Netherlands, the UK and US, on targeting home care services to those who would otherwise need institutional care. This means that people other than the most dependent are unlikely to receive formal services and have to rely on informal care or pay for private services, particularly if they need basic domestic services such as cleaning (Baldock and Evers, 1992).

Table 4.4   *Percentage of population aged 65+ receiving home care*

% of population aged 65+ receiving:	France	Germany[a]	Italy	Netherlands	United Kingdom	United States
home help	3–6[1]	2[1]	1[3]	8[1]	9[4]	0–8[5]
home nursing	0.6[2]	3[1]		15[1]	5[4]	1[6]

[a] former FRG.

Sources: [1] Alber, 1993.
   [2] Jamieson, 1991.
   [3] Florea et al., 1993 (% receiving home care).
   [4] Walker, 1992b.
   [5] OECD, 1994b.
   [6] Keenan, 1989.

The reduction in the role of the state and the development of the mixed economy of care has led to greater fragmentation of services, making it more difficult to coordinate them and to disseminate information about the services available. The increased use of for-profit agencies in the provision of home care for frail older people, for example in Germany and the US, is also a cause for concern about standards of care, as it is difficult to regulate these services (Evers and Olk, 1991). It seems likely that inequalities between groups of older people in the outcomes of domiciliary services will increase (Baldock and Evers, 1992: 306).

The distribution of domiciliary services is uneven both between and within countries. There are wide regional and local variations particularly in social care services on which decisions are made at a local level, and in countries with a high level of decentralisation such as Italy and France. In Italy, there is generally a higher level of services in the north than the south (Florea et al., 1993). In the US, states vary in their eligibility criteria for services and in the extent to which they offer home care services through Medicaid and other programmes. There is a tendency in most countries for urban areas to be better provided with domiciliary services than rural areas.

Social class inequalities in health affect need for domiciliary care; evidence from the GHS, for example, shows that in Great Britain people from lower socio-economic groups report poorer health and have higher levels of disability than those from higher groups (Arber and Ginn, 1991:

122–5). One would expect, therefore, to find a higher proportion of working class people receiving care. Social class, however, also influences the type of care received.

Class differences in use of services occur particularly for social care services such as home help which are means-tested or provided specifically for poor people, for example through Medicaid. Those from lower socio-economic groups are the main recipients of such services. Where there is a mixed economy of care, wealthier older people are able to pay for services of their choice in the private market, rather than rely on often stigmatised means-tested public services. Those who are not poor enough to qualify for free social assistance services, but cannot afford to pay, are disadvantaged in such systems, for example in Germany and the US. In most countries medical and nursing services are covered by health insurance or national health funds and there are fewer social class differences in use. However in the US, for the limited domiciliary services covered by Medicare insurance, there are flat rate co-payments from users, which fall more heavily on people with lower incomes.

The probability of receiving and giving informal care is also influenced by social class: people who can afford to pay for the care they need are less dependent on informal carers; those with dependants needing care are less likely to have to give that care themselves if they are able to pay for formal services. Evidence from the countries studied shows that people from lower socio-economic groups are over-represented among informal carers. For example in Italy 88 per cent of lower to middle class families, compared with 70 per cent of middle to upper class families, provide informal care (Mengani and Gagliardi, 1992: 79). In Germany about two-thirds of carers are from 'blue collar' or 'low to mid-level white collar' backgrounds (Döhner et al., 1992: 22).

As discussed earlier, women represent a higher proportion than men among older people with care needs, because they live longer and have more illness and disability than men. Women form, as expected, a majority of the recipients of domiciliary care, but there are gender differences in the type of care provided, often compounded by social class differences. Women are more likely than men to be in lower socio-economic groups and to depend on social assistance rather than insurance benefits. They are thus disproportionately represented among users of means-tested social care services because they lack financial resources to pay for care. Assumptions about gender roles in the domestic division of labour also affect the care received. Analysis of GHS data for Great Britain shows that for each level of disability there was a 'striking gender difference in help with domestic tasks' in that men received help from more informal and formal sources than women, except at the severest levels of disability (Arber and Ginn, 1991: 147).

Women are more likely than men to be care providers whether as low paid care workers or unpaid carers. The one-third of informal carers who are men are mainly elderly husbands; older spouse carers generally expect to provide care as part of the marital relationship. Among younger generations caring for older people, women predominate; there are also wide social class differences in providing co-resident care, for example in Britain: 'Higher middle class men are least likely to be co-resident carers, whereas semi-skilled and unskilled men are as likely as women in these classes to provide co-resident care' (Arber and Ginn, 1992: 630). As most formal domiciliary services are provided to people living alone, co-resident carers, whether spouses or children, receive little help with their caring tasks. There is, however, evidence from the GHS of gender differences, showing that husbands of disabled spouses are more likely than wives to receive domestic help from formal services (Arber and Ginn, 1991: 149; Bebbington and Davies, 1993: 382).

Inequalities in health, care and caring are also found among people of different 'race'. Data on this topic are more available for the US than for European countries; there is evidence for example that: 'older blacks were much more likely to rate their health as fair or poor (44%) than older whites (28%)' (AARP, 1993: 12). People from black and minority ethnic groups are also more likely than majority populations to have low incomes and depend on means-tested stigmatised services or informal carers. For example in the US one-third of elderly blacks were below the poverty level in 1992, compared with 11 per cent of elderly whites and 22 per cent of elderly hispanics (AARP, 1993: 10). Class and gender inequalities may be compounded with racial inequalities in influencing the type of care received and the likelihood of being a carer, whether low paid or unpaid. In the US system where Medicare insurance benefits the upper and middle classes most, 'out-of pocket health care expenses are disproportionately borne by older blacks and women. The burden is especially high for the poor and near-poor who are sick' (Estes and Harrington, 1985: 265). People from minority ethnic groups and their carers may also have difficulty gaining access both to information about the increasingly fragmented care services available and to assessment systems. The services offered to them may be inappropriate or discriminatory (Atkin, 1991; Valle, 1989); the needs of black carers may be neglected (Walker and Ahmad, 1994: 65).

Poor health, disability and need for care tend to increase with age; those in the oldest age groups are most likely to receive informal and formal domiciliary care. However the interactions of the effects of class, gender and 'race' also affect care needs and the type of care received. Social class differences mean that those from lower socio-economic groups are more likely to have disabilities and need care at a younger age than those from higher social classes (Arber and Ginn, 1991: 124). People in the oldest age groups are more likely to be women and to have few financial resources to allow them to exercise choice in care received or to help them in caring for elderly husbands.

The available evidence suggests, then, that care needs and access to material and caring resources to meet these needs are unevenly distributed (Arber and Ginn, 1991). Policies which aim to increase cost effectiveness by substituting less expensive forms of care for institutional care have not been accompanied by a corresponding development of formal domiciliary services, which are not necessarily less expensive, but by reliance on informal carers whose unpaid work is not included in formal accounting systems. There is abundant research evidence of the multi-faceted costs borne by family carers, especially those caring for parents. These costs include physical and mental health problems; the emotional stress of caring for dementia sufferers; competing demands of other family members; reduced social contacts; and financial consequences including direct costs of caring and indirect costs, for example foregone earnings and pension rights (Glendinning, 1992; Jani-Le Bris, 1993; Jazwiecki, 1989; Lewis and Meredith, 1988; Qureshi and Walker, 1989).

The majority of domiciliary care is given by the informal carers who bear these costs, but the caring role falls unequally, as shown, on women and those from lower social classes. Formal care services and financial support to sustain carers in their role are inadequate and also unevenly distributed between and within countries and social groups. Access to such services depends on their availability and allocation criteria, on knowledge of the systems and skills in negotiating the procedures, on ability to pay the financial and time costs of access, and on willingness to submit to application procedures which may be discriminatory and stigmatising. Social class, gender, 'race' and age all influence the extent to which people have the information, skills and financial resources to gain access to services and to exercise choice.

Rights, responsibilities and choice in domiciliary care

Responsibilities for caring are often clearly designated, particularly in systems based on the subsidiarity principle, but there are fewer rights to domiciliary care. In most systems there are more rights to health care than to social care, especially where there are strong divisions between the medical and social care systems. As emphasised earlier, people with low incomes who depend on residualised means-tested social care services have few rights to services such as home help. In the Netherlands, however, both nursing and home help services are provided through the same compulsory insurance fund and older people assessed as needing care have clear rights to both forms of domiciliary service.

In the US people with disabilities have rights under the Americans with Disabilities Act 1990 to the provision of state or local government services if they are eligible for them (Scott, 1994). There are specific rights for older people with disabilities under the Chronically Sick and Disabled Persons Act 1970 in England and Wales, where local authorities must provide domiciliary services such as practical help and meals for people with assessed needs for them. The existence of these rights does not, however, guarantee provision of services in practice (McEwen, 1992; RADAR, 1994).

The development of non-statutory sectors of the mixed economy of care, entailing the commodification of care and increased reliance on informal care, is likely to reduce rights to care services which may previously have been provided or funded as a right by the statutory sector, for example home help in the UK. As Baldock and Evers (1992: 310) point out, such developments constitute 'a redefinition of the role of governments in the provision of welfare and a renegotiation of the relative balance of obligations and rights between citizen and the state.'

Policies promoting pluralist provision of care based on individual needs emphasise the importance of consumer choice, but fail to acknowledge that people who receive domiciliary care and their carers are rarely in a position to exercise choice. Further, as shown, the possibility of exercising choice depends on social class, gender, 'race' and age, and on the power of professional assessors and allocators. In systems which place responsibilities on individuals and families to provide care for themselves and their dependants, most older people and carers have little choice in whether to accept these responsibilities. Those who are able to choose usually have financial resources to pay for care for themselves or their family members in the private market.

Where care for a frail older person is required, there are also cultural and gendered norms about who should provide the care, beginning with the spouse, then daughter, daughter-in-law, son, other relatives, friends and so on (Qureshi and Walker, 1989); women are expected to become informal carers of elderly relatives to a much greater extent than men. Decisions about which individual within this hierarchy should take on the caring role is negotiated within the family; it is usually one woman who takes the main burden, perhaps because she is less assertive than other family members (Ungerson, 1987; Finch, 1989). Caring may be a positive choice, however, as some carers gain satisfaction from the role. Once a person has taken on the caring task there is little choice about the care they provide, since few support services are offered; the only possibility of help may be for the person receiving care to be admitted to residential care (Finch et al., 1992: 24).

Outcomes from systems of domiciliary care provision

The formal care systems with which older people and carers have to negotiate for domiciliary care are characterised by medical/social divisions in funding systems, organisational structures and professional interests. Differences between countries in the outcomes of domiciliary care arise from varying differentiation between medical and social services, which Alber (1993: 128–30) classifies as 'high' in France, Germany and the UK, 'medium' in the Netherlands, and 'low in theory' in Italy. In countries where services are more easily funded through entitlement to health funding than through discretionary means-tested social services funding, there is an incentive to medicalise people's needs in order to fit the criteria for services (Jamieson, 1991: 114). This is particularly the case in Germany which places strong emphasis on health insurance and where social care services such as home help are underdeveloped. The care systems in the US are also strongly biased towards medical services funded through Medicare and Medicaid and towards nursing homes rather than domiciliary support services (Estes and Lee, 1985: 21–2). Home health care became increasingly medicalised in the 1980s (Estes and Swan, 1993: 104).

The implications of such incentives in the funding systems are that services are provided on a medical model designed to cure rather than a social model geared to care for frail older people with long-term needs. This effect is exacerbated by the powerful role of the medical profession, especially the general practitioner (GP), in referral and assessment systems. Another implication of the medical/social divide is the separation of tasks between care professionals, particularly relevant in domiciliary care in the areas of potential overlap in personal care tasks between nursing and home help workers. In Germany the strict division between levels of nursing means that older people may have several workers, changing over time depending on the criteria for different funding sources (Dieck and Garms-Homolová, 1991: 150–2). In the UK the trend is towards more specialised home care with a focus on personal care rather than the traditional domestic work of the home help. The Netherlands has the 'alpha' system for basic domestic work, while the home help and home nursing services are to be merged, although differentiation of some caring tasks will remain within organisations.

Clearly the long-term health and social care needs of older people will be met more appropriately in systems where domiciliary services are based on individual needs rather than on the funding sources to which people are entitled, and if services are provided flexibly by appropriate workers rather than subject to rigid professional divisions. The appropriate delivery of services also depends crucially on effective coordination of health and welfare services which is impeded by strict medical/social divisions and fragmentation of services between agencies. In the 1990s one strand of policy is moving towards assessment of individual needs for coordinated care packages. Other trends such as the development of non-statutory sectors of provision, however, entail increased fragmentation of services, with consequent difficulties in coordination and regulation, inequalities in access to services, and increased need for information on services. The issues of coordination and information are discussed further in chapter 7.

Summary

Domiciliary care, the cornerstone of community care, embraces a wide range of care tasks and services and care providers, including medical and social agencies and informal carers. Key services such as home nursing and home help developed separately in most countries. As development of home care in response to community care policies was impeded by cost constraints from the 1970s onwards, informal care became the norm with formal care to meet the needs not covered. As institutional care was reduced from the 1980s, domiciliary care services were increasingly targeted to those who might need institutional care and policy moved towards packages of care to meet assessed needs of physically or mentally frail people and their carers. Non-profit and commercial sectors of care, as well as informal care, were promoted as state involvement was reduced. The encouragement of domiciliary care as less expensive than institutional care depends on the contribution of unpaid carers and the assumption that they will continue to care.

Expectations of family carers are most explicit in systems based on the subsidiarity principle, but in all systems informal carers, mainly spouses, daughters and daughters-in-law, provide 75–80 per cent of care, and receive little practical or financial help from formal services.

Components of domiciliary care are organised and funded according to the medical and social systems in different countries and local areas. Evidence suggests an undersupply of services in relation to need and increasing financial and caring burdens on older people and carers. Services are distributed unevenly between and within countries. Access to formal services and the likelihood of receiving and giving informal care are influenced by social class, gender, 'race' and age. Domiciliary care is an area where there are firm responsibilities but few rights to services for older people and carers. There is much policy rhetoric about promoting individual choice, but the extent to which people can exercise choice is unevenly distributed geographically, between social groups, and within families, where caring often falls to one individual with access to little support from others.

5
Health Services Outside the Home

The majority of care for older people with physical or mental health problems or disabilities takes place *at home*, as discussed in chapter 4. More specialised aspects of health care, however, are provided *from home* in the other main type of setting (see chapter 1), when people leave the home where they normally live to receive care in, for example, a hospital, clinic or health centre. Such care may be necessary to enable them to continue to live in their own home. This chapter reviews ways in which older people's acute or chronic health problems are assessed and treated, their health maintained, and therapeutic or rehabilitation services are provided in such settings outside their home. The main services are thus medical care, nursing and rehabilitation, although in the course of receiving such services needs for basic care, counselling, social contacts and information may also be met, and transport services will often be necessary.

Background to health care policies

Hospital, outpatient, ambulatory and primary health services are provided for older people in the context of general health care systems covering all age groups and sections of populations. Health care systems expanded as welfare states developed after the second world war; in all the countries studied, expenditure on health care as a proportion of gross domestic product increased continuously, as shown in Table 2.1. Policies on service provision and funding methods varied, ranging from that based on private health insurance in the 'liberal' welfare regime of the US, to the universal, comprehensive provision under the 'social democratic' British national health service (NHS) set up in 1948. Although policy statements often include some element of promoting positive health and wellbeing, in practice health services have developed with an emphasis on providing cure or care for people with physical or mental illnesses or health problems.

Development of policies on hospital and ambulatory care

The growth of expenditure on health care was perceived as a problem in the 1970s after the economic crises; the emphasis in health policy moved to cost containment (see chapter 2). As hospital care, particularly acute care, was the most expensive item, policies moved towards reducing hospital bed numbers and inpatients' lengths of stay, and promoting outpatient, ambulatory and primary care.

In the 1980s the pursuit of cost-effectiveness, combined with New Right ideology, led in some countries to developing the role of the non-state sectors in health care provision' and stimulating competition between providers. The system in the US changed from being based mainly on private health insurance where items of service are bought from chosen providers, to a system of managed health care organisations such as health maintenance organisations (HMOs). The latter cover over 50 per cent of the population, although the proportion of older people included is small. The HMO receives prepayments through subscriptions from members who are guaranteed access to a package of care provided directly by the HMO or purchased from other providers in a competitive market (Appleby, 1992: 101–2). The governments of the Netherlands and the UK drew on the experience of HMOs in designing health care reforms in the late 1980s and early 1990s; these introduced the idea of 'managed competition' between providers for contracts with purchasers (Appleby, 1992; Abel-Smith, 1992). More generally there has been an increase in the provision of health care through profit-making providers, with whom the non-profit or state providers must compete; this has been the case particularly in the US, but also in the UK and Italy.

Policies on health care for older people developed in this context of cost containment; attention was drawn to the numbers of older people and those with mental health problems considered to be occupying hospital beds unnecessarily or for too long. In many West European countries the numbers of psychiatric hospital beds were substantially reduced during the 1970s and 1980s (Mangen, 1987). Similarly, policies sought to prevent admission of older people to acute hospital care, for example in France by creating medium or long stay units for them or by medicalising residential units to reduce demands for hospital care (see chapter 3). For those admitted to hospital, earlier discharge policies were implemented, for example in the UK.

The development of day hospitals in some countries also helped to reduce both demand for and length of stay in hospital beds. Day hospitals originated in the UK: psychiatric day hospitals in 1946, and geriatric day hospitals in the 1950s, with rapid expansion of both in the 1960s and 1970s (Tester, 1989). In the Netherlands day hospitals based in nursing homes developed in the late 1960s and expanded rapidly in the 1980s (Nies et al., 1991). Day hospital services are, however, much less developed in the other countries studied.

In some countries health care for older people was based on medical specialisms; geriatric medicine was established in the UK in the 1950s and psychogeriatrics in the 1960s. Geriatric medicine is also an established specialism in the US and Italy, whereas in France, Germany and the Netherlands it only became recognised in the 1980s.

Policy development on health services since the 1970s has tended to focus on cost containment and efficiency in the hospital sector. At the same time policy statements often stressed the importance of non-acute and non-hospital care and the need for resources to be shifted to these services from acute care as more demands were placed on them as a result of reductions in hospital beds and earlier discharge. In practice, however, any funds transferred were rarely adequate to meet demands. Further, the development of high technology medicine kept the focus on acute care and led to underinvestment in the low technology solutions often needed by older people. Another trend was the recognition in policy statements of the need to develop self-help, health promotion and disease prevention strategies. Recent policies on health care in the six countries studied are summarised below.

Various measures were taken in *France* from the 1970s to reduce acute, general and psychiatric hospital beds and contain costs. Long-term care for older people was transferred from the medical to the social sector in 1975. Sectorisation of psychiatric services, implemented from the 1970s, provided for development of a range of inpatient and ambulatory services for each area (Barres, 1987). In 1983 annual budgets were introduced for public hospitals, encouraging bed closures and shorter stays. Patient charges for health services were increased. In the early 1990s government planned to create 45,000 medicalised places in homes, financed by reducing acute hospital beds (Guillemard and Argoud, 1992). An agreement in 1991 provided for an extra fee for doctors to undertake health check-ups on insured patients (Rollet, 1991: 199).

In *Germany* a major report on psychiatric services, the Enquête (1975), recommended sectorised community based mental health care with a shift from inpatient to outpatient care (Haerlin, 1987). Concerns about costs led to the 1977 health cost containment act and establishment of the 'Concerted action' commission. Measures were taken to limit doctors' fees, increase charges to patients, and limit the drugs and other items covered by insurance funds. The 1989 health reforms were mainly concerned with such cost containment, but part of the savings were allocated to finance services for very dependent people such as home nursing and respite care. As another concession to public opinion the reforms introduced measures for disease prevention and health promotion, including screening for over-35s (Freeman, 1994).

Italy's national health service was introduced in 1978. Although this reform's main aims included prioritising community care, prevention and health promotion, in practice the system remained 'hospital-centred' (Ferrera, 1989b: 128). The 1978 psychiatric reform (Law 180), however, led to large-scale closures of psychiatric hospitals in some regions, and the development of local mental health centres. Cost containment measures in the late 1970s and early 1980s included increased charges for patients. The 1992 Finance Act increased charges and tightened access criteria (Saraceno and Negri, 1994). The 1991–5 'project for older people' national guidelines stressed preventive measures for over-50s, and implementation of integrated health and welfare services for older people (Florea et al., 1993).

The *Netherlands* government restructured the health care system in 1974, taking on responsibility for administration and planning, although non-profit organisations continued to provide services (Baars et al., 1992). As a cost containment measure acute hospital care was reduced from the early 1980s. In 1983 a unified system for mental health services was introduced with regional institutes for outpatient mental health services (RIAGGs) and 60 community mental health centres (Schra-meijer, 1987). In the late 1980s radical reforms to the health insurance system were planned following the Dekker report (1987), which aimed to introduce managed competition, reduce inpatient care, and encourage community care and health promotion (Ham et al., 1990: 45). After changes in government and resistance to the planned restructuring, many of the proposals were not implemented although insurance funds were merged and a more market-oriented culture was introduced.

The *United Kingdom* government's stated priorities for resources to develop services for older people and those with mental or physical disabilities or illness (DHSS, 1977) were in practice overshadowed by the emphasis from the late 1970s on cost containment measures (Ginsburg, 1992). Following the policy paper *Promoting better health* (HMSO, 1987) the offer of annual health checks by general practitioners (GPs) was introduced in 1990 for all patients over 75. A ministerial review of the NHS in 1988 recommended reforms in *Working for patients* (HMSO, 1989b), implemented in the 1990 NHS and Community Care Act, which introduced managed competition through the separation of purchasing and providing functions. Self-governing NHS trust hospitals and units and fundholding GP practices were set up from 1991 as part of these reforms, which focused on hospitals and GPs, and were not concerned with health promotion (Ham et al., 1990: 19).

The *United States* health care system was based on individual choice of services purchased through health insurance from service providers. The hospital system consisted, until the 1970s, mainly of voluntary non-profit-making and public hospitals. With cost containment policies from the 1970s, public hospitals' budgets were reduced. The development of profit-making hospitals was encouraged; their proportion of hospital beds increased to about 30 per cent by the end of the 1980s; voluntary hospitals had to become more business-like to compete (Ginsburg, 1992: 129). As described above, development of HMOs also stimulated competition between health care providers. Cost containment measures in the 1980s also led to shorter hospital stays for older people, and reductions in Medicare benefits increased the proportion of costs borne by older people themselves.

The emphasis during the 1980s on cost containment and increasing privatisation and competition thus meant that in most countries policies focused on acute care and hospital services. Although some policy documents recognised the importance of chronic care, community services for older people and health promotion, in practice these services received little priority.

Health policies: influences and principles

The health care received by older people in settings outside the home is provided in the context of wider health policies influenced by economic and other factors. The economic crises of the 1970s onwards were significant in prompting policies attempting to contain the rising expenditure on health care in West Europe and North America. As shown in chapter 4, the costs of health care for older people are disproportionately high compared with those for younger groups. The physical and mental health care needs of the rising proportions of very old people were therefore perceived as a burden on younger workers, especially in countries such as France and Germany where sickness insurance schemes were rapidly increasing contribution rates for members. Political and ideological views of the New Right led to attempts to reduce public expenditure and to encourage private markets and competition in health care. The focus in such developments was on the acute sector of hospital care. The interests of older people with chronic illnesses were less well protected as specialists in geriatric or psychiatric medicine generally have lower status than those in acute specialisms.

The main interests which may have conflicting influences over the policy process are those of the state and those of the medical profession. These influences may be exerted at different levels, depending on the organisational structure of a country's health service and the extent of centralisation. In general, health policy decisions are taken at a more centralised level than social care decisions and in most countries health planning takes place and policy guidance is issued at central government and regional levels rather than more locally. For example in Italy regional governments have the power of legislation, planning and budgeting (Vollering, 1991). At a local level, however, other influences such as the power of the medical profession may be exerted over the implementation of policy guidelines. In countries with social insurance systems, different interests are represented by bodies such as health insurance funds and medical professionals' organisations. In Germany the health insurance doctors' associations (KVs), organised at state (*Land*) level, are highly influential (Ginsburg, 1992: 93). The French system, like that in Germany, is based on principles of pluralism of insurers and providers, freedom for doctors to practise and prescribe, and freedom for patients to choose doctors (Rollet, 1991). It is difficult for central government to regulate such systems.

The predominance of economic principles and the pursuit of cost effectiveness rather than equity in outcomes have characterised governments' health policies in the 1980s and 1990s. In the UK some power was shifted from the medical profession to administrators and managers with the introduction to the NHS of market criteria, more explicit forms of rationing, and the rhetoric of consumerism emphasising principles of competition and choice. Some medical professionals, such as fundholding GPs, took on more managerial roles and were expected to work to economic principles. This could lead to conflict between medical values and ethics and the cost effectiveness motive. Although the new system was claimed to provide more choice for the patient, in practice the individual had little choice in where treatment was provided (Jones et al., 1994: 153)

Policy developments in the countries studied have thus taken directions which do not necessarily work in the interests of older people with chronic physical and mental health problems who are not always considered cost effective recipients of treatment. In spite of stated policies of priority to groups needing long-term care, in practice they are given little priority by high status medical professionals seeking to preserve acute hospital services. Further, such older people are in a weak position in health care markets as they are less likely than others to have the necessary information on which to base a choice, or to be in a financial position to exercise choice. Rationing devices discussed later in the chapter also limit the health care choices of older people.

Provision of health services outside the home

Health care systems embrace diverse types of service ranging from basic primary care to highly technical hospital treatment which are often organised under different administrative frameworks. The degree of separation between the acute hospital sector and ambulatory and long-term care services is significant for older people whose overall health care needs cross the boundaries of service delivery systems.

Types of service provided to meet health care needs

The needs of older people with acute or chronic physical and/or mental health problems are met primarily through medical, nursing, para-medical and therapeutic care services. The main aspects of these services are assessment and monitoring, for example by a GP or geriatrician; treatment such as medication, surgery, nursing procedures or supply of prostheses; rehabilitation and the development or maintenance of practical, physical or mental skills, through, for example physiotherapy or reality orientation; and disease prevention through screening, advice and counselling. Such services may be offered on a hospital inpatient basis, in hospital outpatients or emergency departments, or in day care units, clinics or health centres.

Basic care such as meals, laundry, help with washing, dressing and mobility is usually an integral part of health care in hospital or day care settings. Other provision which supports the health care services includes counselling on the effects of disability or illness; arrangements for hospital admission or discharge; social visits and activities; carers support groups, respite care; ambulance and other transport services; and both information about the patient's condition and its management or treatment, and about services and financial benefits. In Table 5.1 the types of need and examples of health care services and professionals are summarised.

Although most older people are healthy and independent, the prevalence of chronic physical diseases and organic mental disorders increases with age; people in their late seventies and over are likely to have one or more long-term conditions requiring medical care. The need for, and costs of, health care thus increase with age, as shown in chapter 4.

There is a lack of cross-national comparative data on the prevalence of older people's health problems, although survey data are available for

Table 5.1 *Health care needs and services outside the home*

Services to meet needs for	Examples of services
physical and mental health care	
assessment and monitoring	GP, specialist clinic, day hospital
treatment, medication, surgery	acute hospital, pharmacy, dentist
nursing, dressings, injections	hospital or clinic nurse
mental health care	psychiatrist, psychiatric nurse
therapy, rehabilitation	physiotherapy, speech therapy
prevention and health promotion	health checks by GP, screening programmes
	older people's nurse, health adviser
basic care	
meals, laundry, bathing	hospital or day care unit
counselling, emotional support, social contacts	
coping with illness, disability, dying	counsellor, self-help group, hospice
arrangements for hospital discharge	hospital social worker
company, social activities	voluntary visitor, day care activities
support for informal carers	carers group, respite care in hospital
transport	
to hospital, GP, clinic, optician	ambulance, transport/escort service
information and advice	
on health problems	health care professionals
on services and benefits available	leaflets, displays in hospital, clinic

individual countries. The chronic physical conditions most commonly reported include cardio-vascular, respiratory and musculo-skeletal diseases and hearing and vision disorders. Surveys show that in Germany and Italy cardio-vascular diseases were the most common among older people, whereas in the UK and US musculo-skeletal conditions such as arthritis occurred most frequently (AARP, 1993; Alber, 1993; Walker, 1992b). Evidence from the General Household Survey in Great Britain shows that older women are more likely than older men, and older people from manual working classes more likely than those from professional classes, to suffer from both acute and longstanding illnesses (Victor, 1991: 73–5).

Estimates of the prevalence of mental disorders in older age also vary, depending on definitions and measures used in surveys. In all countries, however, the prevalence of dementia increases with age. For example in the Netherlands modest and severe dementia was estimated to affect 2.1 per cent of men and 1.4 per cent of women aged 65–69, rising to 17.7 per cent of men and 14 per cent of women aged 80 and over (Baars et al., 1992: 35). Victor concludes that: 'current evidence suggests that the prevalence of this disorder is about 1 per cent for the population aged 65–74 and 10 per cent for those aged 75+' (1991: 93). Surveys find that affective disorders such as depression and anxiety show little difference by age, but that the rates for women are twice those for men. For example, in a sample in South Wales, 3 per cent of men and 8 per cent of women over 70 suffered from depression, and 8 per cent of men and 20 per cent of women from anxiety (Victor, 1991: 88-9). In the Netherlands 3 per cent of men and 6 per cent of women aged 75–84, and 0 per cent of men and 14 per cent of women over 85, suffered endogenous depression (Baars et al., 1992: 34–5).

The higher prevalence of many physical and mental health problems both among the oldest age groups and among women is a cause for concern for policymakers in view of the projected increases in the oldest age groups, the predominance of women in these groups (see Table 4.3), and the likely increased need for health care services for these groups.

Provision of hospital-based and ambulatory services

The hospital-based and ambulatory or community-based services and support are outlined below. Details of the main funding systems for health care are given in chapter 2. Hospital-based services include inpatient, outpatient, emergency and day hospital care; ambulatory services include primary care such as general medical practice, dentistry and chiropody, medical care in specialist doctors' clinics and surgeries, and day care centres. Definitions of day care services usually distinguish between day hospitals with medical and therapeutic aims, and day centres for social care, although in practice their roles overlap (Tester, 1989; Nies et al., 1991). In this chapter day hospitals and specialised day care centres providing health care are included as health services, whereas mainly social day centres are discussed in chapter 6 as social, leisure and educational facilities.

Hospitals in *France* coexist in the public and private sectors: in 1989, 65 per cent of hospitals were public (11 per cent psychiatric); and 35 per cent were private (2.5 per cent psychiatric), 14 per cent non-profit and 18 per cent profit-making (Guillemard and Argoud, 1992). Acute facilities are not provided specifically for older people who constitute a high proportion of hospital patients. Medium stay units for older people offer rehabilitation, medical attention and treatment with the aim of returning people to live in the community. Long-term hospital units are for people who cannot live independently and need constant medical care (Guillemard and Argoud, 1992: 93). Psychiatric hospitals or units provide most inpatient care for older people with mental health problems; the development of small local units has progressed slowly. Specialist outpatients clinics are held in most general and psychiatric hospitals. There are few day hospitals for older people; medical and psychiatric day hospitals serve all age groups.

In *Germany* in 1985 36 per cent of hospitals were in the public sector, 34 per cent non-profit and 30 per cent private profit-making (Dieck, 1989). Older people receive acute or longer-term care in general hospitals; there are few specialist geriatric services: two per cent of hospital beds in 1989 (Alber, 1992). There is legal provision in the 1988 health reform law for rehabilitation hospitals covered by health insurance, but rehabilitation and geriatric hospitals are still rarely provided. Some psychiatric hospitals have geronto-psychiatric sections. Community-based facilities to replace psychiatric hospitals are not yet well established (Mangen, 1987). Outpatient care is not usually provided in German hospitals since ambulatory services are legally separate; there are, however, outpatient clinics at about one-quarter of psychiatric hospitals and some psychiatric day hospitals are linked to hospitals (Haerlin, 1987). Only 14 geriatric or geronto-psychiatric day clinics have been established; these are mainly in university and public hospitals (Dieck, 1989).

Under *Italy's* national health service all residents are entitled to free hospital care in public hospitals or private hospitals under contract to the public sector. There are 162 acute care geriatric wards (120 in public hospitals) and 158 long-term wards (82 public). It is considered, however, that geriatric beds are underprovided and that geriatric medicine is not well recognised or supported with rehabilitation professionals or trained nurses. Outpatient provision is inadequate; this partly contributes to the overuse of inpatient facilities (Florea et al., 1993). Day hospitals for rehabilitation are mainly used by older people; government policy is to develop specialist geriatric day hospitals. Progress in closing psychiatric hospitals and beds varied between regions and was particularly slow in the south. Hospital diagnosis and treatment services set up after the psychiatric reforms are used for inpatient hospital care especially in regions where community facilities are poor (Fasolo and Frisanco, 1991: 223).

In the *Netherlands* most hospitals are run by non-profit organisations. Most people aged over 65 with acute care needs are treated in acute hospitals. Geriatric medicine was recognised as a specialism in 1980 and its development is supported by the government. By 1991 there were ten general hospitals and two teaching hospitals with geriatric wards, 23 geriatricians in general hospitals and seven in psychiatric hospitals and clinics (Baars et al., 1992: 43). The number of hospital beds in each region is limited by the government as part of substitution policy. Outpatient clinics are promoted to reduce hospital inpatient care. Long-term care for older people with physical and mental health problems is provided in nursing homes rather than hospitals. Geriatric and psychogeriatric day hospitals, attached to nursing homes, are well established and their numbers are increasing, as a further measure to reduce hospital care.

The *United Kingdom's* national health service offers hospital care free of charge to patients. Since 1991 district health authorities (DHAs) and fundholding GP practices purchase hospital care from DHA-managed NHS hospitals, self-governing NHS hospital trusts and private hospitals. The numbers of private hospital beds increased during the 1980s to an estimated seven per cent of acute beds in 1988 (Ham, 1992: 47). The private hospital sector is used mainly by those with private health insurance, and covers acute rather than long-term care needs. Older people are mainly treated in NHS acute care wards, but there are also geriatric wards in most district general hospitals. Eighty per cent of health districts have at least one psychogeriatrician (Murphy, 1993: 78). Older people form about one-third of inpatients of psychiatric hospitals (Victor, 1991: 124). NHS hospitals hold outpatient clinics in each of their specialisms. Geriatric and psychogeriatric day hospitals are well established in NHS hospitals in most health districts.

In the *United States* hospitals are mainly in the private sector: 58 per cent owned by non-profit organisations, 15 per cent by for-profit agencies and 27 per cent by state or local government (Ham et al., 1990: 61). Funding for inpatient and outpatient hospital treatment for older people is from Medicare, Medicaid, patients' payments and private insurance or through an HMO. Earlier discharge from acute hospitals has been achieved by Medicare's prospective payment system introduced in 1984, by which hospitals receive a fixed payment based on the patient's classification in a diagnostic related group (Appleby, 1992: 110). Geriatric medicine is an established specialism practised in general hospitals or specialised geriatrics centres. Mental health professionals specialising in geriatric care, however, are in short supply; older people with mental health problems are often unnecessarily placed in nursing homes where appropriate mental health services are not available (AARP, 1990). Day hospitals for rehabilitation of older people are provided by some hospitals, particularly where there are geriatric centres, but they are not widespread.

Turning to the *ambulatory* services, general practitioners (GPs) who mostly work in independent practice play a major part in primary care. This role is particularly important in systems where patients register with a GP who receives a capitation fee, often higher for over-65s; the GP controls referrals to secondary and specialist services, as in Italy, the Netherlands and the UK. In the other main type of system, found in France, Germany and the US, patients choose the GP they consult when they need health care. Under the HMO system in the US, however, the HMO provides or contracts for primary and other care for its members.

Other components of primary care outside the home include dentists, ophthalmologists, pharmacists, chiropodists and physiotherapists, who are also mainly private practitioners in the countries studied. Some practitioners, however, are employed by local or health authorities or non-profit organisations to work in health centres. For example in France primary care may be provided in health centres set up by the commune or in medico-social centres with medical and social work staff. In the UK community dentists and chiropodists may be employed by the health authorities' community units or trusts.

In ambulatory specialist care there are again two main systems. The countries which have outpatient clinics mainly based in hospitals, Italy, the Netherlands and the UK, may also have a minority of private specialists practising in their own clinics. Many NHS consultants in the UK also work part-time in the private sector. In the Netherlands psychiatric diagnosis and treatment is provided mainly by the RIAGG. In France, Germany and the US the main provision of specialist care, including psychiatric care, is by private practioners, to whom patients have direct access. Some French private specialists, however, also work part-time in health centres or public hospitals (Hunter, 1986). In Germany there is much stricter separation of hospital and ambulatory services; specialists diagnose and treat patients in their own clinics. After unification of Germany this separate system was introduced in the new eastern states which previously had an integrated system of hospitals with linked polyclinics providing most primary and outpatient care; polyclinics were allowed to continue until 1995 (Stone, 1991).

Day care centres offering physical and mental health care are well established in the Netherlands and UK. In the Netherlands these centres are often based in residential homes, financed by the government outreach fund to develop the community care role of homes. Day care centre services in the UK are run or purchased by the local authority and operate in residential homes or day centres, sometimes jointly with health authorities, particularly if providing for older people with mental health problems. In France day centres, run by CCASs or non-profit associations, were encouraged in the 1970s to care for the physical and mental health of older people; but health insurance only covers care costs. There are now very few such centres as they did not prove successful and their expansion was not promoted. Day nursing care in Germany also developed slowly as it was not covered by health insurance; it is, however, covered by care insurance from April 1995. There are about 60 day care centres with about 1,000 places, based in nursing homes, community care centres or independent centres (Grossjohann, 1990). In the US some nursing homes offer day care; adult day care for frail older people is also available in some senior centres and other community care facilities.

Although support services for people who are dying are now recognised as an important aspect of care for older people, such services have developed slowly. The hospice movement began in the UK; by 1990 there were 200 charitable hospices in England, caring for terminally ill people and their families (Alber, 1993: 114). Terminal care teams based in NHS health districts also support people who are dying in hospital or at home. The Netherlands has a growing hospice movement with 80 local organisations whose voluntary workers help people to die at home or in homely settings in wards with trained staff;

they also support their relatives (Baars et al., 1992: 58). A French ministerial circular in 1986 promoted services to care for people dying in hospital, institutions or at home, providing support, pain relief and care for families. Such services are provided by trained nurses and by voluntary visitors from non-profit associations. In Germany care for the dying is not covered by health insurance; there were only three hospices and a small number of palliative wards in hospitals in 1990; voluntary agencies are developing services in some cities (Alber 1992). In the US 'hospice care' refers to support services for terminally ill patients and their families in hospital, nursing homes or their own homes (Jazwiecki, 1989).

Transport to hospital and ambulatory care services can present difficulties for older people with disabilities or without access to suitable transport. Emergency ambulances are provided and funded through health insurance or national health services, but non-emergency transport is offered by a variety of means such as ambulances, minibuses, hospital cars or taxis. Transport organised specifically for the clinic or day centre concerned is usually an effective method, but not widely available. Recognition of the difficulties older people have in travelling to medical appointments has led to the development, by local authorities or welfare organisations in the countries studied, of transport services using suitable vehicles to take people to medical services and other venues as detailed in chapter 6.

Coordination between hospital and ambulatory services

Coordination between hospital and ambulatory services is especially important at the time of admission to and discharge from hospital, but is also necessary for long-term management of conditions as well as for prevention of crises that could precipitate hospitalisation. Effective coordination is facilitated particularly when comprehensive geriatric or psychiatric services are provided for a local area. Such services are not widespread, however, and there is evidence in all countries studied of poor coordination between both health care sectors and health and social services. These difficulties are likely to be greatest where the hospital and ambulatory systems operate separately, as in Germany.

Inpatient care may be provided as a planned admission after referral by a GP or by a specialist in a hospital outpatients clinic or private practice. Another frequent route for older people is through a hospital's emergency department, as a result of an accident, crisis or acute health problem such as a stroke or heart attack. A person's admission to inpatient care and the length of their stay may be influenced not only by their medical condition but also by funding criteria and incentives, by pressure from caring relatives, or by reciprocal arrangements between residential or nursing homes over admission and discharge of elderly patients.

Irrespective of the route into inpatient care, the need to plan the person's discharge as early as possible is widely recognised by policy-makers; procedures for coordination with ambulatory and home care services have been devised in the countries studied. In practice, however, satisfactory arrangements are not always made before the patient returns home. For example in Germany community care centres are not necessarily informed that a person needing their services is being discharged from hospital (Alber, 1992: 76). Lack of coordination between hospitals, GPs and social services in the UK prompted the Department of Health to issue circulars to health and local authorities in 1989. These set out discharge procedures, advising early planning of discharge by the NHS hospital departments responsible, and joint planning between local and health authorities, in consultation with the patient and informal carers. These circulars also apply to NHS trust hospitals set up after the 1991 reforms. Under the reformed community care system the special transitional grant made to local authorities from 1993–6 was not paid unless local and health authorities had agreed procedures for linking local authority assessment and hospital discharge procedures (Meredith, 1993: 140). US hospitals have discharge planners to help patients with arrangements including home care; for the limited home health care entitlement under Medicare a doctor must arrange a treatment plan.

The unsatisfactory coordination between hospital and ambulatory services and the uneven provision of health services affect the outcomes of policies and systems which are discussed further below. Issues concerning coordination between all the services and sectors providing care for older people, and other support services such as information, are addressed in chapter 7.

Outcomes of health care systems

Older people with acute or chronic physical or mental health problems receive health services in hospitals, clinics, health centres and day care units usually in addition to domiciliary services. The health services offered to older people are affected by general health policies and systems which in practice place greater priority on acute hospital care and services for younger people than on services to meet long-term care needs of people with disabilities.

Implications of health care policies for different groups of older people and carers

Policies based on economic principles and cost effectiveness are likely to conflict with the interests of older people with chronic health problems. Since the 1970s the main cost containment measures were the control of public expenditure on health care and reductions in hospital beds and lengths of stay. As shown in Table 2.1 total health expenditure as a proportion of GDP continued to rise during the 1970s and 1980s. Public expenditure as a proportion of total health expenditure, however, fell during the 1980s in all the countries studied, apart from the US, where it remained almost the same and much lower than in the other countries, as Table 5.2 shows.

As a result of cost containment measures patients' share of health costs increased. For example in the US in 1987 direct payments amounted to about one-quarter of average expenditure on health care for the over-65s (AARP, 1993). The proportion of total health care costs met by French households rose from 15.6 per cent in 1980 to 18.7 per cent in 1990 (Rollet, 1991: 196). The policy focus on reducing expensive hospital inpatient care has led to closures of hospitals or beds and reduced lengths of stay, entailing increased pressure on community services. The numbers of inpatient hospital beds per 1,000 population and average length of stay in inpatient care fell in the 1970s and/or 1980s in all six countries, as shown in Table 5.3. There were considerable decreases in lengths of stay for the older age groups, for example in the UK and US (Victor, 1991: 118–19).

Table 5.2 *Public expenditure on health as a percentage of total health expenditure, 1970–90*

	France	Germany[a]	Italy	Netherlands	United Kingdom	United States
1970	74.7	69.6	86.4	84.3	87.0	37.2
1980	78.8	75.0	81.1	74.7	89.6	42.0
1990	74.4	71.6	77.6	71.3	83.5	42.2

[a] former FRG.

© OECD, 1993, OECD Health Data Version 1.5. Reproduced by permission of the OECD.

Table 5.3   *Numbers of inpatient hospital beds per 1000 population, and average lengths of stay in inpatient care, 1970–90*

	France	Germany[a]	Italy	Netherlands	United Kingdom	United States
Inpatient beds per 1000 population						
1970	n/a	11.3	10.5	11.4	9.4	7.5
1980	11.1	11.5	9.7	12.3	8.1	5.8
1990	9.7	10.4	n/a	11.5	n/a	4.7
Average lengths of stay (days)						
1970	18.3	24.9	19.1	38.2	25.7	14.9
1980	16.8	19.7	13.5	34.7	19.1	10.0
1990	12.3	16.5	n/a	34.1	14.5	9.1

[a] former FRG.

© OECD, 1993, OECD Health Data Version 1.5. Reproduced by permission of the OECD.

Total expenditure on inpatient care as a proportion of total expenditure on health fell between 1980 and 1990 in France, Italy, the Netherlands and the US, but increased slightly in Germany; total expenditure on ambulatory care as a proportion of total health expenditure increased during the same period in France, Germany and the US, but fell slightly in Italy and the Netherlands, as Table 5.4 shows. Inpatient care, however, still represents the largest proportion of health care costs.

Policies promoting a move from inpatient to ambulatory care were stated along with cost containment measures. A European survey found that in Germany, the Netherlands, England, France and Italy: 'there has been a clear transfer of finance from hospitals to primary health care, a trend that is particularly marked in France and Italy' (Abel-Smith, 1992: 410). Commentators such as Ferrera (1989b) and Rodwin (1989), however, consider that the shift of resources from hospital to community care tended not to compensate for additional demands on community services.

In a climate of cost containment, funding for health care of older people is not necessarily a priority within or outside hospitals, despite

Table 5.4 *Total expenditure on ambulatory care as a percentage of total expenditure on health, 1970–90*

	France	Germany[a]	Italy	Netherlands	United Kingdom	United States
1970	26.6	29.0	36.2	n/a	n/a	26.8
1980	24.8	26.6	29.5	27.7	n/a	26.5
1990	28.4	28.0	27.3	26.9	n/a	29.4

[a] former FRG
© OECD, 1993, OECD Health Data Version 1.5. Reproduced by permission of the OECD.

policy statements about priority for services to older people, for example in the UK (DHSS, 1977). As the proportion of older people in populations increased, reductions in inpatient beds, including geriatric and psychiatric beds, and earlier discharge meant increased pressure on hospital and community services. For example in the UK the numbers of geriatric beds were reduced by 5,000 to 53,000 from 1978–88 (Walker, 1992b: 45) and continued to decrease. In most of the countries studied geriatric care was considered inadequate even where geriatric medicine was an established specialism, for example in Italy (Florea et al., 1993: 101). In countries such as Germany where geriatric medicine was not a specialism there was a lack of expertise to meet older people's needs for physical and mental health care (Dieck, 1989). The provision of day hospital and specialised day care centres for medical treatment and rehabilitation was sparse and uneven, except in the Netherlands and UK. The low status of older people and of those working with them partly explains governments' lack of success in shifting priorities to the community care of older people because at local level more powerful groups may be implementing different policies (Ham, 1992: 210).

The introduction of managed competition and increased privatisation in health services may further disadvantage older people whose care costs are higher than other groups, since preference may be given by budget holders and purchasers to those whose care is less expensive. Although reforms in Europe are in the early stages of implementation, there is some evidence from the US that HMOs select healthier patients and have only recently begun to accept larger numbers of older patients (Appleby, 1992: 112). Competition may also lead to closures of hospitals and mean older people and their visitors have further to travel to hospital. Another concern is that two tier systems may develop in which the better off and healthier patients receive the best quality services (Morris, 1988: 91; Ginsburg, 1992: 129–30; Whitehead, 1994).

Cross-national comparisons between groups in relation to access to and use of health services are more difficult to make than comparisons based on aggregate national data such as the OECD data set used above. There is a lack of comparative or comparable cross-national data on geographical, social class and other differences in distribution of health services; further, such data are not necessarily available for individual countries especially those with federal or regional systems such as Germany, Italy and the US.

In discussing differences between groups in relation to access to health services outside the home, it is important to distinguish between health and health care (Macintyre, 1989). As shown above, inequalities in health affect older people's need for services, but the provision of health care services will not necessarily reduce health inequalities which result from wider socio-economic and environmental factors. The focus below is on differences in access to, or use of, health services which could help older people to remain independent or maintain their daily living abilities despite chronic health problems, which tend to be more prevalent among those from lower socio-economic groups and women.

Differences in expenditure on health services between countries affect the general level of service provision for older people in the context of varying health policies and systems. Within countries there are also differences in expenditure levels which are not necessarily based on differences in need. For example, differences between the countries and regions of the UK, where expenditure per capita in 1988–9 ranged from £320 in the Oxford region to £502 in Scotland and £466 in Northern Ireland (Ham, 1992: 193). Differences between urban and rural areas are reported with generally poorer provision of health services in rural areas, for example in Germany, Italy and the US. Doctors who are independent practitioners tend to choose to practise in the most pleasant areas. In Germany there are also regional differences between the sickness insurance funds in the level of contributions and service provision (Macintyre, 1989: 324; Ginsburg, 1992: 91). Under the Italian health reforms in 1978 universal access to health care was implemented in theory, but there are wide regional and urban/rural differences in the availability and quality of health services (Ferrera, 1989b), and wide inequalities in hospital care for older people (Bianchi, 1991). In the US services available under Medicaid programmes vary between states.

Social class differences are found both in access to and utilisation of services. In the health systems studied, people aged over 65 are covered for basic health care by social insurance, national health or other government programmes. There are, however, costs of using services which bear more heavily on those from lower socio-economic groups. The introduction or increase in co-payments and charges since the late 1970s have increased inequalities in access to health care. For example in Italy the introduction of charges for diagnostic investigations led to lower use of the service, especially by lower socio-economic groups (Townsend et al., 1992: 296–7). In the US older people with lower incomes spend a much higher proportion of their income on health care costs than those with higher incomes (Estes and Harrington, 1985: 264). About 20 per cent of Medicare recipients have no other insurance to cover gaps in Medicare (AARP, 1992).

Studies have found social class inequalities in health services provided. In Germany, for example, sickness funds for white collar workers offer higher quality services than those for blue collar workers (Ginsburg, 1992: 92). HMOs in the US provide poorer treatment to patients from lower socio-economic groups (Appleby, 1992: 113). People from lower socio-economic groups also make less use of health services, as found, for example, in the UK (Townsend et al., 1992). In Germany people on lower incomes visited doctors less often, received less specialised services and used preventive and early diagnostic services less than others (Macintyre, 1989: 326; Ginsburg, 1992: 94). In Italy differences were found 'between professionals and less educated groups in the use of specialist services and admission to top quality hospitals'; in the Netherlands a study of people aged 55–79 found that 'for chronic sickness the highest social group made more frequent use of specialist services and of physiotherapy services' (Townsend et al., 1992: 297, 299).

Such social class inequalities in health care apply particularly to women, especially those in the oldest age groups, who tend to have the most chronic illnesses and use health services most. Older women are more likely than older men to be unable to afford private or additional health insurance or to pay charges for services.

People of different 'race', particularly those in lower socio-economic groups and women, are also likely to lack financial resources or insurance for health care costs, and to receive poorer quality services. There may be additional charges or restricted access to services for people who are not residents or citizens, for example in the UK and Germany. The implementation of such rules can entail racist practice in assessing entitlement of any residents from minority ethnic communities. Evidence of under-use of health services by people from black and ethnic minority groups has been found in many countries (Macintyre, 1989: 326). This may result from lack of knowledge, lack of cultural appropriateness of services, the deterrent effects of charges, or institutional racism.

Rights, responsibilities and choice in health care

Through national health services or social insurance and assistance, people have more rights to health care than to other community care services. In countries with health insurance systems such as France, Germany and the Netherlands, older people are generally entitled to a wide choice of high quality services for which the fees are paid by insurance funds (Ham et al., 1990). In some systems people on low incomes without insurance, however, must apply for means-tested social assistance and their choice of services may be limited. Under national health systems there are in theory universal rights, but rationing devices such as waiting lists in the UK may delay access to services. There are no rights to services not covered by health insurance or national health service, for example specialist day care centres in Germany, for which people had to pay from their own resources or social assistance, before such centres were covered by care insurance in 1995.

Health care reforms from the late 1980s have entailed implementation, or discussion, of rationing devices which are more explicit than those previously used and which may discriminate against people on grounds of age, particularly where high technology procedures are involved. In the UK's NHS the split between purchasers and providers led to greater specification of services that were to be purchased. Chronological age is often used as an arbitrary cut-off point for eligibility, although there is no biological reason for such limits (Medical Research Council, 1994; Royal College of Physicians, 1994). Techniques to assist in rationing have been widely discussed; for example the comparison of costs per QALY (Quality adjusted life year), a measure of outcomes of interventions in expected extra years and quality of life; and the formula devised in Oregon, US, to rank treatments for different conditions so that a limit can be set for care provided under Medicaid (Harrison and Hunter, 1994).

Cost containment measures have reduced people's rights to health care by imposing or increasing charges and restricting the items covered, for example with limited lists of prescription drugs. Older people may be unable to benefit from their entitlement to health care services because of the deterrent effect of charges, rationing devices, or because they are unaware of their rights. In the new eastern states of Germany, older people have particular difficulty adapting to the change from comprehensive free polyclinic services to a system of selecting independent ambulatory practitioners. In the UK NHS continuing care hospital beds are free whereas residential or nursing home care through the local authority is means-tested. Although the health authority has a responsibility to provide free residential nursing care for people who need it, numbers of NHS beds decreased rapidly in the 1980s and 1990s (Laing, 1993; Meredith, 1993). It is unlikely that government guidelines issued in 1994 on the local division of responsibilities between health and local authorities for payment for long-term care for people discharged from hospital will resolve these issues.

Since the introduction of markets and consumerism in health care, together with the encouragement of prevention and health promotion measures, people have increased responsibility for their own health, for providing for themselves through private insurance or payment of charges, and for selecting their health care providers. Those with private insurance and financial resources have greater choice and access to higher quality services, for example through HMOs in the US or private health care in the UK. Many older people with chronic health care needs, however, are less able to exercise such choices because they lack financial resources. They may also have limited access to information about the services which they could choose, and be less able to travel to use such services.

Outcomes from systems of health care provision

Despite policy emphasis on reducing inpatient hospital care and promoting community-based care, incentives in some funding systems lead to over-use of inpatient beds. This is particularly the case in Germany, where hospitals are paid a daily fee for patients and thus have an incentive to keep patients in beds which would otherwise be unoccupied (Ham et al., 1990: 52). Estimates of the proportion of German hospital patients who do not need hospital care include 17 per cent (Abel-Smith, 1992: 405) and 20–30 per cent (Anderson, 1992: 72). The fact that hospital services are free, for example in France, also encourages medicalisation of older people's problems to gain access to care when rehabilitative community-based care may be more appropriate to their long-term needs. In Germany there is an incentive for older people needing long-term care to stay in free hospital beds rather than move to nursing homes for which they must pay. The funding system in the US, however, encourages medicalised long-term care in nursing homes and discourages long hospital stays (Jamieson, 1989).

Unnecessarily long inpatient stays are also caused by either shortage of outpatient and community-based services, for example in Italy (Florea et al., 1993: 52), or by lack of funding for such services, as in Germany where it was difficult to develop services such as specialist day care centres when these were not covered by health insurance. Hospital discharge may be delayed by such shortages and funding problems, or because the person does not have adequate support in her or his home environment (Guillemard and Argoud, 1992). On the other hand, provision of ambulatory and domiciliary services may be easier to arrange for patients being discharged from hospital, for example in Germany, where this provides a further incentive to use hospital care as a route to long-term care services in the community (Dieck, 1989: 112).

Lack of coordination over arrangements for discharge is further reason for delays. Coordination between health services is particularly difficult where there is a strong division between inpatient and ambulatory services and few outpatient services, as in Germany. In France there is a lack of formal arrangements for coordination between private general and specialist practitioners and salaried public hospital doctors (Rodwin, 1989: 269). Such systems do not facilitate follow up of a patient's care after discharge from hospital, or continuity of care for those whose health care needs span different sectors. It seems likely that some of the difficulties in coordination between hospital and ambulatory services could be resolved by the development of specialist geriatric and psychogeriatric services with an emphasis on meeting overall health care needs of older people using a range of hospital and community-based services promoting rehabilitation.

Summary

Health services for older people outside the home in hospital inpatient or outpatient care, day care units, clinics or health centres are part of wider health care systems and policies. These systems often focus on acute care and hospitals, rather than the interests of older people with chronic physical and mental health problems. In the 1970s the emphasis in health policy was on cost containment, and this meant reducing hospital beds and lengths of stay, closing hospital beds for older people and discharging earlier those who were admitted. Although the importance of transferring resources from acute to chronic and non-hospital care was recognised, such policies were not fully implemented, partly because of professional and commercial focus on increasingly high technology medicine. Policy statements encouraged self-help, health promotion and disease prevention and some measures were introduced. The costs of health care for ageing populations were seen as a burden. New Right principles influenced attempts to contain public expenditure and introduce private markets and managed competition in the 1980s. Cost efficiency and economic principles were introduced which may conflict with medical values and ethics. Competition and choice are less relevant to older people who are not in a position to exercise choice.

Specialist geriatric and psychogeriatric services, day care services and support services for terminally ill patients are underdeveloped in most countries. Although basic health services are in theory universally available in the countries studied, evidence suggests that the level and quality of services provided, and access to and use of services, vary according to location, social class, gender, age and 'race' in ways which restrict older people's choices in health care. Cost containment measures have reduced older people's rights to or ability to benefit from, health care services and increased their responsibility for their own health and choice of health care provision. Incentives in funding systems and lack of community-based services lead to over-use of hospital care and delays in discharge from hospitals. Lack of coordination between health care sectors also impedes discharge from hospital and the provision of continuity of care for older people.

6
Day Care, Leisure and Education

Social contacts and leisure activities, crucial to individual wellbeing and quality of life, are pursued by most of the population through a wide variety of social networks, cultural, sports, educational, entertainment and travel facilities. Although many older people continue or increase such activities on retirement, social opportunities are reduced for some people in later life through loss of work contacts, bereavement, disabilities or lack of financial resources. Service providers therefore offer facilities outside the home or in people's homes to compensate for such lack or loss of social contacts, and to help maintain older people's abilities to live independently. The services reviewed in this chapter include social day centres and clubs, leisure and sports activities, educational and cultural opportunities, holidays and volunteering.

Background to policies on social activities for older people

Development of policies on day care and social activities

As policies to promote older people's independent living in their own homes developed from the 1960s onwards, opportunities for social contacts, for example in day centres and clubs, were offered as part of the range of community care services. In all types of welfare state such social facilities tended to be offered at the discretion of local, usually non-statutory agencies as part of general social welfare provision which did not have high priority. These services were usually not mandatory but came under the scope of enabling legislation for agencies to provide facilities with the general aim of social integration of older people. It was recognised that social integration in the community is not simply a matter of residence outside institutions but involves participation in social contacts, which may have to be promoted for older people especially those living alone.

Despite both earlier enthusiasm for developing social and leisure facilities for older people, and rhetoric recognising their importance, funding for such services was restricted as part of cost containment measures from the late 1970s onwards, and responsibilities were increasingly delegated to the informal and independent sectors. Similarly the non-vocational education classes provided for adults by local authorities were reduced in European countries as priority for resources was given to vocational education and training in the context of high levels of unemployment (Norton, 1992: 43–5).

There was also a shift of emphasis from providing social activities *for* older people to promoting their active participation in the social life and organisation of their community, or in residential homes, and empowering them to make decisions, improve their living conditions and develop their own potential. Thus self-help, volunteering and community-based initiatives were encouraged for older people. In the US, organisations of older people such as AARP had a higher political profile than in Europe and lobbied policymakers in the interests of older people. In the early 1990s such participation increased in Europe at an EU level; the EC policy observatory on older people focused on social integration as one of the main issues studied (Walker et al., 1993), and produced a separate report on this (Walker (ed.), 1993).

The extent to which explicit policies on day care, social and leisure activities were developed varied between the countries studied, as shown below.

The promotion of social integration in *France* began in the 1960s with community care policies for people in their third age. The Sixth and Seventh Economic and Social Plans (1971–5 and 1976–80) advocated social opportunities as an essential part of maintaining older people in their own homes and integrating them into the life of the community. Third age clubs and restaurants, promoted in the Seventh Plan, expanded rapidly and were more successful than day centres which were set up on an experimental basis following a ministerial circular in 1974. A national committee of retired and elderly people was instituted in the early 1980s, with a departmental committee (CODERPA) in each *département*. Older people's participation in discussions on service provision and other issues is encouraged through the CODERPA. At local level non-profit associations and/or the CCAS play the main role in organising social and leisure activities. The government has actively encouraged the development of continuing education and cultural activities (Norton, 1992).

In *Germany*, under the Federal Social Assistance Act 1961, assistance may be given 'to maintain the opportunities available to the elderly to participate in the life of the community' (Flamm, 1983: 174), which can include day centres, clubs and educational facilities. Such assistance is, however, means-tested; this has made it difficult to develop services. In the former GDR, *Volkssolidarität*, a state-funded organisation, offered clubs and meeting places with cheap meals and social activities for older people. After unification of Germany *Volkssolidarität* became a welfare organisation and the funding system changed to that of the Federal Republic. In the 1980s and 1990s government policy emphasised self-help and participation; these were focal concerns of the Federal plan for older people in the early 1990s; a similar focus on self-help and participation was adopted in the plans and action programmes of the *Länder* and communes (Alber, 1992: 34–5). The promotion of social, educational and cultural opportunities for older people is the responsibility of welfare organisations at the level of the commune.

In *Italy* state policies on social and leisure provision developed later than in other countries, mainly in the 1980s, as policymakers became concerned about increasing numbers of very old people living alone. Services initiated with the aim of promoting social integration and relieving loneliness include recreational and day centres, cultural and leisure activities and social holidays (Jani-Le Bris, 1993: 41). The social worker was given an increasing role in organising social networks through recreational activities to maintain older people's social, physical and mental wellbeing (Vollering, 1991: 253–4). Provision of such facilities varies according to the policy and resources of the region and local authority and is made by home assistance services or from services centres. The health ministry's plan for 1991–5 includes measures such as transport for older people to social service centres and promoting services which involve older people actively, for example in voluntary activities (Mengani and Gagliardi, 1992: 110–12).

The *Netherlands* traditionally had a high proportion of older people in institutions; social integration and relief of loneliness were reasons for admission to residential care. In the 1970s the emphasis moved to social interaction in the community; leisure and education activities were provided to promote social integration, mainly by associations for coordinated work for older people, funded through municipalities under the social welfare law (Steenvoorden, 1992). Day centres developed rapidly in the 1980s following the policy paper *Outreach activities for older* people (*Nota flankerend bejaardenbeleid*) (Ministerie van Welzijn, 1983) which advocated extending services of residential homes, for example by providing day centres (Nies et al., 1991). The 1990 policy paper *Ageing counts* (*Ouderen in tel*) (Tweede Kamer, 1990) focused on the integration and participation of older people in the community, and included priorities for education and the 'revaluation of old age' (Pijl, 1992: 202). Government policy in the 1980s and 1990s emphasised cost containment and the promotion of self-help and volunteering, rather than direct provision to encourage social integration.

In the *United Kingdom* social day care originated in the voluntary sector which has run day centres and lunch clubs since 1945. Local authorities' power, under the Health Services and Public Health Act 1968, to promote the welfare of elderly people, enabled the provision of statutory sector day care and leisure activities. Local authority day centres expanded rapidly in the 1970s, but there was little policy guidance on the development of these services (Tester, 1989: 2–3). The policy paper *Growing older* recognised the contribution that older people could make through voluntary organisations, and advocated maintaining physical and mental wellbeing through social clubs and local authority leisure facilities and adult education classes (DHSS, 1981). Financial restraints in the 1980s and 1990s, however, led to reductions in or increased charges for some of these services. Although promoting the development of day care was a key objective of the community care reforms in the early 1990s (HMSO, 1989a), few local authorities had resources to implement this. The new system entailed, in many areas, increased or new charges for day centres, meals and transport (Age Concern England, 1993).

Community-based services in the *United States* providing social and leisure facilities to help older people to live independently are funded and developed mainly under Title III of the Older Americans Act (OAA) 1965. Federal funding under OAA is allocated through a structure of State Units on Aging (SUAs) and Area Agencies on Aging (AAAs), which develop services in cooperation with service providers, including voluntary organisations, according to state and local policy. The services include multi-purpose senior centres, meals in such centres, adult day care, transport, physical fitness and recreation, education, volunteer services, and visitors to nursing home residents. Although these services are in theory available to all over 60s, amendments to the OAA in the 1970s and 1980s meant greater emphasis on targeting services to the most disadvantaged and frail older people (Krout, 1989). The OAA also gives SUAs and AAAs an advocacy role, with

130   *Community Care for Older People*

participation by older people, in planning and developing services to meet their needs and improve living conditions.

Influences and principles underlying policies

Policies on day care and social activities developed in the context of wider community care policies influenced by economic factors and the need to contain costs of institutional care. For example, it was considered more cost effective to offer meals and social contacts in centres, which people living in their own homes visited during the day, than to provide full residential care. Further economic pressures were large scale unemployment and redundancy resulting from economic crises and recessions which led to a trend of earlier retirement and increased the numbers of people in their third age. Table 6.1 shows the proportions of older people who were economically active in 1983–91 in the countries studied. At the same time increasing numbers of people in higher socio-economic groups entering retirement with private or earnings-related pensions were perceived as a new market for the leisure and travel industries.

The demographic factor of the rising proportion of older people combined with economic influences to increase the numbers of people in later life who have a potential need for social activities and contacts. Within this heterogeneous population ranging in age from their mid-fifties onwards, different groups were perceived as needing special provision. For example, the increase in numbers of people living alone, particularly widows in the oldest age groups, caused concern as they

Table 6.1   *Percentage of people aged 60+ in the labour force, 1983–91*

	France	Germany[a]	Italy	Netherlands	United Kingdom	United States
% active in labour force						
1983	8.4	9.5	10.0	8.4	14.6	n/a
1991	5.1	8.5	9.8	6.5	13.5	12.0[b]

[a] former FRG.
[b] people aged 65+, 1992.
Sources: Eurostat, 1993: 3.
         AARP, 1993.

were considered at risk of isolation or loneliness. This was particularly the case in Italy where family patterns were changing, especially in the north, and where young people had migrated to the towns, leaving older generations in rural areas (Jani-Le Bris, 1993).

The main principle underlying the aim of promoting social integration is that this will improve or maintain older people's physical and mental wellbeing, to which isolation and/or loneliness may be detrimental. It is also assumed that social networks will provide people with support and thus reduce demands on health and welfare services. Research evidence shows that community-based initiatives which offer social opportunities, such as day centres or involvement in voluntary organisations, can have positive effects on mental and physical health (Checkoway, 1988).

Social policies in the post 1945 period tended to treat older people as a homogeneous group, stereotyped as being in poor health and at risk of isolation and loneliness, whose needs for social contacts could be met by provision of day centres and clubs. Such policies did not distinguish clearly between objective isolation, defined as having few social contacts, and subjective loneliness, a feeling of lack or loss of significant relationships. Research has shown, however, that there is no simple direct association between isolation and loneliness (Townsend, 1968). Loneliness is more likely than isolation to affect people's health and wellbeing and is not easily reduced by providing social contacts which will not necessarily produce close relationships (Tester and Meredith, 1987).

The principles and assumptions on which more recent policies are based differentiate to some extent between the needs of different groups of the older population. Within the overall policy of promoting social integration there are broad divisions between facilities intended for active people in their third age, who are retired and/or have completed raising their families, and provision for those in their fourth age who are more dependent, with physical and/or mental disabilities or health problems. There is also a recognition that individuals' needs for social roles or meaningful activities vary according to personality, circumstances and preferences. Cultural expectations also have an influence on the different activities considered appropriate for older men and women, for example in southern Italy or rural areas (Norton, 1992) or among minority ethnic communities in northern European countries. Recent policies stress more active participation by older people, focusing on the contribution they can make. These assume that it is beneficial for people in their third age to be involved in self-help groups or voluntary work, or for more dependent people such as residents of care homes to participate in committees making decisions about activities and living conditions.

Responsibility for implementation of social integration policies is vested at local levels; few specific policy guidelines are given. Local policymakers and agencies have considerable discretion in determining the level and type of provision. Voluntary agencies and self-help groups play a significant role in initiating and running services at grass roots level.

Provision of day care, leisure and education facilities

Informal networks of family and friends are the main source of social contacts in later life. Wenger (1994) identifies five different types of support network. Although the majority of older people in the countries studied do not live in the same household as younger generations of their family, many have family members living nearby. Surveys show that most older people have frequent and regular contact with family and friends, as shown in Table 6.2. Older people contribute to these networks, for example by offering companionship, practical help with grandchildren or household tasks, advice or emotional support. A minority, however, do not have families. According to opinion surveys, few older people are lonely. A 1992 Eurobarometer survey found that the proportion of over-60s who often feel lonely was 5–9 per cent in Germany, the Netherlands and the UK; 10–14 per cent in France; and 15–19 per cent in Italy (Commission of the European Communities, 1993). Those without family contacts who do not have reciprocal social relationships with friends and neighbours, and experience loneliness, are most likely to have potential needs for social opportunities which could be met by the more formal arrangements outlined below.

Types of service to meet social needs

Although the needs met by the services considered in this chapter are mainly those for social contacts, education and leisure, in the course of using such facilities other care needs may be provided for. An important example is the basic need for nutrition, as well as for company, which the provision of meals in centres and lunch clubs attempts to satisfy. On the other hand domiciliary services offering practical support also provide an important source of social contacts for people with limited social networks or restricted mobility. Thus, as with the other types of

Table 6.2 *Frequency of contacts with family for people aged 60+, 1992*

	France	Germany	Italy	Netherlands	United Kingdom	United States[a]
every day	34.2	46.5	70.7	19.2	21.9	41.0
two or more times a week	16.2	15.6	14.4	26.6	28.3	n/a
once a week	25.1	13.8	7.8	25.4	19.0	20.0
once a fortnight	5.8	9.2	1.2	10.8	6.8	n/a
once a month	6.8	5.4	0.8	8.9	5.6	5.0
less often	9.0	5.5	1.6	5.8	14.5	6.0
never/no family or friends	3.0	3.9	3.4	3.2	4.0	n/a

[a] Data for 1984, people aged 65+ living in community, not living with children.
Sources: Commission of the European Communities, 1993: 11.
         Keenan, 1989: 49.

community care service covered in chapters 4 and 5, the main caring tasks and services identified in chapter 1 are offered by a range of types of provision. Table 6.3 summarises the main social and leisure needs and gives examples of formal services offered to meet them.

The services and facilities provided are reviewed below in four categories: volunteering and self-help; day centres and clubs; education and culture; and active leisure and travel. Examples are given of the facilities available and provision made by statutory and non-statutory sectors, and of the organisation and funding of services in the countries studied.

Volunteering and self-help groups   offer opportunities for older people to contribute to and benefit from support and social interaction. Under-taking unpaid work as a volunteer can provide job satisfaction for people who have retired from employment or no longer have child-rearing responsibilities. There are various structures for the organisation of such work, often within or coordinated by the voluntary non-profit sector. Activities which benefit other older people comprise only part of a very extensive range of volunteering opportunities. Similarly the voluntary organisations and self-help groups in which older people participate include not only those which are exclusively for the older age groups, but also those catering for many other interests.

Table 6.3   *Social and leisure needs and services*

Services to meet needs for	Example of formal services
basic care meals, bathing	lunch clubs, day centres
social contacts company, stimulation	clubs, senior centres, voluntary visits
therapeutic activity keep fit, games, craftwork	sports facilities, classes
education and leisure knowledge, skills, culture	classes, theatre, music, holidays
emotional support friendship, coping with bereavement	peer counsellors, day centre workers
financial support costs of transport, activities	reduced fares, concessions
transport to social facilities, holidays	community transport service
information facilities and services available	information services, professionals

The role of volunteers in social welfare activities increased from the late 1970s onwards in most of the countries studied, since volunteers were encouraged to fill gaps left as state expenditure was contained (Robbins, 1990; Steenvoorden, 1992). Many older people had traditionally played an important role in voluntary work for churches, charities such as the Red Cross, and voluntary organisations. To promote wider opportunities for volunteering and use of volunteer effort, structures were set up at local government level and often with financial support, for example from local authorities in the UK or OAA funding in the US. Such structures help match potential volunteers to the requirements of organisations such as hospitals, day centres or community transport services, and can take the form of volunteer organisers or volunteer bureaux to recruit volunteers and support their activities. There are also special projects through which older people use their skills working with younger people, giving training and advice or helping people with disabilities; such projects include the Retired Senior Volunteer Programme (RSVP) in the UK and US, and the Gilde projects in the Netherlands (Norton, 1992).

Older people may benefit from participation in such activity. Volunteers of all ages also contribute to the social and leisure needs of older people through work in the various health and welfare services. In countries with military service requirements such as Germany and Italy, another source of help in welfare activities is provided by conscientious objectors who choose to do alternative civilian service. Volunteers from churches, voluntary organisations or volunteer programmes also have an important role in visiting the more dependent and/or isolated older people in their homes, residential homes or hospitals, and sometimes also giving them help or taking them out.

Volunteers, however, are not always available or acceptable. In the 1980s and 1990s there was increasing emphasis on the development of self-help groups and community-based initiatives through which people with similar interests or needs could help each other on a more equal and reciprocal basis, for example telephone circles, service exchanges and 'good neighbour' projects. The initiation of such groups was promoted and in some cases given financial support from government sources as part of general welfare or community development programmes. For example in Germany the federal government set up action programmes to promote self-help activities among older people or between generations. In 1992 the German government initiated a model programme of *Senioren-Büros*, at least one in each federal state, to collate information on volunteering opportunities, help place volunteers, promote self-help groups, and develop social networks (Alber, 1992). In Italy new voluntary associations were 'developing services for special needs groups, sometimes in direct partnership with local authorities, in the context of philosophies of self-help or community empowerment' (Robbins, 1990: 118). Volunteer effort thus increased in volume and developed in new directions in the light of policies encouraging social integration during the 1980s and 1990s.

Day centres, social centres and clubs provide for social activities and meals during the day and offer or facilitate access to other services. Definitions of the aims and functions of such centres vary within and between countries. As emphasised in chapter 5, there is overlap in health and social care functions between day hospitals and day centres; similar overlaps occur between day centres providing specialised care and centres which are mainly social in function. In the UK, for example, the term 'day care' is used to embrace specialised day hospitals and centres, and mainly social day centres and lunch clubs, whereas in other countries 'day care' denotes specialised care in day hospitals or centres and the more social facilities are designated as senior centres or social centres for older people. A study of day care services in England and Wales, which found the aims of day care unclear and conflicting, suggested making a conceptual distinction between two types of provision: *day care services* offering specialised assessment, rehabilitation, maintenance and monitoring and relief for carers, and *day facilities* offering company and social activities, including social centres and clubs, educational and leisure opportunities (Tester, 1989: 169).

Although in practice the two types may be combined in one centre and are difficult to distinguish, the review of mainly social day facilities below attempts to identify them separately. The total range of different types of day care services and day facilities in a country or area is also significant, as the availability of other types of care influences decisions on applications for day care and on referral to other services after short-term specialised day care.

As shown in chapter 5, day care centres are well developed in the Netherlands and UK, and are developing in Germany, Italy and the US, but were not successful in France. The aims and activities of such centres vary but are similar in the Netherlands and UK, where most day centres' aims include helping people to remain independent in their own homes; offering social care and company; developing or maintaining skills; and providing relief and support for carers. The activities and care provided comprise a midday meal, social and recreational activities, therapeutic activities, for example crafts and keep fit exercises, and personal care such as hairdressing, bathing and chiropody (Nies et al., 1991). Transport is generally provided for users.

Older people's centres which are mainly social and recreational facilities also offer some of the above services, but are usually intended for fit and active people who can travel independently to them. Such centres aim to provide social contacts and stimulating activity for older people. In France there are drop-in centres that provide restaurant and take-home lunch facilities, newspapers and information, and social, sports and cultural activities. Sheltered housing units are also used as drop-in centres by older people for meals and social activities. Social centres for older people in Germany are meeting places, mainly run by welfare organisations, providing social contacts and a range of leisure activities, education and information. The centres have professional staff who give advice and refer people to other services as appropriate (*Kuratorium Deutsche Altershilfe*, 1993). There are also neighbourhood centres with activities and support for all age groups under one roof.

In Italy social centres for older people are provided to encourage socialisation and offer cultural activities, restaurant, recreation and sport; a minority also offer personal and health care services. They may be linked to home care services, are mainly staffed by volunteers and run by users, and funded through the regions (Costanzi, 1991; Florea et al., 1993). Service centres are provided in many neighbourhoods in the Netherlands; they are mainly used by fit and active people aged over 55 and offer a broad range of social and cultural activities, mainly run by older volunteers, with some paid staff. Some have day care centres for more dependent people on the same premises. These neighbourhood centres are financed through the general welfare budget and users' contributions, and are run by non-profit organisations. In the UK there are drop-in centres for fit and active people, usually organised by the voluntary sector, but the day centre model is more prominent. Senior centres in the US provide meals and social activities for older people and a minority offer adult day care; in addition the centres provide information and a focal point for services for older people (Krout, 1989). Adult day care services also run social and recreational programmes; some people on low incomes may be sponsored by community or religious organisations (AARP, 1992).

A further source of social contact and activity is available through a wide variety of social clubs or lunch clubs for older people, and clubs for mixed age groups or special interests. Such clubs often meet on the premises used by day centres or social centres, are mainly run by the non-profit sector or by their members, and may receive financial subsidies from welfare funding sources. They usually meet at least weekly and offer activities and outings, refreshments and sometimes meals. Clubs for older people are widespread, for example, in France where they are promoted as part of the community care services, mainly for social integration and leisure activities.

Educational and cultural opportunities available to the general population continue to be taken up by older people who previously followed such interests and still have access to them. Special projects and programmes for older people, however, facilitate access in various ways. They encourage participation by those who take up new interests in later life, and provide activities of special relevance to older people, including education for retirement. They can also bring educational and cultural facilities at convenient times to accessible or local venues, including day centres, retirement communities or residential homes, and provide transport or subsidised travel to venues, and concessions on admission prices. For example for the over-65s in the Netherlands a national concession card, the *Pass 65*, gives reduced charges for transport and cultural and educational facilities. Examples of successful projects are given for the countries studied; access to such programmes is unevenly distributed, as discussed later in this chapter.

Although in the early 1990s resources were channelled to vocational courses, general programmes of adult or further education are available to all age groups, offered for example by adult education centres (*Volkshochschulen*) in Germany and adult education institutes in the UK, which make reduced charges for older people. In Italy adult education is free of charge, but mainly focused on vocational qualifications for younger people. Higher education courses are also available to all age groups; distance learning courses, such as those offered by the Open University in the UK, and similar open universities in Germany and the Netherlands, provide an accessible form of education (Norton, 1992).

Programmes to increase participation by older people in further or higher education include holding education classes in clubs, senior centres and residential accommodation, for example in France, Germany and the Netherlands. Special courses for older people are offered, for example in Germany by the Berlin Academy of Further Educational Studies, which runs a summer university for older adults and encourages older people to take part in higher education in colleges and universities (Kramer and Landwehr, undated). Universities of the third age (UTAs), offering a wide range of educational courses and leisure activities, developed in Europe and North America from the 1970s onwards. In France many of the UTAs are part of traditional universities and courses are taught by academics, although older people have an input to the content and running of courses. This model has been taken up in other European countries, for example Italy where UTAs developed rapidly in the 1980s. In the UK, however, UTAs are run on self-help principles, with older people organising and teaching their own courses (Norton, 1992).

In some areas local organisations such as municipalities, voluntary associations or self-help groups promote cultural activities programmes for older people, including guest speakers and visits to concerts, theatres and museums. For example, such programmes are organised in Avignon, France, by a committee initiated by the CCAS, the university, the federation of third age clubs, and cultural organisations. Older people also organise or join groups for specific cultural activities, for example the 'theatre of experience' and similar theatre groups in Berlin, Germany (Kramer and Landwehr, undated). In Michigan, US, the

Turner Geriatric Centre at the University of Michigan runs writing groups which read, discuss and publish members' work; the Michigan Office of Services to the Aging offers a programme of 'enrichment activities' such as creative music making, painting and sculpture for nursing home residents in the state. Similar examples are found in all the countries studied, depending on the availability of interested people to initiate, organise and raise funding for them.

Active leisure and travel opportunities are similarly available to people of all ages who are able to participate in, gain access to and pay for them. Local authorities or private organisations provide swimming pools and sports facilities often with concessionary rates for older people. Clubs for activities such as golf, tennis and walking exist in most areas. For those with reduced mobility or restricted access to such facilities, there are special programmes such as keep fit or swimming classes for older people. Leisure and fitness activities are also offered in day care and residential settings ranging, for example, from music and movement sessions in day centres to extensive on-site facilities such as swimming pools and golf courses in continuing care retirement communities in the US.

Outings and holidays are organised to provide social contacts and activities for older people who otherwise would not have access to such opportunities. In France holidays for older people with disabilities are offered by the CCAS in some communes, with a subsidy from the person's pension fund where appropriate; and voluntary associations organise holidays and outings to places of interest. Holidays may be offered by local authorities as part of the community care services in the UK, with means-tested charges; some voluntary organisations and charities run holidays for people with disabilities. In Italy the provision of summer holidays by local authorities is a well developed service; there are means-tested charges and priority is given according to criteria of need, for example lack of social contacts. There are also day outings to meeting places in parks or at the seaside offering social contacts, leisure and cultural activities (Florea et al., 1993). Holidays and travel opportunities are available, through clubs and organisations for older people, for example, in France and Germany, and through AARP in the US, providing appropriate facilities at advantageous prices.

Older people often have special needs for transport to social and leisure facilities because the transport available is inaccessible, insecure or expensive (Daunt, 1992; Howe et al., 1994). Special transport is thus offered either to specific services such as day centres, or for general social purposes, often using volunteer drivers. Door-to-door services, which eligible users can book by telephone, and which use vehicles equipped for people with disabilities, are organised locally by local authorities or voluntary associations and are well developed in France, Germany, the Netherlands and the UK (Daunt, 1992). In the Netherlands transport services are run by coordinating agencies for services to older people, funded through local authorities from the general welfare budget (Baars et al., 1992). Programmes run with OAA funding in the US provide transport by bus or taxi or specially equipped vehicles to services or for social purposes (AARP, 1992). On public transport there are concessions such as bus and rail passes in European countries; in 1989 the EC recommended a European concession card for over-60s, which has not yet been implemented (Daunt, 1992).

The day care, leisure and education facilities reviewed illustrate the range of services to which older people potentially have access for company, leisure activities and social participation. The full range of possibilities, however, is not universally available, nor are the facilities offered in any area or country equally accessible to all older people and carers.

Outcomes of day care, leisure and education services

Day care, leisure and education services are offered with the general aims of maintaining older people's health and wellbeing by promoting social integration, relieving loneliness and providing stimulating activities. It is difficult to establish how well these services meet their aims because the services are diverse in nature, the aims are unclear, and very few data are collated at national or cross-national level on these areas of community care policy.

Implications of day care, leisure and education provision for older people and carers

The pattern of economic influences on social policy familiar from previous chapters means that, as with other components of community care, economic factors since the 1970s affected or restricted the development of services providing social activities for older people. As there is little public awareness of these services and they are not considered essential, they do not attract high political priority for expenditure, which can easily be reduced without causing protest. In a climate of welfare expenditure restraint, resources are targeted to priority needs; social activities for older people are easily perceived as optional extras, and the possibility that such activities could have a preventive function in reducing longer term demands on health and welfare services is overlooked.

Economic influences have entailed reductions in budgets for social activities, imposition or increase of charges to users, and changes in the nature of services provided to meet funding requirements. For example, in the United States, Krout (1989: 123) identifies three ways in which changes in policy and funding affected senior centres: federal funding for social services was reduced, shorter hospital stays meant increased demand for community-based care, and OAA funding was increasingly focused on the most frail older people. Thus senior centres had to rely more on state and local government finance, fundraising activities and user contributions (Krout, 1989: 146). Similarly in the UK, cuts were made in day care services by local authorities required to reduce social expenditure and, in many areas, charges to users were introduced or increased in the 1990s for day centres and other services under the reformed community care system, and for other local authority services such as education and leisure (Association of Metropolitan Authorities, 1994). Such charges are likely to deter older people and carers from taking up services which they themselves may not consider a priority. Service users are also reluctant to pay for social day care when day hospital care is free of charge.

Funding policy also affects the nature of services that can be provided, particularly in systems where there are strong divisions between medical and social funding, strict criteria for different types of funding, or reliance on short-term or project funding focused on particular priorities. In Germany, for example, day care is affected by the medical/social divide in similar ways to other health and welfare services. Where day care services or facilities are provided for mainly social reasons, health insurance does not cover the costs, and unless potential users have low enough incomes to qualify for social assistance, they face high charges which deter them from using the services. Alternatively service providers have to seek funding or subsidise users from other sources. The care insurance system to be introduced in 1995 will only cover limited aspects of personal care, and is likely to have little impact on the difficulties of funding social day care. Similar constraints are found in France where day centres did not prove successful largely because of problems in funding the social aspects of care. The type of day facilities that can be provided for outside users, for example in sheltered housing, is limited by funding criteria; services are subsidised by the provider.

Funding priorities in the late 1980s and early 1990s changed the nature of services provided by focusing on particular needs and reducing the supply of or demand for lower priority services. The trend to reduce the state's role in the mixed economy of welfare and introduce market criteria also disadvantaged the services providing social and leisure activities for older people with disabilities and health problems, for example in the UK. For the profit-making sector these services are not commercially viable unless purchased under contract from the state. The non-profit sector is similarly limited in providing services purchased by the local authority whereas under the previous grant aid system voluntary organisations had more autonomy over the type of service offered.

Since many policy, practice and funding decisions about day care, leisure and education services are made at local level, there are different systems and inequitable distribution of services within countries. In Germany, for example, in addition to funding difficulties over the medical/social divide, variations in funding systems used in different states affect the distribution of day care. Within countries there is also a wide diversity of provision and varying definitions, aims and roles for each type of service. The lack of clarity in service aims may contribute to the lack of priority and low profile accorded to this type of provision. These factors make it difficult to compare services within or between countries and to assess the effectiveness of the services provided. If the objectives of a service are not clearly defined, the overall need for it cannot be accurately assessed, and conclusions cannot be drawn on the extent to which needs are met. Evidence suggests, however, that there is widespread unmet need for day care in the countries where this service is not yet well developed.

The aims of providing services such as day care for individual users are also often unclear, as it is assumed that users in general will benefit from the package of services, which in practice may not be the most appropriate way of meeting an individual's needs. In the Netherlands and the UK the aim of individualised packages of care is intended to ensure that day care and other social activities are provided as part of a care plan based on the individual's assessed needs, to be monitored and reviewed periodically. The system of purchasing and contracting in the UK should mean that purchasers specify in contracts the appropriate type of care to be provided to meet these needs. However, it is not yet established that such systems are successfully implemented in practice.

Early evidence on the UK system suggests that many local authorities lack coherent strategies for day care and that provision of day care, meals and transport is inadequate and/or inappropriate (Age Concern England, 1993: 15).

There has been little systematic monitoring and evaluation of services such as day care or senior centres on which to base sound conclusions on their effectiveness. Reviews of studies undertaken in the Netherlands, the UK and the US found that they were mainly based on small samples or case studies and tended to rely on consumer opinion (Krout, 1989; Tester, 1989; Nies et al., 1991). Such surveys, for example of day care in the UK, found a high level of satisfaction. Users and carers valued the company and social contacts, the opportunities for activities and the relief of a break for carers; however, there were difficulties over transport and the inflexibility of hours of service (Tester, 1989). Of a sample of 200 senior centre users in the US, 90 per cent thought that the centre 'helped to keep them healthy, active, make new friends, improve their social life, and feel better about themselves' (Krout, 1989: 133). Positive views on education were found from research on older students in Europe (Norton, 1992: 41).

Service users thus tend to have positive opinions about the services. The majority of older people, however, do not take up the day care, leisure and educational opportunities reviewed in this chapter, although policies aim to promote social integration and active participation. The 1992 Eurobarometer survey of over-60s in EC countries found that an average of one in seven had attended a club or centre for senior citizens in the previous seven days; only four per cent had been to cinemas, theatres and concerts; on average eight per cent did voluntary work, including over 10 per cent in France and the UK, and 17 per cent in the Netherlands (Commission of the European Communities, 1993). Low participation rates do not necessarily mean that the facilities are unsuccessful; they may reflect a lack of demand and interest that is also found, to a smaller extent, among the population as a whole. On the other hand, for some older people low participation may indicate inappropriateness of the services offered, lack of knowledge about them, or difficulties over access.

Access, rights and choice in social activities

There are differences between countries in government policy and levels of resources for services such as day care, which is well developed in the

Netherlands and the UK, but not in the other countries studied. Within countries, distribution of services such as day centres, education and leisure facilities, transport and concessionary fares, is very uneven, since these largely depend on regional, federal state or local authority decisions on policy and resources. In Italy, for example, there are wide regional differences in the provision of day centres, with higher levels in the north and centre than in the south (Florea et al., 1993: 56). In the UK there are large differences in the levels of resources for local authorities to spend on the community care system and other services, and wide variations in the charges made for services such as day care (Age Concern England, 1994; Association of Metropolitan Authorities, 1994). Within the countries studied, rural areas tend to be less well provided with social, leisure and education facilities than urban areas.

Older people from higher socio-economic groups who have financial resources and access to transport have greater access to leisure and educational facilities than those who are on low incomes. Those with educational qualifications tend to have a higher rate of uptake, for example of adult education services and universities of the third age, than those with minimal education. As older women generally have lower levels of education than men, and are more likely to be on low incomes, they tend to use educational and cultural facilities less than men (Norton, 1992: 39). Similarly many people from minority ethnic groups are less likely than others to take up these services. The level of volunteer activity is greater among the higher socio-economic groups and among women; it is difficult to recruit volunteers in the areas of greatest need, such as the south of Italy.

Day centres and social centres tend to be used mainly by women, partly because there is a higher proportion of women than men in the older population, and a higher level of disability among women than men. Women also tend to have less access than men to wider leisure opportunities and have to use the special services provided for older people. Day centres and social facilities are often geared to the majority population and do not cater for the dietary, cultural, religious and social needs of black and ethnic minority communities. In the UK, before the community care reforms of the 1990s, local authorities often gave grant aid for minority ethnic groups to provide their own day centres and clubs. Under the reformed system, however, these groups have to compete with other organisations for contracts with the local authority and provide services specified in the contracts, which may disadvantage them in relation to mainstream organisations (Atkin, 1991).

People in the oldest age groups are most likely to need special provision of day care and leisure opportunities, as they tend to have more disabilities and fewer resources than younger groups. However, services such as day care often do not reach those in greatest need, such as the most frail, incontinent, or dementia sufferers, particularly if they have transport needs (Tester, 1989). The social day centres or senior centres in the countries studied are used by, and cater for, fit and active younger senior citizens, and only a minority are able to provide for those with disabilities or health problems (Krout, 1989; Florea et al., 1993). Bus and rail passes and other concessions are also widely used by older people without mobility problems, but are of limited use to those who cannot gain access to these sources of transport (Daunt, 1992: 135).

As for other social welfare services there are few rights for older people to day care, leisure and educational services. Older people with disabilities have more rights under legislation providing for disabled people in countries such as the UK and US, although they are not necessarily aware of these rights. Under the Chronically Sick and Disabled Persons Act 1970 local authorities in England and Wales are required to provide assistance with recreational and educational facilities, travel, holidays and meals for disabled people assessed as needing them. People's rights to these services must be considered in the assessment of need under the reformed community care system; however, early evidence found that older people with disabilities had been denied such rights (Age Concern England, 1993: 14; RADAR, 1994). The Americans with Disabilities Act 1990 gives people with disabilities rights to the provision of state or local government services for which they are eligible and to accessible facilities and transport (Scott, 1994).

Variations in access and rights are reflected in the choices people have in their leisure activities and in the extent to which they are able to exercise choice. Not surprisingly, the better off, healthier older people have the most choice and do not have to depend on services provided for lower income people with disabilities or health problems. When services are means-tested, those on lowest incomes may receive them free of charge, whereas people with slightly higher incomes may find their opportunities restricted if they cannot afford the charges. People in the oldest age groups, on low incomes, with poor health or mobility problems have the least choice, as their opportunities for social contacts and activities outside the home and family are often limited to those provided by the welfare systems, such as day centres and clubs for which transport is provided. The activities in such venues may not be those that the person would choose if other opportunities were available.

Policies which target resources to those in greatest need may improve the provision made for these older people, especially if it is part of a package of care based on people's assessed needs and choices. This may have the effect, however, of limiting the choices of formally provided services for people with lower priority needs who will increasingly have to rely on informal networks and self-help groups. If social integration is to be promoted successfully, policymakers and providers will have to specify objectives more clearly and facilitate service provision and funding sources that are more focused on clear aims at a local level, and thus be able to address the diverse ways in which individual older people may benefit from social participation and activities.

Summary

Government policy statements on care of older people generally include measures to promote social contacts as ways of increasing social integration or reducing isolation or loneliness and helping older people to maintain their health and wellbeing. Legislation exists in all the countries studied to enable day care, social, leisure and educational facilities to be provided and funded, at least for people on low incomes and in greatest need. Decision making on such services is usually vested at local level and non-profit agencies and self-help groups play a significant role in providing facilities.

For most older people informal contacts with family and friends form the main social activity. Although a wide range of facilities is potentially available, a minority of older people participate in day care, leisure and educational activities. It is difficult to assess the effectiveness of these services in meeting policymakers' aims. The services and facilities are diverse, and purposes of service provision unclear or conflicting, and few representative statistical or evaluative studies have been undertaken. Policy trends of cost containment and focusing services on those in greatest need have reduced availability of services and increased charges to the user, thus limiting choices for those unable to provide social and leisure opportunities for themselves. Services and facilities are inequitably distributed both geographically and by socio-economic group, gender, 'race', age and level of disability; there are few rights to these services and few choices for many older people.

7
Coordination of Community Care Services

As the preceding chapters clearly show, care services for older people cover a broad spectrum of functions and are provided and funded by different agencies. There is thus a need for coordination and cooperation between care providers to ensure that services are appropriate to needs and do not overlap. The division between medical and social service provision and funding is a particular obstacle to coordination in some countries. Further difficulties arise from conflicting organisational and professional interests. Commentators on the systems studied identify lack of coordination as a problem which persists in spite of governments' policies to promote structures or measures to facilitate coordination.

Although policy and planning documents at all levels tend to advocate improved coordination as desirable or essential, they rarely define what is meant by coordination or similar concepts used such as collaboration or cooperation. A comprehensive review of definitions and meanings of these concepts by Hallett and Birchall (1992) found that some writers use the terms synonymously, while others distinguish coordination, for example, as more formal than cooperation which involves working together at field level. There are clearly no agreed definitions of the terms. Hallett and Birchall (1992: 11–12) suggest that: 'Inherent in most usages of the terms coordination and collaboration is the idea of working together, cooperatively and in harmony', but point out that: 'cooperation and consensus are not necessary and inevitable components of coordination'. For the policy area of community care, coordination is defined in this chapter as a process of joint working and communication between organisations and individuals, through various formal and informal arrangements, with the aim of providing effective, integrated care services.

Background to policies on coordination

Policies for the care of older people were developed in the post-1945
period in the general context of welfare policies which varied according
to the type of welfare regime. The individual services which contribute
to community care – income maintenance, housing, health and welfare
services, discussed in previous chapters – tended to develop separately,
with little explicit recognition of the desirability of coordination between
them. Most of the stated policy for care of older people focused on
institutional care, on the assumption that people with high levels of
dependence on services would be cared for in this way. With the move
towards community care policies, however, it was intended to maintain
older people with diverse and complex care needs in their own homes by
a variety of community-based health and welfare services. As the extent
of differentiation and fragmentation between these services varied
between countries, there were different perceptions of need for
coordination.

Development of policies on coordination of community care services

Policy documents and research on community care in the 1970s and
1980s identified and reiterated problems in care delivery systems
resulting from poor coordination between and within health, welfare,
housing and other services, and between different sectors of the mixed
economy of welfare. For example in the UK the Audit Commission
(1986: 3) report found services fragmented and community care policies
'in some disarray'; the Dekker report (1987) in the Netherlands and the
Braun report (Braun and Stourm, 1988) in France revealed similar
concerns. In the 1980s policy trends such as reduction in the use of
institutions, development of the mixed economy of care, incorporation of
the role of informal carers into public policy, the focus on individualised
care, and concern about cost effectiveness, increased needs for
coordination. In some respects, however, these trends represented
responses to problems of poor coordination.

Community care policy developments and reforms in the late 1980s
and early 1990s took two main approaches to improving coordination.
First, at strategic level, new management structures or funding systems
were introduced, new responsibilities were allocated, and in some
systems services were decentralised or localised. Second, at the level of
the individual with care needs, systems of assessment and case (or care)
management were developed to provide appropriate 'packages' of care,

sometimes with funding or budgets to span divisions between care-providing agencies. The policies of the six countries on coordination of community care for older people are outlined below.

The strong medical/social divide in *France* is an obstacle to effective coordination of community care. Government policy since the 1970s, for example in the Sixth, Seventh and Eighth Economic and Social Plans, has stressed the need for better coordination between services for older people. A government circular in 1982 (*Ministère des Affaires Sociales*, 1982) introduced a system for local coordination of all agencies and professionals and described the role of local coordinators, for whom 500 posts were created and initially state-funded in 1981. These posts, however, mainly lapsed when state funding ended. The circular also required each *département* to produce a gerontological plan showing existing services and development plans but about half of the *départements* had not done so by the late 1980s. The national committee of retired and elderly people and committees in each *département* (CODERPAs) set up in the early 1980s were also intended to promote coordination.

All these government measures, however, were largely unsuccessful in improving coordination (Braun and Stourm, 1988). In the early 1990s the promotion of coordination between the health and social sectors was one of two main issues on the policy agenda, the other being the question of responsibility for paying for care for people whose needs are covered by different funding agencies and providers (Guillemard and Argoud, 1992: 106; Boulard, 1991; Schopflin, 1991).

In *Germany* a similar problem of divisions between medical and social care, social insurance and social assistance impedes coordination. There are no formal structures for coordination between the different health and social services, each with their own hierarchies and cultures. In the former GDR these services were coordinated at local level but that system was dismantled in the early 1990s and replaced in the new states by the FRG system based on the split between medical insurance and social welfare.

Although the need for better coordination of services for older people is recognised, for example in plans for older people at federal, state and commune level, the main approach taken by federal and state governments has been to encourage coordination at local level rather than introduce more general structures. The main strategy in the 1980s was the development of the local community care centre (*Sozialstation*). Another approach was the funding and initiation, under federal or state plans for older people, of short-term model projects with coordinator posts to stimulate cooperation between agencies working with older people at commune level. Such strategies do not provide for long-term funding of these projects, nor for the wider implementation of successful initiatives. In German policy on care for older people the promotion of coordination has thus received little priority.

The health care reform and introduction of the national health service in *Italy* in 1978 aimed to integrate health and social care services through local health units (USL), but in practice integration is difficult because there are different funding systems for health and social care (Florea et al., 1993). The policy of stimulating the commercial, non-profit and informal sectors of provision in the late 1980s and early 1990s increased the need for coordination. Under the decentralised system initiatives for innovative projects depend on regional and local planning and funding (Vollering, 1991). At national policy level the government's stated aims, through the 1991–5 project for older people, are to promote the integration of health and welfare services for older people (Florea et al., 1993: 51). Local government and health service reforms in the 1990s, however, are likely to increase the separation and fragmentation of health and social services at local level (Saraceno and Negri, 1994: 28).

Coordination of services for older people has been a policy objective in the *Netherlands* since the late 1960s when the government initiated local coordinating agencies for work with older people. These agencies were intended to coordinate existing services and to organise recreational and other services not already provided (Baars et al., 1992: 39). Coordination was needed because health and social services were provided by many different professional organisations. In the 1980s, with the policies of substitution and tailor-made care and the development of outreach functions of residential and nursing homes, the government's policy was for a variety of agencies in a locality to be able to provide integrated community care for individuals. Another strategy following the Dekker report (1987) was to coordinate home help and home nursing services by bringing both into the ambit of one source of funding, the exceptional medical expenses act (AWBZ) and merging the organisations. 'More coordination of policy and practice concerning housing and care' was one of the priorities stated in the 1990 policy paper *Ageing counts* (Tweede Kamer, 1990; Pijl, 1992: 202); this issue is taken up in the Welschen report (Commissie Modernisering Ouderenzorg, 1994).

Difficulties over coordination of health and social services were recognised in *United Kingdom* policy in the 1970s. The Department of Health and Social Security (DHSS) attempted to improve coordination by introducing joint planning arrangements for local and health authorities in 1974 and joint finance in 1977, but these arrangements did not prove very successful. The need for coordination between services for older people was stressed in the policy paper *Growing older* (DHSS, 1981) and in policy documents and reports throughout the 1980s (see, for example, Audit Commission, 1985, 1986; HMSO, 1987). The Griffiths report (1988: vi) urged that: 'there must be a clear framework within which local and health authorities are working out their own process of coordination'. Key changes in the policy paper *Caring for people* (HMSO, 1989a: para. 1.12) included new responsibilities for local authorities 'in collaboration with medical, nursing and other interests, for assessing individual need, designing care arrangements and securing their delivery within available resources'; local authorities were also to be 'expected to produce and publish clear plans for the development of community care services, consistent with the plans of health authorities and other interested agencies'. The 1990 National Health Service and Community Care Act legislated for local authorities' duties to carry out these functions.

In the *United States* services for older people are very fragmented, making coordination difficult to achieve. Under the Older Americans Act (1965) the US has a structure, at various levels, for the administration of services for older people. At federal government level the Administration on Aging (AoA), located in the Department of Health and Human Services, has interagency agreements with other relevant departments. Each state must designate a State Unit on Aging (SUA) to implement the OAA and form a focal point for policy on services for older people. Each SUA must divide the state into geographic planning and service areas and, for each, appoint an Area Agency on Aging (AAA) which focuses on planning, development and coordination of services for older people. Another main policy approach to coordinating services for the individual older person was the development of case management through demonstration projects funded by the Health Care Financing Administration (HCFA) in the late 1970s, and the wider implementation of large case management projects through waivers for Medicaid funding in the 1980s. By the 1990s case management had become the key method of developing individual packages of long-term care, recommended, for example in the Pepper Commission (1990) report (Davies, 1992).

Coordination policies: influences and principles

Policies on coordination developed in response to perceived problems in coordinating health and welfare services. In some cases reforms in community care, such as the development of individualised care and case (or care) management, were also designed to promote closer coordination. Other general trends in social policy and community care, however, such as cost containment measures or the encouragement of non-statutory sectors of provision, often conflict with the aim of promoting coordination.

Policies to improve coordination of community care were influenced by economic factors such as reports that uncoordinated, often over-lapping services, wasted resources. Service coordination could thus be promoted as a cost effectiveness measure. Similarly care management could be used to organise coordinated packages of community-based care for people who would otherwise receive more expensive care in institutions. The development of policies on innovative methods of coordinated care delivery such as care management was also influenced by experimental projects funded by governments to evaluate commu-nity-based care. Such projects included the Channeling experiments in the US, the Personal Social Services Research Unit (PSSRU) community care projects which influenced the UK government's community care reforms (Davies, 1992), and the six local experiments commissioned by the Netherlands government in the 1980s to evaluate ways of substituting community care for expensive institutional care (Coolen, ed., 1993; Romijn and Miltenburg, 1993).

The formulation and implementation of coordination policies also depends on the levels at which policymaking and planning take place, in addition to general national planning. A major obstacle to coordination in France is the split between health and welfare planning: the *département* is responsible for planning social and socio-medical services, while the state, at regional level, is responsible for health planning (Henrard et al., 1991). In Germany plans for older people are produced at federal, state and commune level. Under the Italian decentralised system, planning for health and social services takes place at regional level. In the Netherlands responsibilities for planning of services are taken at national, provincial and local levels. The NHS and Community Care Act 1990 gives local authorities in the UK the duty to produce, monitor and review community care plans in consultation with local health and housing authorities, voluntary housing agencies and voluntary organisations. At national level these plans are monitored by the Social Services Inspectorate (SSI). Local and health authorities also negotiate planning agreements on divisions of responsibilities for people with health and social care needs. Under the OAA in the US, the area level is the focus of responsibility for planning services for older people; each AAA must develop an annual area plan on aging, with details of services for each county.

It is clear from previous chapters that where community care is concerned there are no easy solutions to the difficulties of achieving coordination. Obstacles to coordination identified in the literature include structural or boundary difficulties, different or conflicting organisational and professional interests, and low priority for devoting resources and time to interagency coordination. Hallett and Birchall (1992: 60–5) identify five main factors that may facilitate coordination: the 'external environment' including, for example, policy guidance; the 'degree of consensus' between agencies on the purpose of coordination; the 'role of reticulists', that is key individuals with commitment to coordination; 'co-terminous boundaries'; and the 'role of incentives', such as funding for coordinative projects. The factors which facilitate or inhibit coordination are, however, complex and the context in which interagency working takes place should always be considered.

General obstacles to coordination combine with the effects for interagency working of different systems and the principles and assumptions on which they are based. For example in the German system there are many impediments to coordination and few of the facilitating factors are evident. As a 'conservative–corporatist' welfare regime it is based on the social insurance model, with a strong divide between medical and nursing services covered by health insurance and social care services supported through the social assistance system (Dieck and Garms-Homolová, 1991). The systems have different statuses and cultures and there is little interest in developing formal links between them. The principle of subsidiarity further ensures a fragmented system which works against the integrated planning and provision of community care services (Tester, 1994).

Policies promoting coordination are put forward on the assumption that a coordinated approach will overcome such difficulties in inter-agency working. They also aim for results which could not be achieved by any one agency alone. The values underlying coordination policies include both organisational and humanitarian aims which may not be compatible. Cost effectiveness and efficiency are sought through joint working and the elimination of wasteful overlaps, using methods such as organisational structures and allocated responsibilities. From a huma-nitarian perspective coordinated responses aim to focus on individuals' needs, providing flexible individualised services and continuity of care through methods such as multi-disciplinary teams and care manage-ment.

Methods of coordinating community care

Coordination between organisations and individuals takes place at different levels of government and service provision, between different parts of the same organisation, between statutory and non-statutory service providers and funders, and between the formal sectors and informal carers. The processes can take place through different types of arrangements and procedures in a variety of settings and forms, as well as through different levels of formal and informal communication.

Types of arrangements for coordination between services and sectors of provision

As stressed throughout this book, coordination is needed between all those supplying components of community care for older people, so that appropriate services can be provided effectively to individuals and carers. The methods of seeking coordination serve different functions all of which may be necessary to achieve the desired outcomes (Tester, 1985).

First, general procedures are needed for joint working or communication between the organisations and actors involved in planning services, sharing responsibilities, making referrals and assessments, and communicating with users and carers. Second, arrangements are necessary to facilitate joint working and communication concerning provision of a range of services to individuals. Third, the exchange and dissemination of information are essential for policymakers, service providers, care workers, service users and carers to ensure access to information about the range of services offered and the entitlement criteria and conditions of service provision. Fourth, for individuals to work effectively together and generate commitment to coordination, training and experience in other agencies' structures, services, aims and cultures are desirable. Social contacts and informal meetings provide further opportunities for developing mutual understanding. Table 7.1 summarises these types of arrangements and procedures for coordination.

The extent to which any of these arrangements exists in practice varies between and within countries. Structures for interagency coordination to serve the main functions are examined below.

Strategic planning for care services for older people takes place at different levels of central, regional and local government as described above. In unitary states such as the UK the central government has the

Table 7.1 *Coordination arrangements and procedures*

Function of coordination	Examples of arrangements
general procedures, communication	
policy guidance on coordination	guidance manuals
agreed procedures	for assessment, hospital discharge
points of contact	coordinator, case manager
joint planning	multi-agency committees
communication with carers	carers groups
communication, assessment at individual level	
geographical proximity	agencies/services located on one site, resource centres, community care centres
joint assessment	multi-disciplinary assessment committees
joint working	multi-disciplinary units, teams
designing care package	case manager
information exchange, dissemination	
joint discussion	interagency meetings
information for service planning	confidential access to databases
information for users and carers	information brochures, displays
information for care workers	resource centres, information packs
training, developing mutual understanding, social contact	
multi-disciplinary training	joint seminars, in-service training
experience of other agencies' work	placements, exchange visits
social contacts	informal meetings, social events

potential to coordinate all policies that impinge on community care for older people; such rational coordination would be more difficult in federal states such as the US. In practice, policies are not coordinated rationally in this way in the UK. Thus, although local authorities have the responsibility to draw up community care plans for their area, these plans cannot compensate for irrational or conflicting central government policies on social security, housing, fuel and so on. Further, the local authority's responsibility for community care planning does not give the authority any power to change health or housing provision.

Responsibilities for delivery of care services are located at different levels of administration and the extent to which the coordination of services is addressed varies between countries and areas. For example in Germany there are administrative structures at federal, state and local levels with responsibility for different aspects of services for older people, but no structures for coordination between the different health and social services. The relationships between levels of government and between formal agencies and informal sectors of provision are based on the principle of subsidiarity, with responsibilities placed at the lowest possible level (Tester, 1994). In the United States a coordination role is designated through the OAA structure to State Units and Area Agencies on Aging (SUAs and AAAs). The National Association of State Units on Aging (NASUA) provides resource, networking and coordination functions for the SUAs and represents them in consultations with government departments. States such as Oregon have combined most long-term care services for older people in one state department with the aim of improving coordination (Justice et al., 1988). The Italian national health service provides in theory for coordination between health and welfare services at local health unit level; in some regions there are combined units to administer both services, or departments to provide for health and welfare services to older people. Where there are no such structures, agreement protocols on responsibilities for health and social services for older people are drawn up between local health units and communes (Florea et al., 1993: 49–50).

At *département* level in France the sector (*circonscription*) structures for social services attempt to promote coordination, for example by basing social workers in medico-social centres. A recent approach in some states in Germany is the development, with funding incentives, of 'networks of help' such as local cooperatives or joint councils of service providing agencies to exchange information and coordinate their work (Alber, 1992: 76–7).

In the late 1960s the Netherlands government attempted to promote local coordination through the initiation of coordinating agencies for work with older people (*Gecoördineerd ouderenwerk*). These agencies were intended to coordinate local services, to organise leisure, education and information services, and promote the interests and integration of older people (Steenvoorden, 1992). The policy paper *Nota flankerend bejaardenbeleid (Outreach activities for older people)* (Ministerie van Welzijn, 1983) extended the law on residential homes to promote the development of outreach services from care homes. Government guidelines in 1989 introduced 'substitution' funding for nursing homes to provide care in the community for people eligible for nursing home care. From the late 1980s, as part of substitution policy in the Netherlands, mechanisms for coordination between the home help and home nursing services were developed through cooperation and working arrangements for the division of tasks.

Another approach to working level coordination is the combination of different services or professionals on one site, which also provides opportunities for social contact and the development of mutual understanding. The community care centre in Germany, for example, is intended to coordinate services by locating them together. The development of service centres with residential home, community care centre and mobile social services is planned, for example, in Bonn. In the Highland region of Scotland, the local authority social work department offers a flexible range of residential, domiciliary and day care services from a network of locally based resource centres which provide short and long-term residential care and day care on site, and a base for services such as home care, meals delivery and alarm systems. The On-Lok progamme in San Francisco, California, provides a comprehensive range of health and social support services to help frail older people to remain in their own homes (Minkler, 1988).

The importance of coordination between institutions and community-based services is emphasised in earlier chapters. Mechanisms for coordination between hospital and ambulatory services are described in chapter 5. Integrated multi-disciplinary systems of assessment for admission to residential and nursing home care are operated in the Netherlands and the UK, as outlined in chapter 3. Under the reformed community care system, there is a common assessment procedure in the UK for residential and community-based care. In the Netherlands the Welschen report recommends integrated, client orientated assessment for welfare, housing and care services (Commissie Modernisering Ouderenzorg, 1994).

Coordination between formal and informal care

Formal services only constitute a minor part of the care received by older people; these services may substitute for family care if none is available, or complement and support the informal care given to an individual. With policy emphasis on supporting informal carers and on providing individualised care, the importance of the relationship between the formal and informal sectors has become increasingly recognised. The relationship is, however, affected by the conflicting aims of community care; on the one hand informal carers are considered to save public expenditure by providing more care themselves, whereas on the other hand they are to be offered services and support. They may be viewed as 'resources', 'co-workers', 'co-clients' or 'superseded carers' (Twigg and Atkin, 1993). Perhaps because of such conflicts, there are, in practice, few structured arrangements for coordination between the formal and informal sectors in the six countries. Coordination between the sectors tends to be seen as the role of the social worker, which is increasingly that of organising care services and caring networks, whether or not as part of formal care management processes. It is also recognised that many informal carers perform a care management role for their dependants and should therefore be included in formal assessment and care management procedures.

Support services for carers form part of the relationship between the sectors. The development of such services is at an early stage even in countries with policy commitments to them, for example the Netherlands and the UK, as shown in chapter 4. Instrumental or practical support for carers includes services provided mainly for the older person, such as home care, and respite services provided to benefit both carer and cared-for. Respite services include respite in the home such as that given by care attendants or night sitters, and services outside the home such as day care or short-term residential care (Twigg, 1992). The extent of financial support for carers is summarised in chapter 4.

Emotional or psychological support for carers may be offered by social workers and other professionals in the various formal structures of the six countries, through individual counselling or support groups. The main emotional support, however, often comes from the wider informal sector of family, friends and neighbours who support the main carer but contribute more in social relations than in practical tasks (Daatland, 1983). Emotional support has also developed as a key role of non-statutory, voluntary and self-help groups. For example in the UK, the Carers National Association and its local branches provide carers groups or telephone support. Voluntary and self-help groups concerned with sufferers of Alzheimer's disease are active in organising support groups for carers in, for example, Germany, the Netherlands, the UK and the US. In the US there are counsellors in some private sector companies to advise employees who are carers.

Information on services available is crucial to coordinated community care services for older people and their carers, particularly where systems are complex, fragmented or in process of change, for example under the community care reforms in the UK, or in the new states of Germany. In all the countries studied, however, many older people and carers lack information which could help them gain access to support. Information is communicated to older people through a continuum of impersonal and personal methods (Tester, 1992). Organisations such as local authorities, non-profit welfare agencies and self-help groups produce leaflets, directories and other written impersonal information made available in central locations and sometimes in mobile displays. Information is also disseminated to people's homes through the press, radio and television. New technology through which people access by telephone information on computer terminal is a developing method of providing information for disabled people at home. The Minitel system is widely used for this purpose in France (Haldane and Ruppol, 1992).

Informing older people in person about services available is often the role of social workers and other specialist workers with older people. For example in Germany the social worker or older people's nurse advises people about services, and helps with applications. Professionals and care workers with older people thus need to be well informed about the services in order to give accurate advice and, where appropriate, devise care packages (Tester and Meredith, 1987). Information and advice centres and telephone advice services also provide centralised resources for both personal and impersonal information. Advice centres for older people and carers are a recent development in Germany (Döhner et al., 1992). Home care centres in Italy are increasingly used as advice and information centres (Costanzi, 1991), as are senior centres in the US (Krout, 1989). The AAA also plays a key role in information-giving in the US. For example the mid-Florida AAA's Center for Aging Resources, with OAA funding, provides information packs, a free telephone line, and specialist resource workers, using computerised data bases of all service-providing agencies for older people in the area.

The importance of information is generally recognised in the six countries and projects have been set up to develop more effective ways of ensuring that information reaches those who need it. For example in 1991 in England the Department of Health initiated a three-year pilot project, the National Disability Information Project, to evaluate different methods of providing integrated information services (Hinkley and Steele, 1992).

Coordination in funding, organisation and procedures

Since many coordination difficulties arise from the existence of different agencies and funding sources for community care, attempts have been made to improve coordination by combining or reorganising funding sources, agencies or departments and designating clear responsibilities and lines of accountability. An early example was the introduction in the UK in 1977 of joint funding for health and social services projects as an incentive for joint planning. The UK's reformed funding system for community care in the 1990s was a more fundamental reallocation of finance from the central government social security budget to the local social services authority. In the Netherlands the approach since the late 1980s has been to unite health and social care under the same funding system.

Reorganisation of government departments at different levels in the 1980s also attempted to promote local coordination by decentralising administrative systems and providing more localised offices covering a combination of services, for example housing and social services were combined in some UK local authorities. There was also a trend in the UK to reorganise local authority social services management on a localised basis, so that residential, domiciliary and day care were combined under the same decentralised management. Subsequently further reorganisation was recommended under the 1990 community care reforms to separate the purchasing and service provision functions.

At operational level, mechanisms to promote coordination have involved multi-disciplinary teams and care management systems. Multi-disciplinary teams take a variety of forms and serve different purposes. Ovretveit (1993: 55) defines a community multi-disciplinary team as:

a small group of people, usually from different professions and agencies, who relate to each other to contribute to the common goal of meeting the health and social needs of one client, or those of a client population in the community.

Teams, whose functions include direct service provision, assessment and care management, range from the loosely related group of workers serving one client, to groups meeting to discuss issues and make referrals, and to more structured and formal assessment panels for residential and community care.

Neighbourhood support units, developed in Sheffield, England, exemplify locally organised, 24 hour flexible social service provision by community support workers in people's own homes, ranging 'from routine domiciliary assistance through to comprehensive care equivalent to that available in a residential setting' (Walker, 1992b: 51). In the Netherlands, home teams have been set up in some localities; they consist of health and social service workers, such as GPs, district nurses, home helps and social workers. Based, for example, in a neighbourhood health centre, they form a team voluntarily to work together and discuss services for clients (Tunissen and Knapen, 1991). In more formal teams members from different professions are managed by a team manager as, for example, in Northern Ireland the 'patch' team manager manages the team's health and social services workers directly (Ovretveit, 1993: 65–6).

Care (or case) management has been widely adopted as a method of coordinating a range of services, or care package, designed to meet individual needs. Care management takes different forms, has varying aims and uses different methods, but usually includes the following core tasks:

> case-finding, screening for eligibility, and assessment which is as purposive, skilled and comprehensive as is appropriate for the case; care planning and arranging, ongoing monitoring, review and the adjustment of care plans. (Davies, 1992: 8)

The arrangements for care management may be made by a care manager and/or care management team, depending on the model adopted. Case management developed in the US in the late 1970s, and was initiated in the 1970s and 1980s in innovative projects in the UK and later in the Netherlands.

In the US a wide variety of case management models is used in different programmes across the states and counties, with Medicaid or OAA funding. For example Oregon state has an advanced model of case management. At state level community-based 'aging adult' services and Medicaid are based in one department with one director. Within each local area there is an agency, usually an AAA, with a case management function, staff who can provide subsidy payments, and a three-pronged service-delivery system for nursing homes, community-based care, and preventive programmes under the OAA. The case manager chooses the best setting for the individual and purchases services across all three types, after assessment of eligibility for Medicaid and other funding sources (Justice et al., 1988).

One of the objectives of the UK community care reforms is: 'to make proper assessment of need and good case management the cornerstone of high quality care' (HMSO, 1989a: 5). From 1993 local social services authorities began to implement assessment and care management systems, following government guidance for managers and practitioners (Department of Health and Scottish Office, 1991a; 1991b), but using different types of arrangement. In general, where individuals have multiple or complex needs, a multi-disciplinary 'comprehensive' assessment is made; the local authority decides which needs are to be met and draws up a care plan. Depending on the local authority system care managers may be involved in assessing needs and arranging packages of care, and may have a 'devolved budget' within which they purchase services (Meredith, 1993: 77). Joint training of health and social services staff and of workers from statutory and non-statutory sectors is promoted in government guidance on implementation of the community care reforms and monitored, in England, by the SSI and regional health authority (Department of Health SSI, 1991).

Approaches to coordination such as care management or integrated community care services were developed in North America and Western Europe through demonstration projects, such as the Channeling projects in the US, and the community care projects evaluated by the PSSRU at the University of Kent, England (Davies, 1992). Six experimental community care projects initiated by the Netherlands government in the 1980s used different methods of coordination, including case management for the Rotterdam project, integrated intake systems in Nieuwegein and Venlo, experiments with existing systems in Zeeland and Groningen, and a residential/nursing home and sheltered housing scheme in the Hague (Coolen ed., 1993; Romijn and Miltenburg, 1993).

The approach taken by federal and state governments in Germany has been to develop model projects, financed in the short-term through the plans for older people funds. For example in the early 1990s in Nordrhein–Westfalen a coordinator based in the local authority social welfare office in Cologne was funded for three years, to encourage cooperation between all agencies, groups and institutions working with older people in the city and to develop their involvement in planning policies for older people. In Berlin a coordination and case management team for the rehabilitation of older people was set up, financed by the federal and state governments. The team assesses people in hospital and prepares a care plan for home based services, which is then implemented by the community care centre. In Germany such projects have not yet been integrated into mainstream services, as has been the case under the UK reforms.

The above review of approaches and mechanisms for promoting effective coordination gives a brief indication and some key examples of types of arrangements and procedures in the six countries. It was not possible to provide a systematic account of coordination procedures, nor to cover all the systems in detail, as resources and materials were not available for such research. The main point to be emphasised is that, although these approaches and procedures vary within and between countries, they all attempt, in theory, to remedy some of the problems in the provision of community care arising from poor coordination between the agencies and actors involved.

Outcomes of systems of coordination

Promoting coordination is frequently advocated at the level of policy rhetoric in West European and North American countries, but evidence of successful outcomes of coordination in practice is sparse and often inconclusive. Previous chapters have stressed the difficulties in assessing outcomes of various aspects of community care, arising both from lack of data and from the complex nature of the services. These difficulties are compounded when attempting to assess the outcomes of coordination, since it may not be possible to attribute any positive effects of a programme specifically to coordination. Evaluative studies of projects to promote coordination tend to be biased towards favourable accounts. The desired outcomes of coordination may also vary for the different groups of policymakers, service providers, users and carers involved (Hallett and Birchall, 1992: 73–7).

Impact of coordination methods for older people and carers

In policy documents and research reports from the 1970s onwards, most attention was given to the problems of coordination rather than to any successful outcomes of initiatives to promote it. Such reports led to reforms designed to improve coordination. Evidence from EC-wide studies in the early 1990s suggests, however, that the problems of poor coordination and lack of information persist. For older people and carers these difficulties may mean that they receive uncoordinated, over-lapping services from different agencies, or that the services they receive do not meet all their needs appropriately, or that they do not receive services from which they could benefit.

A study of family care in the EC found that coordination was: 'a major missing element factor in the systems which operate in Europe' (Jani-Le Bris, 1993: 122); coordination was lacking at organisation level, between services and sectors, and at the level of the individual older person and carer. Similar problems were revealed by national studies for the EC Observatory on ageing. In France, for example, the services were fragmented, were not based on people's needs and were neither efficient nor effective (Guillemard and Argoud, 1992: 108). In Germany there was little coordination between hospital and ambulatory services, between the different health and welfare services or even between the community care centres run by different non-profit or commercial organisations (Alber, 1992: 76).

Evidence of poor information provision was also widespread. Family carers in most European countries experienced lack of information, especially if they became carers as the result of a crisis (Jani-Le Bris, 1993: 108). For older people and carers it was difficult to find information about services in countries such as France (Jani-Le Bris, 1992), Germany (Alber, 1992; Döhner et al., 1992), and Italy (Vollering, 1991). Formal workers and professionals were often also inadequately informed about the range of services for older people. General practitioners are potentially a key source of information for older people, yet their lack of knowledge, especially of social welfare services, received frequent comment (for example, Henrard et al., 1990).

Research in the UK shows that although much information is produced in the form of leaflets, booklets and so on, it does not necessarily reach those who need it most, because strategies for communicating information effectively are not clearly devised (Mullings, 1989). Multi-agency coordinated approaches to information provision for workers, older people and carers have proved effective in improving the dissemination of accurate information, particularly through personal contact rather than impersonal information. Such initiatives, however, are usually dependent on short-term funding; it is difficult to generate commitment to resourcing effective information-giving as part of mainstream services (Tester, 1992).

As described above, reforms to promote coordination consist of those concerned with changes to overall systems and structures, mainly initiated 'top-down' by governments and policymakers, and locally based experimental projects, the initiative for which may be 'bottom-up' and which may not lead to longer term structural changes (Baldock and Evers, 1991: 88–90). Structural changes introduced in the countries studied, did not always entail improved coordination. As Hallett and Birchall (1992: 13) point out: 'The existence of coordination machinery does not necessarily mean that coordination exists'.

In France, for example, in the sector (*circonscription*) structures for social work, the role of '*responsable de conscription*' in coordination with other agencies had not proved very successful and was not given high priority, although there was potential in this role for achieving improved coordination (Henderson and Scott, 1990). At *département* level, few had used the gerontological plan as a vehicle for promoting coordination (Guillemard and Argoud, 1992). Although the community care centre was set up in Germany as an approach to achieving coordination at local level, there were still problems of coordination with hospitals and other health and welfare services (Dieck and Garms-Homolová, 1991).

The coordinating agencies for work with older people in the Netherlands were less successful in their coordinating roles than as service providers and information resources. They lacked the power necessary to coordinate the work of other agencies which were keen to preserve their own interests (Baars et al., 1992: 39).

The 1990s community care reforms in the UK gave local authority social services authorities a lead role in organising community care and a new financial structure for payment for residential and community-based care organised through the local authority. The reforms, however, mainly concerned the organisation and funding of social care, and did not integrate the provision or funding of health, housing and social care in the NHS and local authority systems. The fundamental medical/social divide which thus remains in the system is a major obstacle to effective coordination (Walker, 1992b: 50). Another aspect of the reforms was the expectation in policy guidance (HMSO, 1990) that local authorities should show in their community care plans 'what arrangements they intend to make to inform service users and their carers about services' (p.19) and that the information should be accessible, using, if appropriate, braille, tape and ethnic minority languages. Early research on implementation of the reforms, however, showed that information on services was not easily understood, and that people from minority ethnic groups found it difficult to gain information on the community care system (Age Concern England, 1993: 6). A study commissioned by the Department of Health in 1993 found that users and carers were not well informed about services available nor about the assessment system (Department of Health, 1994c). Guidance was issued on the production of local community care charters in England to give information to users and carers about services, procedures and performance standards (Department of Health, 1994d).

Another strategy for promoting coordination has been the use of experimental projects. Such initiatives usually have some integral form of evaluation. This was the case with the above-mentioned government-funded community care projects in the Netherlands, the UK and the US. Evaluations of the Channeling projects in the US, which used case management models, found that they were less successful than expected in improving cost-effectiveness and access to services (Davies, 1992: 81–4). These and many other experiments and models tested in the US in the 1970s and 1980s did not provide evidence that the use of institutional care and the level of public expenditure could be reduced through case management and other innovative schemes which targeted home-based care on those most at risk of institutional care (Weissert et al., 1988). The use of case management to coordinate community-based care was, however, widely implemented with varying aims and models throughout the federal states.

Community care projects funded by the UK government in the 1980s were evaluated by PSSRU, University of Kent (Davies, 1992). The Kent community care project, for example, proved successful in reducing admissions to institutions and in providing services that were more responsive to individuals' and carers' needs than the services usually offered (Challis and Davies, 1986: 219–24). The results of these projects strongly influenced the initiation of local authority care management and assessment systems under the 1990 reforms. Early evidence of the implementation of these systems, however, shows varied outcomes across the country (Baldock and Ungerson, 1993; Department of Health, 1994a; Means and Smith, 1994). Difficulties included, in some areas, delays in carrying out assessments and inappropriate discharges from hospital (Age Concern England, 1993; 1994). The findings of the carers survey mentioned above suggested that the assessment system had not helped meet the needs of most carers and those they cared for (Warner, 1994: 5–6). There was little liaison between assessment procedures for community care and housing (Department of Health, 1994b: 3).

Evaluation of the demonstration projects on methods of substituting community care for institutional care in the Netherlands found that, although better care could sometimes be provided, it was not necessarily less expensive than institutional care (Coolen, ed., 1993). The individual care subsidy project in Rotterdam, based on the Kent project, was successful in postponing admission to residential care and in providing care at lower costs than for the control group, but there were no clear benefits in terms of health problems, social isolation and mental wellbeing (Koedoot and Hommel, 1993). The six experiments stimulated many other projects which were able to develop more quickly. Another programme which led to wider implementation consisted of intensive nursing projects set up in three regions by the public health insurance company with a subsidy from AWBZ (Tunissen and Knapen, 1991). In spite of progress made as a result of such projects, however, there is not yet an integrated system of assessment and coordinated care provision for older people in the Netherlands (Baars et al., 1992: 53). This may indicate a lack of political will to adopt new policies in line with the findings of the experiments.

Community care projects and other reforms to health and social welfare systems do not aim solely to promote coordination. There are other aspects of policy trends and reforms which conflict with the aim of coordinated services. Economic principles such as cost-effectiveness and efficiency underly most social policy reforms of the 1980s and 1990s, even when these reforms also have humanitarian aims. For example, the reduction in the use of institutions and the development of more varied and flexible forms of less expensive community-based care by different providers in the mixed economy of welfare increased fragmentation of services, such as in France and the UK.

The development of care management and individualised care was promoted by governments as a way of reducing expenditure on institutional care and eliminating wasteful overlaps of services to the individual. Care management and tailored packages of care are potentially effective ways of providing appropriate services to individuals and carers. If the main aim is to reduce costs, however, budgetary constraints may prevent the care manager from organising the most suitable services. Targeting of the assessment and care management process to those most in need may entail reductions in services for those with lower priority (Age Concern England, 1994: 15–16). The effect of such changes may be to transfer costs from the state to individuals and carers. Although policies increasing the role of informal carers assume that carers will provide the required services, research has shown that: 'Encouraging the informal sector to take on additional loads may merely lead to a reduction in the willingness to care' (Baldock and Evers, 1992: 301).

Differences in access, rights, responsibilities and choice

Access to coordinated systems and to information about the services available and eligibility for them varies geographically between and within countries. Even where there are national systems and structures for coordination, implementation varies at local level. Where coordination is promoted through special projects, only those in the relevant catchment area will benefit. Such projects depend on short-term funding, with no guarantee of continuity.

Access to integrated care also varies between groups. People from higher socio-economic groups have greater access to resources and information, and are thus most able to organise and finance their own package of care. Other groups are more dependent on public provision, which in many systems is being reduced, substituted by the informal sector. Women and those from lower social classes are most likely to take on the duties of informal caring (Arber and Ginn, 1992: 623–4). Carers of older people need information to gain access to support services. As a full time carer, however, or as a very frail or disabled person, it is difficult to reach information in centralised locations. The provision of services is also influenced by both the gender of the older person and the carer, and their relationship, in the extent to which it is expected that different formal services, such as domestic or personal help, are substituted by informal care (Arber et al., 1988).

People from minority ethnic communities are also more likely to be expected to give and receive informal care because of generalised assumptions about extended family caring (Walker and Ahmad, 1994). They are less likely than others to know about services, particularly if they speak a minority language. It is difficult to ensure that information, even when translated, reaches older people from minority ethnic groups. Gaining access to the services and assessment systems may also necessitate interpreting services which are not readily available. These issues have not yet been successfully addressed in the countries studied, even where they are recognised, as in the reformed UK system (Age Concern England, 1993; 1994).

With widely varying provision of, and access to, coordinated care systems and information, it is not surprising that there are few rights to these aspects of care. In the UK older people with disabilities have rights to information and to assessment under the Disabled Persons Act 1986, which local authorities must take into consideration under the community care assessment system (Meredith, 1993: 66). However, evidence suggests that some local authorities have not respected these rights, of which older people are not always aware (Age Concern England, 1993: 7, 14). Where coordination between the formal and informal sectors is concerned, policy trends in some countries have placed greater responsibilities on informal carers. Recognition of carers' roles, consultation with carers and policies on support for carers have not yet compensated in practice for these additional responsibilities, which are borne more by certain groups, as discussed above.

Although policies of developing a mixed economy of care and moving to more individualised care are based on the ideological principles of promoting choice and participation, the increased responsibility of informal carers in such provision can reduce choices for older people and carers. People with care needs do not necessarily prefer to receive personal care from relatives or friends (Begum, 1990). The aim of assessment for care which takes account of users' and carers' choices, for example in the UK system, may conflict with the aim of providing services within the resources available; the decision rests with the local authority assessor based on local authority criteria rather than with the older person (Meredith, 1993: 80–2). The use of assessment and care management as rationing devices and the targeting of public resources to priority needs have reduced choices for less dependent groups who have had publicly provided services such as home help withdrawn (Age Concern England, 1994; RADAR, 1994). In such systems it is only the advantaged groups who are likely to be able to exercise choice, partly because they are able to bypass assessment systems for state-supported services. A higher level of choice for the older population as a whole would entail empowerment so that disadvantaged groups could also exercise choice (Johnson, 1993: 53).

Of the six countries studied, the UK's reformed community care system has potentially the most effective methods of providing coordinated care to meet users' and carers' needs. Yet evidence suggests that, partly because of conflicting aims of community care, there remain wide variations in access to such care and in rights, responsibilities and choice for different groups of older people and carers. In spite of policy rhetoric and reforms there is much progress to be made before coordination as defined in this chapter is achieved in practice in the community care systems studied.

Summary

Problems in care delivery systems resulting from poor coordination between and within health, welfare and other services, and between statutory and non-statutory sectors of provision were identified in the 1970s and 1980s. Community care policy developments in the late 1980s and early 1990s took two main approaches to improving coordination: strategic changes in management structures and funding systems; and the development of assessment and care management systems to provide appropriate care to individuals. Other trends in community care, influenced by economic and ideological factors, conflict with the aim of promoting coordination. In addition to general obstacles to coordination, such as different organisational and professional interests, the effects of specific systems based on varying types of welfare regime and different principles and values, can work against coordinated community care provision. Coordination processes take place through different types of arrangements and procedures serving different functions as reviewed in the chapter.

Despite the policy initiatives and processes implemented to promote coordination, there is little evidence that coordinated community care has been achieved. Reports of poor coordination, gaps and overlaps in services and lack of information in the countries studied continued to appear in the early 1990s. Structural changes had not necessarily succeeded in improving coordination between health and welfare services. Locally based experimental projects using care management models had achieved some positive outcomes but did not always lead to more general implementation. There was wide variability across the countries in access to coordinated care and information and in rights, responsibilities and choices for different groups of older people and carers.

8
Summary and Conclusions

The book reviews a wide range of areas of provision of community care for older people, defined broadly as care for people who live in their own homes, whether in ordinary, specialised or residential settings. In providing a background understanding to the policies, systems, procedures and outcomes of community care in Europe and North America, a critical approach is taken, and effects of policies and procedures for different groups of older people and carers are identified.

Although resources have not allowed purpose-designed comparative research, comparisons are made between the six countries studied, drawing on available published material and study visits. Systematic comparisons of the topics covered have been hampered by a paucity of comparative data on community care services and on differences in outcomes by socio-economic class, gender, 'race' and age; caution should thus be exercised in drawing conclusions from the data. Further, the breadth of coverage entails generalisations at a national level, which often mask wide differences within countries, between regions, states and even within local areas. As a basis for more detailed comparative policy analysis of community care, a framework has been developed (see Table 1.3), covering three key components: origins, substance and outcomes (Ginsburg, 1992). Using this framework, the main findings and conclusions on each component are summarised below.

Background to community care policies

Policies on caring for older people gradually became more explicit during the second half of the twentieth century, in response to economic crises, demographic change, the perceived 'burden' of the ageing population, and changing perceptions of institutional care. In tracing the development of policies, it must be recognised that stated policies may consist mainly of rhetoric; such policies may not be fully

implemented; and the outcomes of policy and practice may not be those
intended by policymakers.

Development of policies on aspects of care for older people

After the second world war, in a period of economic growth, low
inflation and low unemployment, welfare states expanded in terms both
of expenditure and of the services offered. The roles of the state, market
and family in welfare systems varied according to the type of welfare
regime. Three main types identified by Esping-Andersen (1990) are the
'liberal', 'conservative–corporatist' and 'social democratic' welfare
regimes (see chapter 1). Such models help to identify the broad
background to a country's policies on pensions, or health and welfare,
but rarely address issues of gender, 'race' and age which affect people's
experiences of welfare services and community care. Nor do they take
account of unpaid caring work mainly undertaken by women (Langan
and Ostner, 1991; Taylor-Gooby, 1991; Lewis, 1992).

Policies for older people received little priority in the post-1945
period; where such policies were stated they were mainly concerned with
institutional care. Little policy attention was paid to the housing needs
of older people or to domiciliary care services. In the 1960s the main
response to care needs was to rehouse older people in specialised or
institutional settings; sheltered housing tended to be seen as a panacea
for meeting older people's housing and social needs. Domiciliary services
such as home help and home nursing expanded in the 1960s and 1970s
and were promoted to suppport older people with care needs living in
their own homes, as community care policies became established.
Countries varied in the level of care offered, with lower provision in
'liberal' or 'conservative–corporatist' than in 'social democratic'
regimes.

Pensions, housing, health, social care and leisure services for older
people developed separately with different statutory frameworks and
funding sources. Policy documents in the 1970s and 1980s identified
problems in care provision arising from poor coordination between
services (Audit Commission, 1986; Dekker, 1987; Braun and Stourm,
1988). Although there was little integrated approach, policy trends
across the different areas of provision had implications for all
components of community care for older people.

The mid to late 1970s marked a turning point for policies in the
countries studied, as policymakers responded to economic crises and to

the political influence of the New Right. By the late 1980s and early 1990s the main issues concerning funding of services and controlling public expenditure were, first, methods of paying for pensions, health and social care, especially long-term care which was not covered by the systems established in the post 1945 period (Laing, 1993); and second, developing the mixed economy of care. Reforms to funding and/or care delivery systems were considered, implemented or, in some cases, postponed following major reviews, policy papers and legislation. These included the Boulard (1991) and Schopflin (1991) reports in France; the German health service reform Act (1988) and legislation for compulsory care insurance by 1995–6; the Italian national health service reform (Law 421 and Decree 502, 1992); the Dekker report (1987) and Welschen report (1994) in the Netherlands; the Griffiths review (1988) and National Health Service and Community Care Act (1990) in the UK; the Pepper Commission report (1990) and Clinton health security plan in the US.

The overriding policy trend affecting care for older people from the mid 1970s onwards was economic, resulting in a new concentration on cost containment and cost effectiveness. This entailed restrictions on public expenditure, changes in the type and distribution of services, and increased targeting of services, using economic criteria and market practices (Jamieson, ed. 1991; Baldock and Evers, 1992). Methods of expenditure restraint included cash limits or reduced budgets for health and welfare services, tightening eligibility criteria for pensions or services and increasing insurance contributions or direct charges.

The types and range of services for older people changed as policies emphasised reducing institutional care and developing home-based care, for both economic and humanitarian reasons (Jamieson, 1989), except in Italy where residential care is increasing. The policy of 'substitution', formalised in the Netherlands and also practised elsewhere, entailed a move from institutional care to less formal, ostensibly less expensive, more social (rather than medical) forms of community-based care (Baldock and Evers, 1992: 297; Coolen, ed., 1993). In some countries institutions began to change in nature with a move to more localised units, providing resources such as day care to the local community, whereas some forms of health care became more centralised into larger units. Numbers of hospital beds and lengths of stay were reduced, and policies advocated shifting funds to non-hospital care, although the extent to which this happened in practice was limited. Domiciliary health and welfare services, considered to be less expensive than inpatient and residential care, were increasingly targeted to people who would otherwise need institutional care.

A second major trend was to reduce the direct role of the state and develop the commercial, non-profit and informal sectors of service provision in the welfare mix. Private markets and competition were introduced or increased in fields such as pensions, housing and health care. Care became refocused on informal carers and there was a move towards incorporating the role of carers into the stated policies and procedures of community care (Baldock and Evers, 1992: 299).

Third, there was a trend towards promoting individualised care, with more flexible services and greater choice. Although this ideal has not yet been widely implemented, policy recommendations, for example in the Netherlands and the UK, include treating housing and care needs as separate, offering tailored 'packages' of care to people in their homes, and promoting participation in self-help and community-based initiatives. The ideal of individualised care necessitates effective coordination between care providers. Policy statements of the late 1980s and 1990s promoted ways of bridging the medical/social divide, for example by combining funding sources, as in the Netherlands; by allocating responsibilities for planning services, assessing needs and arranging care, as in the UK; and, in several countries, initiating assessment and care management systems to coordinate care at individual level.

Community care policies: influences and principles

As identified above, economic influences pervaded all aspects of care for older people, with policy emphasis on cost containment following the 1973 oil crisis and subsequent recession. The need to control public expenditure and reduce public deficits persisted during the 1980s and early 1990s. The high costs of pensions, health and welfare services, and especially of institutional care were a cause for concern. Cost containment policies limited the housing, health and welfare services available for older people in non-institutional settings. Economic pressures also promoted the aim of better coordinated services to reduce wasteful overlaps and target services more cost effectively.

Demographic forecasts of increasing numbers in the oldest age groups, on whom health and welfare expenditure is disproportionately high, influenced policymakers' motivation to control expenditure on these groups. Other trends such as the increase in older people living alone, particularly widows, affected the number and type of housing units needed, and promoted policies to encourage social participation and reduce the risk of social isolation or loneliness. Policymakers were also concerned about demographic trends which reduced the potential availability of family carers, for example smaller families, rising divorce rates, and increased paid employment of women.

Political influences on policy originate first in the political and ideological context of a country's welfare regime type and in the cultural and religious perspectives that affect welfare systems and social preferences for types of care. Changes in political power or influential ideologies modify these systems over time. The most powerful influence since the 1970s in the countries studied was that of the New Right, which sought to reduce the role of government, increase welfare pluralism and promote individual responsibility for welfare. This had a direct effect on policies for older people in the fields of housing, health care and domiciliary services. Other dominant interests include those of professionals, especially medical professionals whose power was a major factor in retaining the medical/social divide and in focusing services on the medical model rather than on long-term social care. Differing interests of professionals and organisations also constitute obstacles to the effective coordination of services.

Community care policies and their implementation are influenced by the levels of government at which planning and policymaking take place. Policies vary within countries, especially where systems are decentralised. The level at which policymaking occurs also varies for different services. Health policy decisions tend to be taken at a more centralised level than social care decisions, which can mean that greater government control is exercised over health care, although at a local level medical professionals may affect the implementation of policy. Social care and leisure services are often more variable and more subject to local political decisions than health services. The location of planning and policymaking at different levels for health and social care constitutes a further impediment to coordination of services.

Policies are based on principles and assumptions which vary between systems and reflect predominant influences. Unfounded assumptions about the dependence, poor health and isolation of older people tend to persist despite recognition since the 1970s of the heterogeneity of this group and of differences between the active majority and dependent minority with multiple care needs (Alber, 1992: 12–13). Care systems are based on the principles underpinning a country's welfare regime type. For example expectations about family care are strongest in 'liberal' regimes which stress family and individual responsibilities, and in 'conservative–corporatist' regimes in which the principle of subsidiarity places explicit duties on families. There are fewer expectations of carers in 'social democratic' regimes, but informal care is increasingly promoted as part of substitution policy. In practice most community care policies operate on the assumption that informal carers will provide most of the care. This means that the broad categorisation of welfare regime types is useful mainly as an indicator of the overall welfare system, but is of limited relevance to the production of services for older people with care needs.

Community care policies are based on potentially incompatible 'organisational' and 'humanitarian' principles (Macintyre, 1977). The predominant economic principle of cost effectiveness underlies substitution policies which assume that community care is less expensive than institutional care, which is not necessarily the case. Humanitarian aims stated in community care policies are based on negative assumptions about institutional care and positive values of social integration and the promotion of independence, choice and individualised services, which can rarely be implemented in the context of cost effectiveness goals.

Policies on community care thus developed from the 1970s onwards in a political context in which the humanitarian needs of older people were afforded little priority in practice. The welfare systems of the countries studied varied in the political and cultural origins of their different welfare regime types established in the post-1945 period. Background factors, such as the preservation of status differences and the principle of subsidiarity underpinning the German system, account for some of the main differences in community care policies and service provision. These basic systems changed to some extent in response to wider economic, demographic and political factors which cross national boundaries. Policy trends common to the countries studied are identified in their approaches to major issues in the financing and provision of care for older people. Trends such as cost containment, substitution of community-based for institutional care, and development of the mixed economy of care suggest a certain amount of convergence in community care policies, although distinctive features based on longstanding welfare cultures remain embedded in the systems.

Provision of community care services

Details of provision of the main areas of community care services are given in chapters 2 to 7. This section reviews the main components of community care and summarises the principal features of funding and organisation of services by different sectors of the mixed economy of welfare in each country studied. Developments in patterns of care provision resulting from the changing policies, influences and principles discussed above are also identified. In order to compare provision of community care in its widest sense, in countries with differing definitions of the concept, distinctions are made between the services, the settings in which they are provided, and those who provide and finance the services.

Community care: components and settings

The basic components of community care, the services to support older people or tasks to be done, vary little cross-nationally. In chapter 1 types of services or tasks contributing to community care are identified, and settings in which they are provided are categorised as either *in the home* where the person usually lives, whether ordinary, specialised or institutional; or *from home* (Higgins, 1989), that is in venues such as hospitals, health centres, day care units, clubs or cultural facilities to which people go to receive services before returning home. The types of services are summarised below, with examples from the wide variety of provisions to meet the complex range of needs identified (see also Tables 4.1, 5.1, 6.3).

Financial support consists either of direct cash benefits through state, occupational and private pensions and social assistance systems (chapter 2), housing benefits and benefits for caring (chapters 3 and 4); or of services in kind through the funding of health and social care (chapter 2). *Suitable housing* may be achieved through options for moving to grouped or sheltered housing or institutional care; or for staying put, aided by adaptations, home alarm services, care and repair schemes, or intensive home care (chapter 3). *Basic care* to help with daily living, mobility and self care is provided in the home by informal carers, home helps, home nurses and ADL equipment (chapter 4); meals, help with laundry and bathing are also received in hospital and day care settings (chapters 5 and 6). *Medical and nursing care* for physical and mental health problems are offered by doctors and nurses in the home or in hospitals or health centres and clinics (chapters 4 and 5). *Therapy and rehabilitation services* are also provided in the home, in health care premises and sometimes in day care settings (chapters 4, 5 and 6).

Counselling or emotional support for older people and carers are offered by social workers, self-help groups, counsellors, hospice workers or day centre workers in the home or in health and social care venues (chapters 4, 5 and 6). Access to *social, leisure and educational activities* may be gained through voluntary visitors, day care services, clubs, educational and cultural facilities, or volunteering opportunities (chapter 6). *Transport* is provided by ambulance or community transport services to health care or day care venues or for wider leisure activities (chapters 5 and 6). *Information* about the range of services and opportunities is available from professionals providing or organising care, through the media, leaflets and displays, and information and advice services (chapters 4, 5, 6 and 7).

The ways in which these basic components of community care are organised and funded differ according to countries' welfare policies and systems, and the balance of the welfare mix, as outlined below. The importance of the informal sector as provider of at least three-quarters of community care in all systems must be emphasised, as must the role of older people in self-care, before turning to the informal or formal sectors (Wilson, 1994).

Community care: provision, funding and organisation

France, with a social insurance system based on solidarity, has a 'conservative-corporatist' welfare regime, influenced by the Catholic church and applying the principle of subsidiarity. However, it also has a high level of social spending (Jones, 1985), and a strong role for the state in welfare provision. Most services, for example low income housing, residential care, domiciliary care and hospitals, are provided either by the statutory sector or by non-profit associations; the pattern of welfare mix varies by area. There are small profit-making sectors in hospital and residential care provision.

Through the social security system there is compulsory insurance for pensions and health care. A guaranteed minimum income is provided for those aged over 60. Means-tested social assistance has a minor role in funding medical care for those not insured, and home help and residential care for people on low incomes; children and grandchildren are obliged to contribute for some costs. Health insurance pays for care costs in residential settings with medical care sections; the individual or social assistance meets board costs. There is a compensatory allowance for caring costs of people with disabilities in their own homes. A strong medical/social divide in administration and funding of health and social care impedes effective coordination of services. A proposed dependence allowance which would cross this divide is under discussion.

Germany developed a 'conservative–corporatist' welfare regime, influenced by conservative politics and Catholic teachings. The principles of subsidiarity and self-help are applied, limiting the role of the central state and of statutory organisations and giving first responsibility for welfare to the individual and family. This model, however, is beginning to lose legitimacy (Evers and Olk, 1991: 93). Most formal service provision, such as social rented housing, sheltered housing, residential homes and domiciliary care is by non-profit welfare organisations. Inpatient hospital care is provided by the public, non-profit and commercial sectors. There is a small, growing commercial sector in domiciliary care. The system is strongly divided between compulsory social insurance for pensions and health care, and means-tested cash and care services from social assistance for people on low incomes. Funding for home nursing and home care is through health insurance for strictly defined categories; other social care, including long-term residential care, is funded by the individual or through social assistance, with children's obligation to contribute. There are pension contribution credits for family carers and a care allowance through social assistance. Compulsory care insurance introduced from 1995–6 will cover some costs previously met by social assistance. The main approach to coordination is the location of health and social care services together in community care centres. However, there are serious obstacles to coordinated community care in the strong divisions in organisation and funding between hospital and ambulatory services, health and social care.

Italy also has a 'conservative–corporatist' welfare regime influenced by the Catholic church and the principle of subsidiarity, and relying considerably on the family and church to provide care. In the late 1970s there was a move to a more 'social democratic' system with the introduction of a national health service in 1978; planning and provision of health and welfare services were decentralised to regions and communes. Although there is free hospital care in public hospitals or private hospitals under contract, private provision and insurance expanded in the 1980s as the health service was not fully implemented. In the 1980s and 1990s increased emphasis was placed on self-help and volunteer effort. Reforms in 1995 introduced an internal market to the health service.

Pensions are funded through a compulsory state earnings-related pension scheme and there are means-tested social pensions for people aged over 65 on low incomes. Means-tested social care is mainly organised by the communes. Companion payments are available for some carers. A high proportion of older people own their homes. There is a low level of institutionalisation; over two-thirds of residential accommodation is in the private sector. Local health units, introduced with the health service, are in theory responsible for all health and welfare services but in practice there is poor coordination with the social services provided by the commune. Forms of provision, organisation and coordination of services vary widely throughout the country.

The *Netherlands* has a 'social democratic' welfare regime with social security benefits and comprehensive welfare services. The system is influenced by Catholic and Protestant churches and the principle of subsidiarity. Although state-funded, most services, including social rented housing, sheltered housing and residential homes, domiciliary care and hospitals, are provided by non-profit organisations. There is a small commercial sector in sheltered housing. Day hospitals and day centres are well established.

There are compulsory universal basic rate pensions and occupational earnings-related supplementary pensions. As the basic pension is set above social assistance level, such means-tested assistance plays a minor part, mainly in funding residential care for people on low incomes. Small tax concessions are made for informal caring costs. Most health care is provided through social health insurance or through AWBZ, which covers all residents for long-term care, and funds nursing home care, domiciliary nursing and home care. Other social welfare services are financed through the municipality's general welfare budget and organised by coordinating agencies for work with older people. Local multi-disciplinary committees assess all residential and nursing home applications. Since the late 1980s, close working relationships were developed between home nursing and home care, residential homes and community-based services.

The *United Kingdom's* mainly 'social democratic' welfare regime with universal services set up after 1945 gradually became more 'liberal' as greater selectivity was introduced. Traditionally the public sector dominated the provision of social rented housing, residential care, domiciliary services, health care and day care. Conservative governments since 1979 encouraged greater use of non-statutory sectors. The proportion of for-profit residential care rose to over 50 per cent by 1990. Non-profit housing associations took an increasing role in social housing. Community care reforms promoted greater involvement of the commercial and non-profit sectors in domiciliary and day care in the 1990s.

National insurance provides universal basic pensions with a small earnings-related addition. These pensions are supplemented by occupational and private pension schemes, or by means-tested social assistance.

There are cash benefits for informal care. Health care is free under the NHS which covers home nursing and long-stay hospital care. However, numbers of long-stay beds have been much reduced, leaving people with long-term care needs to pay for care in nursing homes. Under the community care reforms implemented in 1993, local authorities assess needs for residential and nursing homes and social care services for which means-tested charges are made. The needs assessment and care management system is intended to target services efficiently and to coordinate 'packages' of care to meet individual needs.

The *United States* has a 'liberal' welfare regime, influenced by different religious, ethnic and professional groups. The state takes a minimal role, relying on the market and family to supply care; means-tested state assistance is a last resort. Most service provision, for example nursing homes, domiciliary care and hospitals, is by the private commercial or non-profit sectors. Since the 1980s the role of the federal state has decreased and that of the for-profit sector has increased.

A compulsory federal social security system provides small earnings-related pensions; supplementary company or private pensions play a large role. There is means-tested supplemental security income for people aged over 65 and those with disabilities. Health care is funded through private health insurance, Medicare insurance for those over 65, and Medicaid for people with very low incomes and assets. Medicare provides for skilled nursing but not for home care. For those eligible, Medicaid funds nursing home, hospital and medical care. Other health and welfare services may be funded by Medicaid or OAA funding depending on the federal state's programme. The Veterans Administration provides health care and benefits for eligible veterans. There is no national programme or funding system for long-term care. The existence of many different providing and funding agencies hinders service coordination. Different models of case management are used to target and coordinate local services.

The main changes identified in patterns of service provision arise from the promotion of non-statutory sectors of the mixed economy of welfare, increasing welfare pluralism in the six countries. Changing demographic and employment conditions have resulted in greater divisions between services with insurance or national health entitlements, and those funded through means-tested social assistance. The aims of individual responsibility and greater flexibility have produced a greater diversity of housing solutions and providers. Reductions in hospital care have meant increased use of residential and day care, ambulatory and domiciliary health and social care. The fields of leisure and cultural activities have placed more emphasis on participation through self-help and volunteering initiatives rather than the direct provision of home visitor, centres and clubs. Community-based care has begun to move towards greater coordination between services and more focus on individuals' overall needs, introducing multi-disciplinary teams and committees, assessment and care management systems.

Outcomes of community care systems

The intrinsic role of rhetoric in community care policy is a recurrent feature of the preceding chapters. The gap between rhetoric and reality identified by writers such as Titmuss (1968) and Griffiths (1988) persists. A proliferation of policy research, statements and recommendations has shown ways of improving community care in, for example, the Netherlands (Pijl, 1992), the UK and the US. Evidence suggests, however, that the policy aims identified above have not necessarily been implemented and that any successful outcomes of community care are unevenly distributed. Implications of community care systems in the early 1990s for older people and carers, and issues of access, rights and choice are discussed below.

Implications of community care systems for older people and carers

The levels of resources allocated to welfare and to the various components of community care are basic determinants of outcomes of systems. Overall levels of provision vary, to some extent according to the type of welfare regime, with higher provision of financial support and community care services in 'social democratic' regimes such as the Netherlands, and lower levels in 'liberal' regimes. In the US, and increasingly in the UK, there is no safety net for long-term care until the person becomes impoverished enough to be eligible for social assistance. In the new states of Germany the former GDR's 'bureaucratic state collectivist' system (Deacon, 1992) was replaced after unification in 1990 by the FRG's 'conservative–corporatist' social insurance based system, with substantial federal government subsidies, but no guaranteed continuation of funding for care services.

Cost containment policies from the late 1970s restricted the levels of resources available for community care services in the six countries.

Housing, health, welfare and leisure services could not be developed adequately to compensate for increased needs arising from reductions in hospital and institutional care and increases in the oldest age groups. There is evidence of underprovision of these services, greater financial costs and caring responsibilities for individuals and families, and costs to carers in terms of physical and mental health problems, reduced social contacts and financial costs (Jani-Le Bris, 1993). There is little support for family carers in any of the six countries.

Outcomes of systems are also determined by the methods of distribution of the available resources. Policies of reducing institutionalisation and substitution of ostensibly less expensive community-based services entailed restrictions in eligibility for and increased targeting of publicly financed services. Institutional care and specialised housing were focused on those in greatest need, with lowest incomes and no family support, while domiciliary care was concentrated on those living alone who would otherwise need institutional care. The implication of such rationing is that those with less priority could have state services withdrawn and would have to rely on private or informal care (Baldock and Evers, 1992). These changes took place in the context of policies promoting the non-statutory sectors of the mixed economy of welfare, greater fragmentation of services and increased privatisation. Thus divisions in dual welfare systems were intensified: those on the insurance side of the insurance/assistance divide (see Table 2.5) received benefits and services through entitlement or purchase on the market, whereas others relied increasingly on means-tested discretionary services or assistance and informal carers.

Another significant division affecting the outcomes of community care systems is that between health and social services in terms of funding, organisation and professional interests. Although the strength of the medical/social divide varies, in most countries there are separate funding sources for health and social care which provide incentives to transfer people to services covered by other budgets (Jamieson, 1989). A further difficulty arises where medical services such as inpatient hospital care or day hospital are free of charge to the user through insurance or health service entitlement, whereas the user must meet means-tested charges for social services such as residential or home care or day centres. In such cases there is an incentive for older people to medicalise their problems and use the health services when these may not be most appropriate to their needs (Jamieson, 1989). Similarly where there are family duties to contribute financially for residential or social care funded through social assistance, there are incentives for family members to care for the person at home or to request hospital care, and disincentives to apply for stigmatised social assistance.

Organisational and professional interests in the medical/social divide also work against the provision of appropriate care for individuals. Where there is strict separation between services and tasks, such as there is in Germany between hospital and ambulatory services and between nursing and home care tasks, people may receive the services allowed by the criteria and funding sources rather than those suited to their overall needs (Dieck and Garms-Homolová, 1991). Different professional statuses and cultures help to perpetuate the medical/social divide since, in most countries, medical professionals generally have higher status and more power than social care workers, and less motivation to work together in the interests of coordinated services for older people. The continuing emphasis on the medical model of service provision which stresses cure rather than care, means that services are not geared to the chronic health conditions and disabilities of frail older people.

The medical/social divide, the provision of services through diverse structures and complex financing systems, and the increasing fragmentation of services through development of the commercial and non-profit sectors, all contribute to a lack of coordination identified in all six countries. Coordination between housing, health and social services is essential for effective community care which is appropriate to individual needs rather than based on funding criteria and professional divisions. The more positive policy trends towards assessment of individual needs and care management have potential for providing flexible integrated care, but are only in the early stages of implementation. Further, the conflict between the aims of cost-effectiveness and of individualised care works against the provision of coordinated packages of care based on assessed needs and user choice. The coordination involved, for example, in the UK's reformed system mainly focuses on the various social care services; the policy and funding systems do not allow for full integration with housing and health care systems.

Poor coordination of services entails delays, overlaps or gaps in services supplied to users. In some cases people do not request support services because information about the range of services does not reach them. There is evidence of lack of information for older people and carers in all six countries. Although information is a key component of coordinated community care services, resources are not generally allocated to initiate and maintain coordinated information systems (Tester, 1992). Access to services often depends crucially on accurate information being available when needed.

Community care: access, rights and choice

Wide variations in access to community care services result from geographical differences and inequalities between social groups. Generalisations about countries' systems at the level of aggregated national data mask uneven distribution of services between areas within countries, for example between federal states in the US, or local authorities in the UK. There is evidence of inequitable distribution of housing services, residential and domiciliary care, health care and leisure facilities, and of poorer services in rural rather than in urban areas. There are, in all six countries, examples of good practice, where high standard community care is available, in some cases only to those who can afford to purchase it. Much depends on local decisions on policy and finance, and on the existence of specially funded projects or well motivated individuals, since the provision of high quality community care is neither a feature of mainstream services, nor a high political priority in most areas.

Access to services and to relevant information also depends on the socio-economic class, gender, 'race' and age of both the older person and the carer, and on interactions between these factors. Socio-economic group is often the crucial determinant of financial and other resources which facilitate access to long-term or social care, as advantages from earlier life are carried through into older age. People from higher socio-economic groups are more likely than others to have the resources to organise and finance their own package of care and to choose their housing, care services and leisure activities. Those from the poorest groups are most likely to depend on means-tested, stigmatised public services. The middle income groups may be disadvantaged by having inadequate means to purchase services but be ineligible for state support, for example in Germany and the US.

Gender differences are highly significant to community care because women tend to live longer than men, to have more disabilities and greater care needs, and are also more likely than men to be care providers, usually low paid or unpaid. Expectations about gender roles lead to differences in the care services received by men and women. Women are less likely than men to have the financial resources to facilitate access to services of their choice in housing, care or leisure activities, and are thus more likely to depend on means-tested social assistance services. These differences are exacerbated in the oldest age groups when women tend to have greatest housing and care needs and fewest resources. People from black and minority ethnic communities are also more likely to be disadvantaged by lack of financial resources and access to information, and to have to depend on informal care or on services which are means-tested, of poor quality and/or inappropriate to their cultural needs.

Differences in access occur partly because there are few rights to community care, particularly to housing services and social care. Trends such as increased duality in welfare systems, the reduced role of the state in service provision, increases in charges and explicit rationing of services, have led to diminished rights, especially for the marginalised groups most dependent on state support. Those who are most advantaged, with substantial pensions and insurance rights, are also better able to purchase privatised services, and more likely to be well informed about their rights. In the limited areas of community care where there are legal rights, for example for people with disabilities or people in residential care, older people are not necessarily aware of these rights.

Although rights have decreased since the 1980s, additional respon- sibilities have been placed on individuals to purchase insurance or services for themselves and their families. In countries such as Germany that apply the principle of subsidiarity there are explicit duties on children to provide care and to contribute financially for services for which their parents require social assistance. With reductions in institutional care and greater reliance on the informal sector of the mixed economy of welfare, increased responsibilities have been placed on carers, usually spouses, daughters or daughters in law, to provide care. These responsibilities, however, are more likely to be taken on by working class than middle class carers, who may have other options.

As discussed above, people who are most advantaged, for example white middle class men, have the greatest choice in caring solutions for themselves and their families. The lower socio-economic groups, especially people with most disabilities and care needs, are rarely able to choose to purchase or select services and may not have access to information on which to base choices. They are often dependent on professionals to assess their needs and allocate services, and must usually accept the services offered, which may not be those they would prefer. Although policies advocating user-led community care services based on assessed individual need are alleged to promote choice, for example in the UK, the exercise of such choice is rarely possible in practice.

Comparative data on outcomes of community care systems are rarely collected; conclusions, therefore, can only be tentative. However, the review of different components of community care systems and consideration of their implications for different groups in the six countries indicate wide inequalities between areas and groups in the care received. Further, the evidence suggests that changing policies and patterns of services in the 1980s and 1990s have increased these inequalities between advantaged and disadvantaged older people and carers.

Summary of main conclusions

The book provides a framework for cross-national comparative analysis of community care for older people. The study is exploratory, since few comparative data on this topic are available. Further systematic cross-national research and comparative data collation are necessary to provide evidence for decision making on the pressing issues of paying for long-term care and providing effective integrated care for increasing numbers of frail older people. The study illustrates the complex patterns of policies, service provision and differential outcomes in community care systems.

Comparison of systems in the six countries shows that similar components of community care are available and that there are common trends in the issues addressed and in the factors that influence policies on these issues, suggesting a certain degree of convergence. There are also examples of policy diffusion where policies such as care management are directly borrowed from other countries. The systems of organising and funding financial support and care services are, however, specific to the countries concerned, and are determined largely by the historical background of the welfare regime and by political and cultural influences on policy. For example the strong social insurance system in Germany provides excellent pensions and medical care for those fully covered, but social care remains underdeveloped, based on expectations of family care under the principle of subsidiarity, and on the means-tested social assistance system. In the Netherlands, on the other hand, both medical and social care are well developed and home nursing and home help are integrated through a common funding source (AWBZ). This represents an attempt to bridge the medical/social divide which is a major obstacle to the implementation of community care policies and integrated care provision.

Although the different areas of community care developed separately, in all six countries the need for better coordination is widely recognised and integration of health, social care and housing services is advocated in policy statements. Separate systems of funding and service provision, however, inhibit the successful implementation of coordinated flexible solutions. The emphasis on medical funding and the medical model persists, with the effect that the long-term and social care needs of many older people are inadequately met. Any successful outcomes are found mainly at a local level and often depend on the existence of special projects or funding and the motivation of key individuals in service-providing agencies.

Government policies based on official reviews, research and demonstration projects advocate community care as a humanitarian way of supporting older people with care needs. Positive approaches such as individualised care packages and care management have been initiated. However, such policies have not yet been widely implemented largely because of the conflicting economic aims of cost containment and cost effectiveness, and the development of non-statutory sectors of the mixed economy of welfare, which have entailed wider inequalities in access to care services and additional demands on informal carers. A shift in the balance of political priorities in favour of the humanitarian aims of community care is necessary if integrated care for older people and carers is to be resourced and implemented effectively.

References

B. Abel-Smith (1992) 'Cost containment and new priorities in the European Community', *The Milbank Quarterly*, 70, 3, 393–416.

P. Abrahamson (1992) 'Welfare pluralism: towards a new consensus for a European social policy', in L. Hantrais et al. (eds), *The mixed economy of welfare* (Loughborough: European Research Centre, Loughborough University).

Age Concern England (1993) *No time to lose: first impressions of the community care reforms* (London: Age Concern England).

Age Concern England (1994) *The next steps: lessons for the future of community care* (London: Age Concern England).

J. Alber (1986) 'Germany', in P. Flora (ed.) *Growth to limits: the Western European welfare states since world war II. Vol. 2.* (Berlin: Walter de Gruyter).

J. Alber (1992) *Older people in Europe: social and economic policies. National report Germany* (Konstanz: University of Konstanz).

J. Alber (1993) 'Health and social services', in A. Walker, J. Alber and A.-M. Guillemard, *Older people in Europe: social and economic policies* (Brussels: Commission of the European Communities).

American Association of Retired Persons (1990) *Toward a just and caring society: the AARP public policy agenda. Long-term care* (Washington DC: AARP).

American Association of Retired Persons (1992) *A handbook about care in the home: information on home care services* (Washington DC: AARP).

American Association of Retired Persons and Administration on Aging (1993) *A profile of older Americans: 1993* (Washington DC: AARP/AoA).

R. Anderson (1992) 'Health and community care', in Age Concern England, *The coming of age in Europe: older people in the European Community* (London: Age Concern England).

J. Appleby (1992) *Financing health care in the 1990s* (Buckingham: Open University Press).

S. Arber and N. Gilbert (1989) 'Men: the forgotten carers', *Sociology*, 23, 1, 111–18.

S. Arber, N. Gilbert and M. Evandrou (1988) 'Gender, household composition and receipt of domiciliary services by elderly disabled people', *Journal of Social Policy*, 17, 2, 153–75.

S. Arber and J. Ginn (1990) 'The meaning of informal care: gender and the contribution of elderly people', *Ageing and Society*, 10, 429–54.

S. Arber and J. Ginn (1991) *Gender and later life: a sociological analysis of resources and constraints* (London: Sage).

S. Arber and J. Ginn (1992) 'Class and caring: a forgotten dimension', *Sociology*, 26, 4, 619–34.

U. Ascoli (1988) 'The Italian welfare system in the 1980s: less state and more market', in R. Morris (ed.) *Testing the limits of social welfare: international perspectives on policy changes in nine countries* (Hanover: University Press of New England).

Assemblée Nationale (1991) *Rapport d'information déposé en application de l'article 145 du Règlement par la commission des affaires culturelles familiales et sociales sur les personnes âgées dépendantes* (Paris: Documentation Française).

Association of Metropolitan Authorities (1994) *A survey of social services charging policies 1992–94* (London: AMA).

K. Atkin (1991) 'Community care in a multi-racial society: incorporating the user view', *Policy and Politics*, 19, 3, 159–66.

Audit Commission (1985) *Managing social services for the elderly more effectively: a report by the Audit Commission* (London: HMSO).

Audit Commission (1986) *Making a reality of community care* (London: HMSO).

J. Baars, K. Knipscheer, E. Breebaart (1992) *Older people in Europe: social and economic policies. National report Netherlands* (Amsterdam: Vrije Universiteit).

J. Baldock (1993) 'Patterns of change in the delivery of welfare in Europe', in P. Taylor-Gooby and R. Lawson (eds), *Markets and managers: new issues in the delivery of welfare* (Buckingham, Open University Press).

J. Baldock and A. Evers (1991) 'On social innovation: a short introduction', in R. Kraan et al., *Care for the elderly: significant innovations in three European countries* (Frankfurt am Main: Campus Verlag).

J. Baldock and A. Evers (1992) 'Innovations and care of the elderly: the cutting edge of change for social welfare systems. Examples from Sweden, the Netherlands and the United Kingdom', *Ageing and Society*, 12, 289–312.

J. Baldock and C. Ungerson (1993) 'Consumer perceptions of an emerging mixed economy of care', in A. Evers and I. Svetlik (eds), *Balancing pluralism: new welfare mixes in care for the elderly* (Aldershot: Avebury).

M. Barres (1987) 'Sectorisation and overcapacity in France', *International Journal of Social Psychiatry*, 33, 2, 140–3.

A. Bebbington and B. Davies (1993) 'Efficient targeting of community care: the case of the home help service', *Journal of Social Policy*, 22, 3, 373–91.

N. Begum (1990) *Burden of gratitude: women with disabilities receiving personal care* (Warwick: University of Warwick, Social Care Practice Centre).

M. Bianchi (1991) 'Policy for the elderly in Italy: innovation or modernization?', in A. Evers and I. Svetlik, *New welfare mixes in care for the elderly* (Vienna: European Centre for Social Welfare Policy and Research).

H. Bolderson (1988) 'Comparing social policies: some problems of method and the case of social security benefits in Australia, Britain and the USA', *Journal of Social Policy*, 17, 3, 267–88.

J. C. Boulard (1991) *Vivre ensemble: rapport de la mission parlementaire*. Publication de l'Assemblée Nationale no. 2135 (Paris: Assemblée Nationale).

T. Braun and M. Stourm (1988) *Les personnes âgées dépendantes* (Paris: Documentation Française).

R. Brooke-Ross (1987) 'Elderly people's care in Germany', *Social Policy and Administration*, 21, 3, 244–51.

J. Bull and L. Poole (1989) *Not rich: not poor. A study of housing options for elderly people on middle incomes* (London: SHAC and Anchor Housing Trust).

Bundesministerium für Familie und Senioren (1990) *1. Teilbericht der Sachverständigenkommission zur Erstellung des 1. Altenberichts der Bundesregierung* (Bonn: BMFuS).

A. Butler (1986) 'Housing and the elderly in Europe', *Social Policy and Administration*, 20, 2, 136–52.

A. Butler, C. Oldman and J. Greve (1983) *Sheltered housing for the elderly* (London: Allen and Unwin).

H. Carlin (1994) *The housing needs of older people from ethnic minorities: evidence from Glasgow* (Stirling: University of Stirling, Housing Policy and Practice Unit).

Centraal Bureau voor de Statistiek (1993) *Ouderworden in Nederland 1993* (Voorburg: CBS).

D. Challis and B. Davies (1986) *Case management in community care* (Aldershot: Gower).

P. Chamberlayne (1991/2) 'New directions in welfare? France, West Germany, Italy and Britain in the 1980s', *Critical Social Policy*, 33, Winter, 5–21.

B. Checkoway (1988) 'Community-based initiatives to improve health of the elderly', *Danish Medical Bulletin*, Gerontology special supplement series No. 6, 30–6.

Commissie Modernisering Ouderenzorg (Welschen committee) (1994) *Ouderenzorg met toekomst* (Care for older people in the future) (The Hague: Ministry of Welfare, Health and Cultural Affairs).

Commission of the European Communities (1993) *Age and attitudes: main results from a Eurobarometer survey* (Brussels: CEC).

J. Coolen (ed.) (1993) *Changing care in the Netherlands: experience and research findings from policy experiments* (Assen/Maastricht: Van Gorcum).

C. Costanzi (1991) 'Home care services in Italy (with special reference to Genoa)', in A. Jamieson (ed.), *Home care for older people in Europe* (Oxford: Oxford University Press).

S. Daatland (1983) 'Care systems', *Ageing and Society* 3, 1, 1–21.

G. Dalley (1988) *Ideologies of caring: rethinking community and collectivism* (Basingstoke: Macmillan).

P. Daunt (1992) 'Transport and mobility: a European overview', in Age Concern England, *The coming of age in Europe* (London: ACE).

B. Davies (1991) *A universal challenge: making the best use of community-based and residential-based care modes*, Discussion paper 778 (Canterbury: PSSRU, University of Kent).

B. Davies (1992) *Care management, equity and efficiency: the international experience* (Canterbury: PSSRU, University of Kent at Canterbury).

B. Deacon (ed.) (1992) *The new eastern Europe: social policy past, present and future* (London: Sage).

Dekker Committee (Commissie Structuur en Financiering Gezondheidszorg) (1987) *Willingness to change* (Bereidheid tot verandering) (The Hague: DOP).

Department of Health (1994a) *Implementing caring for people: care management* (London: Department of Health).

Department of Health (1994b) *Implementing caring for people: housing and homelessness* (London: Department of Health).

Department of Health (1994c) *Implementing caring for people: informing users and carers* (London: Department of Health).

Department of Health (1994d) *A framework for local community care charters in England* (London: Department of Health).

Department of Health SSI and Scottish Office SWSG (1991a) *Care management and assessment: managers' guide* (London: HMSO).

Department of Health SSI and Scottish Office SWSG (1991b) *Care management and assessment: practitioners' guide* (London: HMSO).

Department of Health and Social Security (1977) *Priorities in the health and social services: the way forward* (London: HMSO).

Department of Health and Social Security (1981) *Growing older* (CMND 8173 London: HMSO).

Department of Health Social Services Inspectorate (1991) *Training for community care: a joint approach* (London, HMSO).

Department of Health and Social Security for Northern Ireland (1990) *People first: community care in Northern Ireland* (London: HMSO).

M. Dieck (1989) 'Long-term care for the elderly in the Federal Republic of Germany', in T. Schwab (ed.), *Caring for an aging world* (New York: McGraw Hill).

M. Dieck (1992) 'Besondere Perspectiven des Alterns und des Alters im vereinten Deutschland', in P. Baltes, J. Mittelstrass, *Zukunft des Alterns und gesellschaftliche Entwicklung* (Berlin: Akademie der Wissenschaften zu Berlin, Walter de Gruyter).

M. Dieck (1994) 'Reforming against the grain: longterm care in Germany', in R. Page and J. Baldock (eds), *Social Policy Review 6* (Canterbury: Social Policy Association, University of Kent).

M. Dieck and V. Garms-Homolová (1991) 'Home-care services in the Federal Republic of Germany', in A. Jamieson (ed.), *Home care for older people in Europe: a comparison of policies and practices* (Oxford: Oxford University Press).

H. Döhner, H. Rüss and B. Schick (1992) *Family care of the older elderly: Germany* Dublin: European Foundation for the Improvement of Living and Working Conditions).

D. Döring, R. Hauser, G. Rolf and F. Tibitanzl (1994) 'Old-age security for women in the twelve EC countries, *Journal of European Social Policy*, 4, 1, 1–18.

P. Doty (1988) Long-term care in international perspective, *Health Care Financing Review* 1988 Annual Supplement, 145–55.

P. Doty and A. Mizrahi (1989) 'Long-term care for the elderly in France', in T. Schwab (ed.), *Caring for an aging world* (New York: McGraw Hill).

P. Emms (1990) *Social housing: a European dilemma* (Bristol: School of Advanced Urban Studies).

G. Esping-Andersen (1990) *The three worlds of welfare capitalism* (Cambridge: Polity).

C. Estes and C. Harrington (1985) 'Future directions for long term care', in C. Harrington, R. Newcomer and C. Estes, *Long term care of the elderly: public policy issues* (London: Sage).

C. Estes and P. Lee (1985) 'Social, political and economic background of long term care policy', in C. Harrington, R. Newcomer and C. Estes (eds.), *Long term care of the elderly: public policy issues* (London: Sage).

C. Estes, J. Swan and Associates (1993) *The long-term care crisis: elders trapped in the no-care zone* (London: Sage).

Eurostat (1993) *Rapid reports: population and social conditions* (Luxembourg: Office for Official Publications of the European Communities).

A. Evers (1993) 'The welfare mix approach: understanding the pluralism of welfare systems', in A. Evers and I. Svetlik (eds), *Balancing pluralism: new welfare mixes in care for the elderly* (Aldershot: Avebury).

A. Evers and T. Olk (1991) 'The mix of care provision for the frail elderly in the Federal Republic of Germany: deficits, changes and prospects of reform', in A. Evers and I. Svetlik, *New welfare mixes in care for the elderly*, Vol. 3., (Vienna: European Centre for Social Welfare Policy and Research).

A. Evers and I. Svetlik (eds) (1993) *Balancing pluralism: new welfare mixes in care for the elderly* (Aldershot: Avebury).

A. Evers and G. van der Zanden (eds) (1993) *Better care for dependent people living at home: meeting the new agenda in services for the elderly* (Bunnik: Netherlands Institute of Gerontology).

E. Fasolo and R. Frisanco (1991) 'Mental health care in Italy', *Social Policy and Administration*, 25, 3, 218–27.

M. Ferrera (1986) 'Italy', in P. Flora (ed.) *Growth to limits: the Western European welfare states since world war II. Vol. 2.* (Berlin: Walter de Gruyter).

M. Ferrera (1989a) 'Italy', in J. Dixon and R. Scheurell (eds) *Social welfare in developed market countries* (London: Routledge).

M. Ferrera (1989b) 'The politics of health reform: origins and performance of the Italian health service in comparative perspective', in G. Freddi and J. Bjorkman (eds) *Controlling medical professionals: the comparative politics of health governance* (London: Sage).

J. Finch (1984) 'Community care: developing non-sexist alternatives', *Critical Social Policy*, 9, 6–18.

J. Finch (1989) *Family obligations and social change* (Cambridge: Polity Press).

J. Finch and D. Groves (1980) 'Community care and the family: a case for equal opportunities?', *Journal of Social Policy*, 9, 4, 487–511.

J. Finch and D. Groves (eds) (1983) *A labour of love: women, work and caring* (London: Routledge and Kegan Paul).

J. Finch, R. Hugman, J. Carter (1992) *Family care of the older elderly: United Kingdom* (Dublin: European Foundation for the Improvement of Living and Working Conditions).

F. Flamm (1983) *The social system and welfare work in the Federal Republic of Germany* (2nd English edition Frankfurt/Main: Eigenverlag des Deutschen Vereins für Offentliche und Private Fürsorge).

A. Florea, L. Colombini, A. Costanzo and A. Cuneo (1993) *Social and economic policies and older people 1992: national report Italy* (Prepared for the European Commission Observatory on Ageing) (Rome: Institute for the Study of Social Services, ISTISSS).

P. Foster (1991) 'Residential care of frail elderly people: a positive reassessment', *Social Policy and Administration*, 25, 2, 108–20.

R. Freeman (1994) 'Prevention in health policy in the Federal Republic of Germany', *Policy and Politics*, 22, 1, 3–16.

J. Fries (1989) 'Reduction of the national morbidity', in S. Lewis (ed.), *Aging and health* (Michigan: Lewis).

J. Ginn and S. Arber (1992) 'Towards women's independence: pension systems in three contrasting European welfare states', *Journal of European Social Policy*, 2, 4, 255–77.

N. Ginsburg (1992) *Divisions of welfare: a critical introduction to comparative social policy* (London: Sage).

C. Glendinning (1992) *The costs of informal care: looking inside the household* (London: HMSO).

C. Glendinning and E. McLaughlin (1993) *Paying for care: lessons from Europe* (London: HMSO).

H. Glennerster (1992) *Paying for welfare: the 1990s* (Hemel Hempstead: Harvester Wheatsheaf).

E. Goffman (1961) *Asylums: essays on the social situation of mental patients and other inmates* (Harmondsworth: Penguin).

H. Green (1988) *Informal carers*, OPCS Series GHS, Supplement A (London: HMSO).

R. Griffiths (1988) *Community care: agenda for action* (London: HMSO).

K. Grossjohann (1990) *Tagespflege in der Bundesrepublik Deutschland* (Stuttgart: Verlag W. Kohlhammer).

E. Grundy and A. Harrop (1992) 'Demographic aspects of ageing in Europe', in Age Concern England, *The coming of age in Europe: older people in the European Community* (London: Age Concern England).

A.-M. Guillemard and D. Argoud (1992) *Les personnes âgées en Europe: les politiques économiques et sociales: rapport national France* (Paris: Centre d'Etude de Mouvements Sociaux).

C. Haerlin (1987) 'Community care in West Germany: concept and reality', *International Journal of Social Psychiatry*, 33, 2, 105–10.

C. Haldane and P. Ruppol (1992) 'Information technology', in Department of Health, *Inform '92: meeting the information needs of disabled people in Europe* (London: Department of Health).

C. Hallett and E. Birchall (1992) *Coordination and child protection: a review of the literature* (Edinburgh: HMSO).

C. Ham (1992) *Health policy in Britain: the politics and organisation of the National Health Service* (Basingstoke: Macmillan).

C. Ham, R. Robinson and M. Benzeval (1990) *Health check: health care reforms in an international context* (London: King's Fund Institute).

L. Hantrais (1989) 'Approaches to cross-national comparisons', in L. Hantrais (ed.) *Franco-British comparisons of family and employment careers* Cross-national research papers (Birmingham: Aston University).

S. Harrison and D. Hunter (1994) *Rationing health care* (London: Institute for Public Policy Research).

A. Heidenheimer, H. Heclo and C. Adams (1983) *Comparative public policy: the politics of social choice in Europe and America* (2nd edition) (London: Macmillan).

P. Henderson and T. Scott (1990) 'Making the most of 1992', *Insight*, 5, 4, 20–2.

J.-C. Henrard and A.-M. Brocas (1990) 'Financial barriers to health', in A. Jamieson and R. Illsley (eds) *Contrasting European policies for the care of older people* (Aldershot: Avebury).

J.-C. Henrard, B. Cassou and D. Le Disert (1990) 'The effects of system characteristics on policy implementation and functioning of care for the elderly in France', *International Journal of Health Services*, 20, 1, 125–39.

J.-C. Henrard, J. Ankri and M.-C. Isnard (1991) 'Home care services in France', in A. Jamieson (ed.), *Home care for older people in Europe: a comparison of policies and practices* (Oxford: Oxford University Press).

J. Higgins (1981) *States of welfare* (Oxford: Blackwell/ Martin Robertson).

J. Higgins (1986) 'Comparative social policy', *The Quarterly Journal of Social Affairs*, 2, 3, 221–42.

J. Higgins (1989) 'Defining community care: realities and myths', *Social Policy and Administration*, 23, 1, 3–15.

J. Hills and B. Mullings (1991) 'Housing: a decent home for all at a price within their means?', in J. Hills (ed.), *The state of welfare: the welfare state in Britain since 1974* (Oxford: Oxford University Press).

P. Hinkley and J. Steele (1992) *National disability information provision: sources and issues* (London: Policy Studies Institute).

HMSO (1987) *Promoting better health: the government's programme for improving primary health care* Cm. 249 (London: HMSO).

HMSO (1989a) *Caring for people: community care in the next decade and beyond* Cm. 849 (London: HMSO).

HMSO (1989b) *Working for patients* Cm. 555 (London: HMSO).

HMSO (1990) *Community care in the next decade and beyond: policy guidance* (London: HMSO).

D. Howe, N. Chapman and S. Baggett (1994) *Planning for an aging society* (Chicago: American Planning Association).

R. Hugman (1994) *Ageing and the care of older people in Europe* (Basingstoke: Macmillan).

D. Hunter (1986) *Care delivery systems for the elderly: inter-nation review of policies and services* (Bath: Age Care Research Europe, University of Bath).

R. Illsley and A. Jamieson (1990) 'Contextual and structural influences on adaptation to change', in A. Jamieson and R. Illsley (eds) *Contrasting European policies for the care of older people* (Aldershot: Avebury).

A. Jamieson (1989) 'A new age for older people? Policy shifts in health and social care', *Social Science and Medicine*, 29, 3, 445–54.

A. Jamieson (ed.) (1991) *Home care for older people in Europe: a comparison of policies and practices* (Oxford: Oxford University Press).

H. Jani-Le Bris (1992) *Family care of the older elderly: France* (Dublin: European Foundation for the Improvement of Living and Working Conditions).

H. Jani-Le Bris (1993) *Family care of dependent older people in the European Community* (Luxembourg: Office for Official Publications of the European Communities).

D. Jarré (1991)' Subsidiarity in social services provision in Germany', *Social Policy and Administration*, 25, 3, 211–17.

T. Jazwiecki (1989) 'Long-term care for the elderly in the United States', in T. Schwab (ed.), *Caring for an aging world* (New York: McGraw Hill).

N. Johnson (1993) 'Welfare pluralism: opportunities and risks', in A. Evers and I. Svetlik (eds), *Balancing pluralism: new welfare mixes in care for the elderly* (Aldershot: Avebury).

C. Jones (1985) *Patterns of social policy: an introduction to comparative analysis* (London: Tavistock).

D. Jones, C. Lester and R. West (1994) 'Monitoring changes in health services for older people', in R. Robinson and J. Le Grand (eds), *Evaluating the NHS reforms* (London: King's Fund Institute).

D. Justice with L. Etheredge, I. Luehrs and B. Burwell (1988) *State long term care reform: development of community care systems in six states* (Washington DC: Center for Policy Research, National Governors' Association).

M. Keenan (1989) *Changing needs for long-term care: a chartbook* (Washington DC: American Association of Retired Persons).

K. van Kersbergen and U. Becker (1988) 'The Netherlands: a passive social democratic welfare state in a Christian democratic ruled society', *Journal of Social Policy*, 17, 4, 477–99.

M. Kleinman (1992) 'Policy responses to changing housing markets: towards a European housing policy?', in L. Hantrais et al. (eds) *The mixed economy of welfare* (Loughborough: Cross National Research Group, European Research Centre, Loughborough University).

N. Koedoot and A. Hommel (1993) 'Case management and incentives for the elderly: findings from the Rotterdam experiment', in J. Coolen (ed.), *Changing care in the Netherlands: experience and research findings from policy experiments* (Assen/Maastricht: Van Gorcum).

D. Kramer and R. Landwehr (undated) *Soziales Berlin* (Berlin: Senator for Health and Social Affairs in connection with the Senator for Youth and Family).

J. Krout (1989) *Senior centers in America* (New York: Greenwood Press).

Kuratorium Deutsche Altershilfe (KDA) (1993) *Arbeitshilfen für die Planung und den Betrieb von Tagespflege–Einrightungen* Köln: KDA).

W. Laing (1993) *Financing long-term care: the crucial debate* (London: Age Concern England).

M. Langan and I. Ostner (1991) 'Gender and welfare: towards a comparative framework', in G. Room (ed.), *Towards a European welfare state?* (Bristol: School of Advanced Urban Studies).

P. Laroque (1962) *Rapport de la commission d'étude des problèmes de la vieillesse* (Paris: Documentation Française).

S. Leibfried (1993) 'Towards a European welfare state?', in C. Jones (ed.), *New perspectives on the welfare state in Europe* (London: Routledge).

J. Lewis (1992) 'Gender and the development of welfare regimes', *Journal of European Social Policy*, 2, 3, 159–73.

J. Lewis and B. Meredith (1988) *Daughters who care: daughters caring for mothers at home* (London: Routledge).

S. Macintyre (1977) 'Old age as a social problem', in R. Dingwall et al (eds), *Health care and health knowledge* (London: Croom Helm).

S. Macintyre (1989) 'The role of health services in relation to inequalities in health in Europe', in J. Fox (ed.), *Health inequalities in European countries* (Aldershot: Gower).

S. Mackintosh, R. Means and P. Leather (1990) *Housing in later life: the housing finance implications of an ageing society* (Bristol: School of Advanced Urban Studies).

S. Mangen (1987) 'Mental health policies in Europe: an analysis of priorities and problems', *International Journal of Social Psychiatry*, 33, 2, 76–82.

S. Mangen (1991) 'Social policy, the radical right and the German welfare state', in H. Glennerster and J. Midgley (eds), *The radical right and the welfare state* (Hemel Hempstead: Harvester Wheatsheaf).

M. Mayo (1994) *Communities and caring: the mixed economy of welfare* (Basingstoke: Macmillan).

E. McEwen (1992) *Home help and care: rights, charging and reality* (London: Age Concern England).

R. Means (1990) 'Community care, housing and older people: continuity or change?', *Housing Studies*, 6, 4, 273–84.

R. Means and R. Smith (1994) *Community care: policy and practice* (Basingstoke: Macmillan).

Medical Research Council (1994) *The health of the UK's elderly people* (London: MRC).

M. Mengani and C. Gagliardi (1992) *Family care of the older elderly: Italy* (Dublin: European Foundation for the Improvement of Living and Working Conditions).

B. Meredith (1993) *The community care handbook: the new system explained* (London: Age Concern England).

B. Meredith (1995) *The community care handbook: the reormed system explained* (London: Age Concern England).

O. von Mering and L. Neff (1993) 'Joining a life care community: an alternative to 'frailing' into a nursing home in the USA', *Generations Review*, 3, 4, 5–8.

Ministère des Affaires Sociales et de la Solidarité Nationale (1972) *Circulaire relative au maintien à domicile des personnes âgées* (Paris: Documentation Française).

Ministère des Affaires Sociales et de la Solidarité Nationale (1982) *Circulaire du 7 avril 1982 relative à la politique sociale et médico-sociale pour les retraités et personnes âgées* (Paris: Documentation Française).

Ministerie van Welzijn, Volksgezondheid en Cultuur (1983) *Nota flankerend bejaardenbeleid* Rijswijk: MWVC).

M. Minkler (1988) 'Community-based initiatives to reduce isolation and enhance empowerment of the elderly: case studies from the US', *Danish Medical Bulletin*, Gerontology special supplement series No. 6, 52–6.

R. Mishra (1990) *The welfare state in capitalist society: policies of retrenchment and maintenance in Europe, North America and Australia* (Hemel Hempstead: Harvester Wheatsheaf).

R. Mishra (1993) 'Social policy in the postmodern world: the welfare state in Europe by comparison with North America', in C. Jones (ed.) *New perspectives on the welfare state in Europe* (London: Routledge).

D. Mitchell (1991) *Income transfers in ten welfare states* (Aldershot: Avebury).

R. Morris (ed.) (1988) *Testing the limits of social welfare: international perspectives on policy changes in nine countries* (Hanover: University Press of New England).

C. Mullings (1989) *Famine among plenty: the paradox of information use by the elderly* (Bath: University of Bath).

E. Murphy (1993) *Dementia and mental illness in older people: a practical guide* (London: Papermac).

National Institute for Social Work (1988) *Residential care: a positive choice?* (Wagner Report) (London: HMSO).

H. Nies, S. Tester and J.-M. Nuijens (1991) 'Day care in the United Kingdom and the Netherlands: a comparative study', *Ageing and Society*, 11, 245–73.

P. Nijkamp et al., (1991) *Services for the elderly in Europe: a cross-national comparative study* (Leuven: Katholieke Universiteit).

A. Norman (1985) *Triple jeopardy: growing old in a second homeland* (London: Centre for Policy on Ageing).

D. Norton (1992) 'Social provision for older people in Europe: in education and leisure', in Age Concern England, *The coming of age in Europe: older people in the European Community* (London: Age Concern England).

J. van Nostrand, R. Clark and T. Romoren (1993) 'Nursing home care in five nations', *Ageing International*, XX, 2, 1–5.

Office of Population Censuses and Surveys (OPCS) (1993) *General Household Survey* (London: HMSO).

C. Oldman (1990) *Moving in old age: new directions in housing policies* (London: HMSO).

Organisation for Economic Cooperation and Development (1987) *Financing and delivering health care: a comparative analysis of OECD countries* (Paris: OECD).

Organisation for Economic Cooperation and Development (1988a) *Ageing populations: the social policy implications* (Paris: OECD).

Organisation for Economic Cooperation and Development (1988b) *Reforming public pensions* (Paris: OECD).

Organisation for Economic Cooperation and Development (1994a) *New orientations for social policy* (Paris: OECD).

Organisation for Economic Cooperation and Development (1994b) *Caring for frail elderly people: new directions in care* (Paris: OECD).

J. Ovretveit (1993) *Coordinating community care: multidisciplinary teams and care management* (Buckingham: Open University Press).

Pepper Commission (1990) *US bipartisan commission on comprehensive health care: a call for action* (Washington DC: US Government Printing Office).

J. Petersen (1991) 'Problems of pension policy: American, British, Danish and German ideas', *Social Policy and Administration*, 25, 3, 249–60.

M. Pijl (1992) 'Netherlands policies for elderly people', *Social Policy and Administration*, 26, 3, 201–08.

P. Potter and G. Zill (1992) 'Older households and their housing situation', in Age Concern England, *The coming of age in Europe: older people in the European community* (London: Age Concern England).

H. Qureshi and A. Walker (1989) *The caring relationship: elderly people and their families* (Basingstoke: Macmillan).

D. Robbins (1990) 'Voluntary organisations and the social state in the European Community', *Voluntas*, 1, 2, 98–128.

V. Rodwin (1989) 'New ideas for health policy in France, Canada and Britain', in M. Field (ed.), *Success and crisis in national health systems: a comparative approach* (London: Routledge).

J. Roebroek (1989) 'Netherlands', in J. Dixon and R. Scheurell (eds), *Social welfare in developed market countries* (London: Routledge).

C. Rollet (1991) 'Problems of health services finance in France', *Social Policy and Administration*, 25, 3, 193–201.

C. Romijn and T. Miltenburg (1993) *Monitored innovations in the care for the elderly in the Netherlands* (Nijmegen: Institute for Applied Social Sciences).

I. Rosow (1967) *Social integration of the aged* (New York: Free Press).

Royal Association for Disability and Rehabilitation (1994) *Disabled people have rights* (London: RADAR).

Royal College of Physicians (1994) *Ensuring equity and quality of care for elderly people* (London: RCOP).

D. Sainsbury (1993) 'Dual welfare and sex segregation of access to social benefits: income maintenance policies in the UK, the US, the Netherlands and Sweden', *Journal of Social Policy*, 22, 1, 69–98.

C. Saraceno and N. Negri (1994) 'The changing Italian welfare state', *Journal of European Social Policy*, 4, 1, 19–34.

P. Schopflin (1991) *Dépendance et solidarité: rapport de la Commission du Commisariat Général au Plan* (Paris: Documentation Française).

F. Schrameijer (1987) 'New comprehensive mental health authorities in the Netherlands', *International Journal of Social Psychiatry*, 33, 2, 132–6.

V. Scott (1994) *Lessons from America: a study of the Americans with Disabilities Act* (London: Royal Association for Disability and Rehabilitation).

P. Spicker (1991) 'The principle of subsidiarity and the social policy of the European Community', *Journal of European Social Policy*, 1, 1, 3–14.

M. Steenvoorden (1992) *Family care of the older elderly: the Netherlands* (Dublin: European Foundation for the Improvement of Living and Working Conditions).

D. Stone (1991) 'German unification: east meets west in the doctor's office', *Journal of Health Politics, Policy and Law*, 16, 2, 401–12.

P. Taylor-Gooby (1991) 'Welfare state regimes and welfare citizenship', *Journal of European Social Policy*, 1, 2, 93–105.

S. Tester (1985) *Cash and care: the relations between Supplementary Benefit and other agencies* (London: Bedford Square Press).

S. Tester (1989) *Caring by day: a study of day care services for older people* (London: Centre for Policy on Ageing).

S. Tester (1992) *Common knowledge: a coordinated approach to information-giving* (London: Centre for Policy on Ageing).

S. Tester (1994) 'Implications of subsidiarity for the care of older people in Germany', *Social Policy and Administration*, 28, 3, 251–62.

S. Tester and B. Meredith (1987) *Ill-informed?: a study of information and support for elderly people in the inner city* (London: Policy Studies Institute).

A. Tinker (1989) *An evaluation of very sheltered housing* (London: HMSO).

A. Tinker (1992) *Elderly people in modern society* (Third edition) (Harlow: Longman).

R. M. Titmuss (1968) *Commitment to welfare* (London: Allen and Unwin).

R. M. Titmuss (1974) *Social policy* (London: Allen and Unwin).

H. Tomann (1990) 'Housing in West Germany', in D. Maclennan and R. Williams (eds) *Affordable housing in Europe* (York: Joseph Rowntree Foundation).

P. Townsend (1962) *The last refuge* (London: Routledge and Kegan Paul).

P. Townsend (1968) 'Isolation, desolation and loneliness', in E. Shanas et al., *Old people in three industrial societies* (London: Routledge and Kegan Paul).

P. Townsend, N. Davidson and M. Whitehead (1992) *Inequalities in health: the Black Report, the Health Divide* (Harmondsworth: Penguin Books).

C. Tunissen and M. Knapen (1991) 'The Netherlands', in R. Kraan et al., *Care for the elderly: significant innovations in three European countries* (Frankfurt am Main: Campus Verlag).

Tweede Kamer der Staten Generaal (1990) *Ouderen in tel: beeld en beleid rond ouderen 1990–1994 (Ageing counts)* (The Hague: Staatsuitgeverij).

J. Twigg (1992) 'Carers in the service system', in J. Twigg (ed.), *Carers: research and practice* (London: HMSO).

J. Twigg and K. Atkin (1993) *Carers perceived: policy and practice in informal care* (Buckingham: Open University Press).

C. Ungerson (1987) *Policy is personal: sex, gender and informal care* (London: Tavistock).

United Nations (1991) *World population prospects 1990* (New York: United Nations).

US Bureau of the Census (1992) *Statistical Abstract of the United States: 1992* (112th edition) (Washington DC: US Bureau).

US Department of Health and Human Services Social Security Administration (1991) *Social Security Bulletin*, 54, 9. (Washington DC: US DHHS).

R. Valle (1989) 'US ethnic minority group access to long-term care', in T. Schwab (ed.), *Caring for an aging world* (New York: McGraw Hill).

C. Victor (1991) *Health and health care in later life* (Buckingham: Open University Press).

A. Vollering (1991) 'Italy', in P. Nijkamp et al., *Services for the elderly in Europe: a cross-national comparative study* (Leuven: Katholieke Universiteit).

A. Walker (1981) 'Towards a political economy of old age', *Ageing and Society*, 1, 1, 73–94.

A. Walker (1989) 'Community care', in M. McCarthy (ed.), *The new politics of welfare* (London: Macmillan).

A. Walker (1992a) 'Pensions and the living standards of pensioners in the EC', in Age Concern England, *The coming of age in Europe: older people in the European Community* (London: Age Concern England).

A. Walker (1992b) *Older people in Europe: social and economic policies. National report United Kingdom* (Sheffield: University of Sheffield).

A. Walker (1993) 'Living standards and way of life', in A. Walker, J. Alber and A.-M. Guillemard, *Older people in Europe: social and economic policies* (Brussels: Commission of the European Communities).

A. Walker (ed.) (1993) *Older people in Europe: social integration* (Brussels: Commission of the European Communities).

A. Walker, J. Alber and A.-M. Guillemard (1993) *Older people in Europe: social and economic policies* (Brussels: Commission of the European Communities).

R. Walker and W. Ahmad (1994) 'Windows of opportunity in rotting frames? Care providers' perspectives on community care and black communities', *Critical Social Policy*, 40, 46–69.

R. Wall (1989) 'The living arrangements of the elderly in Europe in the 1980s', in B. Bytheway et al. (eds), *Becoming and being old: sociological approaches to later life* (London: Sage).

N. Warner (1994) *Community care: just a fairy tale?* (London: Carers National Association).

H. A. Waxman (1990) 'The forgotten catastrophe: financing long-term care', *Journal of Aging and Social Policy*, 2, 1, 11–13.

W. Weissert, C. Cready and J. Pawelak (1988) 'The past and future of home and community-based long-term care', *The Milbank Quarterly*, 66, 2, 309–88.

G. C. Wenger (1994) *Understanding support networks and community care: network assessment for elderly people* (Aldershot: Avebury).

M. Whitehead (1994) 'Is it fair?: evaluating the equity implications of the NHS reforms', in R. Robinson and J. Le Grand (eds), *Evaluating the NHS reforms* (London: King's Fund Institute).

F. Williams (1989) *Social policy: a critical introduction* (Cambridge: Polity).

G. Wilson (1991) 'Models of ageing and their relation to policy formation and service provision', *Policy and Politics*, 19, 1, 37–47.

G. Wilson (1993) 'The challenge of an ageing electorate: changes in the formation of social policy in Europe?', *Journal of European Social Policy*, 3, 2, 91–105.

G. Wilson (1994) 'Co-production and self-care: new approaches to managing community care services for older people', *Social Policy and Administration*, 28, 3, 236–50.

Index

202